*The Virtuous Journalist*

# The Virtuous Journalist

*Stephen Klaidman*

*Tom L. Beauchamp*

*New York Oxford*
Oxford University Press
*1987*

Oxford University Press

Oxford   New York   Toronto
Delhi   Bombay   Calcutta   Madras   Karachi
Petaling Jaya   Singapore   Hong Kong   Tokyo
Nairobi   Dar es Salaam   Cape Town
Melbourne   Auckland

and associated companies in
Beirut   Berlin   Ibadan   Nicosia

Copyright © 1987 by Klaidman & Beauchamp

Published by Oxford University Press, Inc.,
200 Madison Avenue, New York, New York 10016

Oxford is a registered trademark of Oxford University Press

Library of Congress Cataloging-in-Publication Data
Klaidman, Stephen.
The virtuous journalist.
Includes bibliographies and index.
1. Journalistic ethics.   I. Beauchamp, Tom L.   II. Title.
PN4756.K43   1987   174'.9097   86-23852
ISBN 0-19-504205-0 (alk. paper)

*174.9097*
*K66v*
*14 4302*
*may 1988*

9 8 7 6 5 4 3 2 1

Printed in the United States of America
on acid-free paper

*For Kitty, Lisi, and Danny*
*For Ruthie and Karine*

# Preface

This book is for anyone interested in the subject of moral integrity in journalism, whether they are journalists, the subjects and sources of news stories, or consumers of news. Each chapter provides an analytical framework for examining fundamental concepts such as truth, bias, harm, trust, manipulation, and accountability. The principles developed in this framework are used throughout the book to analyze concrete cases.

*The Virtuous Journalist* was not written as a comprehensive account of every conceivable subject in journalism ethics, but only to offer some insights, raise some new questions, and undermine a few entrenched assumptions.

Many of the examples of morally questionable journalism found in this book are atypical of the work of the news organizations they represent, but they do typify the kinds of moral problems journalists face daily.

*Washington, D.C.*                                          S.K.
*August 1986*                                               T.L.B.

# Acknowledgments

This book would still be unfinished and its future far from certain without the help of a great many people and two institutions. We are indebted to the National Endowment for the Humanities, which provided the funding that made the project possible (grant no. RO-20684-84), and to the Kennedy Institute of Ethics, whose scholars, fellows, and staff provided a full measure of intellectual and practical support. Specifically, we want to thank the research assistants who helped us in innumerable ways to gather material and prepare the manuscript. They are Gregory Acs, Quin Hillyer, Robin Bourjaily, and Jeffrey Kahn. We are also grateful to Mary Ellen Timbol, without whose efforts our early work would never have been delivered to the endowment on time, and Denise Brooks and Manuel Fernandez, who worked on the manuscript with cheer and diligence.

# Contents

*The Virtuous Journalist*

# Chapter 1

# The Idea of Ethics in Journalism

Political columnist David Broder once criticized George Will for helping President Ronald Reagan prepare for a debate and then praising Reagan's performance on the air without disclosing his role in its preparation. But before taking his well-aimed shot at Will, Broder observed, accurately, that "it is difficult to write about 'journalism ethics' without sounding like a jerk." Broder's integrity transcended his concern over sounding jerkish, however, and he finished the column.[1]

Broder risked sounding like a jerk for only about eight hundred words. We have done so for about three hundred pages. On virtually every page some reader is likely to find us arrogant, utopian, holier-than-thou—or just plain jerks. CBS producer George Crile, in private correspondence, has described some of our criticisms of his work in these pages as "shrill" and "outrageous." He said that he has "had the experience now of defending 'The Uncounted Enemy' [a documentary about the Vietnam War over which Gen. William C. Westmoreland sued CBS for $120 million] for nine days of hostile examination from Dan Burt [Westmoreland's lawyer] before an 18-man federal jury. . . . But far more difficult has been the challenge of answering the horde of press judges with all of their prejudices and varying points of view and varying levels of competence. . . ."[2] The implicit question Crile directs at us and at his other critics is, "Do you meet your own standards?" The question is fair, and we expect to be judged by our own criteria.

Under these or any criteria, however, it would be fatuous to suggest that everyone will agree with the way we analyze problems in journalism ethics. Our analytical framework derives from modern moral philosophy, which we recognize as having a language and approach that may make journalists slightly uncomfortable. We appeal to what is often called in philosophy "our considered moral intuitions and judgments." But "our" shared intuitions and judgments are not always entirely shared, and not always consistent when they are shared. Part of the exercise is to render them as coherent and consistent as possible, while appreciating the inevitability of some disagreement. We believe, however, that underlying our disagreements is a common core of consistent and widely shared moral beliefs that save us from purely subjective preferences.

Using these shared moral beliefs for shaping and developing an ethics in journalism is a formidable and fragile undertaking. Meg Greenfield, editor of *The Washington Post*'s editorial and op-ed pages, once wrote a column in which she argued that Washington "is a place that talks endlessly of moral issues, but . . . is essentially confused, selective, frightened, skittish, unhappy and unsuccessful in dealing with them."[3] The years we have devoted to journalism ethics have led us to conclude that this comment applies as fully to journalists as to politicians and civil servants in the federal city.

Journalists, of course, are not unexposed to moral problems. They have been examining moral problems in their own and other professions for decades. Some journalists have written series and even books on moral problems in medicine, such as the treatment of handicapped newborns, euthanasia, abortion, and the use of experimental cancer therapies. Other journalists have written about business and political ethics, exploring at length such problems as conflict of interest and corporate responsibility. A good case can even be made that journalists have anointed themselves the public's guardians against the moral failures of professionals. For example, our survey of one year's issues of *The Wall Street Journal* turned up more than a thousand articles on moral problems (largely confined to business).

Because journalism touches almost everyone's life, and because it benefits substantially from our liberal tradition of press freedom, moral standards and conduct in journalism deserve at least as much attention as the standards and conduct of lawyers, physicians, or business persons. We do not mean to imply that journalists are a morally defective lot. American journalists, both print and electronic, are often fair, competent, even altogether virtuous. They are sometimes criticized indiscriminately, perhaps as a result of inflated expectations, and many of their failures are understandable in context. Given the catch-it-on-the-fly nature of daily journalism, it would be unreasonable to expect the total output of even a generally competent and fair-minded group of professionals to be uniformly satisfactory. Journalism being what it is, even the most virtuous journalists, operating from what they view as the best of motives, inevitably will produce some morally unsatisfactory results. In either case it is worth understanding what went wrong and how to prevent its recurrence.

We offer several central moral concepts in this first chapter as a framework from which to evaluate journalistic conduct. Much of the rest of the book flows from this framework. In particular, we examine freedom, morality, rules of duty, virtue, competence, and fairness. The natural starting point is freedom, because of its historical and ongoing significance. We examine this concept together with certain values with which it sometimes clashes and competes such as the avoidance of harm and public service.

## Freedom and the Weight of Competing Values

The expectation in the United States and most Western democracies is that journalists will provide information the public needs to carry out the duties of citizenship and that the media will provide a forum for the circulation of ideas and opinions. To help realize this expectation, the press has been given special legal privileges and protections to gather and publish or broadcast news and other information and opinion free of intimidation. Although the issues and arguments that concern us throughout this book are almost entirely moral, the tradition of a legally protected free press forms an indispensable background against which we will interpret the moral rights and responsibilities of journalists.

*The History and Relevance of Legal Protections.* Former Supreme Court Justice Potter Stewart rightly points out that in drafting and ratifying the First Amendment, James Madison and the other framers of the Constitution were thoughtful, precise, and farsighted—not verbose—when they included the word *press* along with *speech* in the phrase, "Congress shall make no law . . . abridging the freedom of speech, or of the press. . . ." But Leonard W. Levy is no less correct to point out that the framers of the Constitution had only a vague idea of what they meant by freedom of the press and that it remains unconfirmed that they intended the First Amendment's press clause to rule out prosecution for "seditious libel," an eighteenth-century euphemism for criticizing public officials.[4]

Much of the debate surrounding the drafting of the First Amendment consisted of an untidy mix of ill-defined expressions of support for free speech and freedom of the press. The "press" was composed largely of commercially oriented printers and self-promoting politicians who often hid behind pseudonyms such as Leonidas, Craftsman, and Father of Candor. The pseudonyms allowed these men to present views that did indeed seem to border on "seditious libel," despite the vagueness that surrounded this notion. Some writers of the period were the spiritual descendants of John Trenchard and Thomas Gordon, jointly known as Cato, who wrote a series of 138 "letters" on constitutional government and the rights of Englishmen that were published in London newspapers between 1720 and 1723. A principal reason for using pseudonyms at the time Cato was writing, and indeed into the beginning of the nineteenth century, was that the doctrine of libel entailed that truth was no defense; libel was considered worse if truthful. The reason was that a libel or slanderous accusation against government was considered more likely to incite to violence or to other crime if true.

Few had the foresight in the eighteenth century to see that press freedom was incompatible with a preference for falsity over truth. Cato represents the first popular recognition that truth should be taken into consideration in matters of libel, especially seditious libel. In the essay, "Of Freedom of Speech: That the same is inseparable from Publick Liberty," Cato wrote the following: "That men ought to speak well of their Governors, is true, while their Governors deserve to be well spoken of; but to do publick Mischief, without hearing of it, is only the Prerogative and Felicity of Tyranny; A free People will be shewing that they are so, by their Freedom of Speech."[5] Cato's message was that the press should be free to speak the truth about government and its officials even if the truth was unflattering. Cato wrote elsewhere, however, that in suits between private parties a true statement could conceivably be libelous.[6]

Despite Cato's campaign for truth as a defense in cases of seditious libel, little of substance happened to change the landscape of law until 1735, a year that in some ways is as important in the American struggle for liberty as 1776. It was in 1735 that German-born printer John Peter Zenger, who had emigrated to America in 1710, was tried for seditious libel against the governor of New York, William Cosby, whose policies Zenger had truculently opposed in his paper, *Weekly Journal*. In this landmark case a brilliant brief written by James Alexander, and delivered in court no less brilliantly by Andrew Hamilton, persuaded a jury that despite the existing and applicable common law, truth should be admitted as a defense in libel. The precedent was thus established that the truth was not libelous. Although the national debate on the issue was not terminated, Zenger's acquittal was a vital step toward freedom of the press in America.

By the time the Bill of Rights was drafted, Americans had passed from subjects of a limited monarchy to citizens of a free republic. It was appropriate, even necessary, for such citizens to have a press that was free to report on the actions of a government of and by the people. There was no raging debate on that point between the Revolutionary War and the Constitutional Convention of 1787 or the drafting of the Bill of Rights in 1789. Virtually everyone accepted the principle of press freedom, as a rejection of precensorship and licensing. However, the context of the principle was unsettled. The idea that there should be no prior restraints on publication was supported almost unanimously, but so was the principle that there should be legal recourse for anyone damaged by licentious publication.

This historical sketch shows that late-eighteenth-century Americans were grappling with issues about press freedom that resemble those with which we struggle today. At present considerable controversy surrounds the question of what limitations, if any, should be placed on press freedom. The power of the press, some argue, is as great as that of the judiciary and the executive branches of government, and the press has continually come under fire in recent years on charges of abuse of liberty and violation of the public trust. Even some journalists maintain that mistrust of the press is growing into open hostility that threatens traditional press freedom. "We are getting to the point," wrote Daniel Schorr, "where a politician will be able to run against the news media as he used to run against Communism, crime or corruption—issues no longer available to some of them."[7]

Schorr's comment may be an overstatement, but it is consistent with questions now raised with increasing frequency. What should be done, for example, when the press publishes something injurious to government or something defamatory about a public official? The jury concluded in the case of *Gen. Ariel Sharon* v. *Time, Inc.* that although false and defamatory statements had been published, nothing could be done under law unless *Time* had intentionally published the information knowing that it was false or published it in reckless disregard of whether it was true. Not everyone agrees that this legal principle should control libel cases. Many critics of the press think the press is too free to libel public persons as the result of an overgenerous interpretation of the First Amendment. Others counter that abuse of press freedom is the inevitable price for having it.

We acknowledge throughout this book that the press should retain its traditional legal freedoms, with only minimal legal constraints; but we also insist that there is no evidence that the Founding Fathers intended conflicts involving press freedom to be resolved by an absolute principle of freedom and that they were right to stop short of endorsing such sweeping freedom. They proposed only that as few legal obstacles as possible—consistent with respect for other values—be placed in the way of press freedom.[8] For this reason, federal, state, and local governments have traditionally given the press an extensive and privileged set of liberties—including relatively easy access to officials, documents, and restricted areas—but never freedom that would amount to license.

As an example of the nature of the freedom and protections provided to the press and how they have been balanced in court opinions, consider the current state of libel in the United States. Libel laws have in large part been written and interpreted by courts to protect news organizations from being successfully sued by public officials and public figures, many of whose legal actions in recent years have been far from frivolous. When the press is threatened by an unfavorable libel ruling, the issue of whether the rights of a free press should override some competing value that deserves to be balanced against the value of a free press plays the central role.

A 1985 decision in the case of *Tavoulareas* v. *The Washington Post* provides an instructive example because of the attempts by one judge after another to balance protections for subjects who might be libeled against press freedoms. A three-judge panel of the U.S. Court of Appeals for the District of Columbia reinstated a libel verdict against the *Post* in a suit brought by William P. Tavoulareas, president of Mobil Oil. The *Post* article had alleged that Tavoulareas had abused his position and misappropriated Mobil's corporate assets to "set up his son" in the shipping business.[9] The Tavoulareases said the story was false and had held them up to ridicule. A jury found in July 1982 that the *Post* had published false material with "actual malice"—that is, either with knowledge of its falsity or with reckless disregard of its truth or falsity—and set an award of over $2 million. Trial judge Oliver Gasch then overturned the jury verdict in May 1983, writing: "The article in question falls far short of being a model of fair, unbiased investigative journalism. There is no evidence in the record, however, to show that it contained knowing lies or statements made in reckless disregard of the truth."[10] The court of appeals panel, in a two-to-one ruling, reversed Gasch two years later and found that the evidence *was* sufficient to establish "actual malice."[11] Judge J. Skelly Wright dissented, finding that only "flimsy facts" supported an "excessive jury verdict" in this "extremely important First Amendment case."[12] (In June 1985, the full court of appeals threw out the panel's ruling in order to reach its own decision.[13])

Judge Wright noted—correctly, we think—that the negative effect on freedom of expression of the appeals court decision would be "incalculable" because the court was sending a message to the media that it must steer clear of unpleasant, hard-hitting, investigative reporting.[14] The American press predictably, but properly, supported Wright's dissent. There was a consensus in the media that the *Post* should, if necessary, battle all the way to the Supreme Court, despite the risk of an unfavorable ruling.[15] *The New York Times*'s Alex Jones interviewed a number of editors on the appeals court verdict, including Jean Otto, editorial page editor of *The Rocky Mountain News* in Denver, and John Emmerich, editor and publisher of *The Greenwood Commonwealth,* a 9,000-circulation paper in Mississippi. Otto and Emmerich said, respectively, "I think we know the public is hostile, but when the courts reflect that kind of hostility and disregard, I think every big and little newspaper in the country will have a problem deciding what to print and what not to print," and, "Ultimately does the American public win when newspapers are intimidated and caused to be less aggressive?"[16] In a full page of coverage, the *Times* did not present a single journalist—although it found plenty of lawyers—in favor of the majority decision.

Journalists often write as if the First Amendment justifies unrestrained freedom rather than a freedom that must be balanced against other values, because, like Otto and Emmerich, they worry that public concern over competing values such as the need to avoid harm and to keep information confidential can be fashioned into a club by government to intimidate the press. They also argue that other freedoms, such as freedom of religion and freedom of assembly, would wither without freedom of the press. These claims are often augmented by the contention that the press has internal mechanisms of control calculated to produce restraint; but the brunt of the argument is almost always that permitting virtually any government regulation will put the press and thereby the public on a slippery slope. The following excerpt from a *Wall Street Journal* editorial entitled "Free Speech" typifies this view:

> If one gives government officials responsibility for monitoring what institutions or individuals say in public, they will do precisely that, with the result that speech that was once free will become less free. The often-held belief that such limitations will be marginal or insignificant is not true. By its nature, government regulation accretes; it grows larger and it spreads wider.[17]

There is little immediate reason to think that the courts in the United States have been chipping away at free speech in the sense that concerns this editorial writer, which is government regulation. The legal right to free speech and a free press remains solidly protected, although in recent years the courts have been more inclined to impose penalties for defamation, a "restriction" on speech imposed after the fact.

*The Moral Limits to Freedom.*   Our own approach to values that compete with press freedom is independent of all distinctly legal considerations, because we are assessing the moral rights and responsibilities of the press. But the two are not so different in this respect. The problem of valid limits on press liberty is viewed in ethical theory as in legal theory in terms of competing moral rights. Freedom of speech and of the press are rights that—like all moral rights, without exception—are constrained by other rights with which they may compete on occasion. The press has a right to express beliefs and judgments about persons, but if the press violates someone's moral right not to be defamed, then the latter's right *might override* the press's right to free expression. President Theodore Roosevelt, who took the word *muckrake* from John Bunyan's *Pilgrim's Progress* and first applied it to the press, put the point tersely, and we think properly: "Men with the muckrake are often indispensable to the well-being of society, but only if they know when to stop raking the muck."[18] On this general point there should be no fundamental difference between law and morals, despite their different limitations and applications.

The defenses of unrestrained press freedom found in contemporary journalism seldom explicitly consider the range of moral rights and responsibilities that confront the press, and these defenses often amount to a demand for privileged treatment that moral analysis will not support. Journalists need not be moral philosophers, of course, but they should be aware that competing values may have moral weight equal to or greater than press freedom. Of course, which values should be put in the balance and how much weight they should be given will often be controversial, and a consensus may not emerge. A former president of CBS News, Fred W. Friendly, said, in a discussion of priorities for journalists, "I have decided in my 70th year that I am a citizen first and a journalist second."[19] We have no doubt that responsibilities of citizenship can, on occasion, outweigh journalistic objectives and even restrain freedom of the press, but Friendly's generalization is destined for everlasting controversy because it was stated in such an unqualified form that it permits no balancing of competing values in specific contexts.

John Stuart Mill's celebrated thesis that a maximally free press serves the public interest better than any system of press control, on grounds that truth most consistently emerges from a free marketplace of ideas, is now widely accepted. But Mill was not a free speech absolutist. He argued that no one should be free to wantonly violate someone else's rights, unjustly damage another's reputation, disclose secrets vital to the public interest, and so on.[20] Some of the most committed utilitarians (including Mill) and libertarians have advocated placing some restraints—moral and legal—on the press. They recognize, as do we, that even highly valued privileges of the press such as the protection of confidential sources may have to yield to other moral claims in some circumstances.

Even in the kinds of cases that are usually considered by journalists to be clear-cut, a reporter is not necessarily morally vindicated because of the legal privilege to withhold information. For example, in May 1985 a reporter for *The Patriot Ledger* in Quincy, Massachusetts, was ordered by a court to testify at the trial of a vice-president of Rockland Trust Company. During an interview, the bank official apparently made incriminating statements about Rockland's failures to report cash transactions to the IRS. The reporter and his attorney took the view—now almost universally accepted in journalism—that testimony by the reporter at the bank official's trial would have a "chilling effect" on investigative reporting, and therefore the First Amendment protected the reporter against being compelled to testify. The judge rejected this claim; he said that while he disliked interfering with the press, he also had to "consider the interests of justice."[21] We agree in principle with the judge, although, again, our perspective is moral rather than legal. (In this case the reporter interviewed the vice-president after an indictment had already been brought, and both were fully aware of the charges. The reporter's actions could not therefore be construed as a cause of the indictment or as a betrayal of a source. This mitigates the possibility of a chilling effect, a factor that should be weighed along with other considerations.)

From the perspective of moral analysis, it is worth reflecting on questions such as whether a journalist who obtains the confidential diary of a Supreme Court justice that contains information vital to the public interest has a moral right to publish the diary any more than the police have a moral right to search the journalist's files if they contain vital information. Similarly, it is an open question whether in every case the protection of a reporter's sources is more valuable than effective law enforcement, which may be promoted by giving the police access to a journalist's confidential files.

Both the objectives of journalism and the public interest will be served if journalists learn to weigh and balance competing moral considerations in their work, rather than leaving such balancing to the courts or leaving it aside completely as if it were a purely legal matter. The ABC television network seemed to agree with this principle when it took out an advertisement in American newspapers in April 1985 that was, in effect, a brief position paper on a specific problem of moral balancing. It dealt with the press's "freedom and responsibility" in suppressing information about certain kinds of "sensitive issues." These are issues that, in ABC's estimation, we should not ignore as a society and yet seem too sensitive to "confront" on television. The examples given by ABC were discovering homosexuality in a family and the psychological and emotional effects of incest. The network argued that "broadcasters must be extraordinarily sensitive to the balance between the public's freedom to be informed on an important subject and the sensitivity of the topic."[22] ABC here correctly appreciates that even if television is legally free to produce vital and compelling information, and even if society has a legal right to hear it, there may nonetheless be valid reasons for not airing the information. ABC's statement captures our general thesis: The press must be keenly sensitive to the need to make these decisions and must develop procedures to improve the chances that the balancing will be done wisely.

A *Washington Post* reader apparently disagreed with this conclusion in a letter to the editor. Scott Wood was responding to a column by the *Post*'s ombudsman, Sam Zagoria, who questioned whether it is ethically proper for newspapers to publish betting lines. Wood wrote: "It seems to me highly arrogant and downright unethical for editors to withhold information that people demonstrably want just because they don't think such information is 'proper.' Newspapers have no more and no less of an obligation to print what their readers are interested in knowing, and leave the ethical judgments to the reader."[23] We disagree profoundly with Wood. It is a part of the press's responsibility to exercise moral judgment about what it is improper to publish or broadcast. The pertinent question is how to frame a justifiable account of what is improper.

In summary, the issues that concern us are not those involving the press's legal entitlements to publish free from most constraints, although we support those entitlements. We are primarily interested in the press's moral obligations not to libel, not to invade privacy, to publish as fact only what can be confirmed, to be tasteful, and so on. Although the law is often concerned with moral problems, it is not the basic repository of our moral standards and values. A law-abiding person is not necessarily morally virtuous, and if an act is legally acceptable that fact alone does not make it morally acceptable. If a journalist is legally innocent of libel, for example, it does not follow that the journalist is morally innocent of defamation. Similarly, if a reporter invents facts and includes them in a story, the fact that this dishonesty is not illegal does not make it morally acceptable. We are opposed to enforcing many of these moral requirements by law, but legal protections that permit irresponsible journalism do not imply that journalists have no moral responsibility. Quite the reverse is true: freedom from legal constraints is a special privilege that demands increased awareness of moral obligation.

*Keeping the Moral and the Legal Distinct.* The need to keep the moral and the legal distinct can be further illustrated by returning to the Tavoulareas case and examining some reactions to it by journalists. *The New York Times* published a column by Anthony Lewis in which he wrote: "As it happens, I personally thought the Tavoulareas story was an overblown and unconvincing tale not worth the play or space. *But.* . . . The press could not operate with any semblance of freedom if judges made a practice of second-guessing editorial decisions."[24] This comment is typical of dozens we have seen in the press: it moves from a negative moral evaluation to a "but" transition, followed by a positive evaluation of the freedoms the press should enjoy under the law. Many journalists typically address the issues in this way: they argue that a news story and the reporter's performance may be seriously flawed, but neither the product nor the conduct must be subject to legal sanctions because of the threat to freedom of expression. This conclusion supposedly settles the issue.

Journalists often judge the work of their colleagues "acceptable" when they do not admire it, or even respect it, because of the overwhelming importance they attach to press freedoms and because moral standards seem trivial by comparison. A column by Haynes Johnson on the Tavoulareas case published one week after the decision provides an example.[25] Johnson's initial premise resembles ours in the previous section: The press has "historically" been granted an "extraordinary legal license to examine and report, criticize and praise," deriving from "the touchstone of First Amendment jurisprudence." Johnson then writes as if this legal protection were also a moral license. He defends muckraking, which he asserts to have "relentlessly exposed pervasive corruption"; even if the work of the muckraker "offends and startles," there is "nothing to fear," because it may serve to wake up "absent-minded citizens." There is not a word in this column about the press's responsibilities for moral evaluation or for any form of self-restraint.

We should not overstate our thesis that there is a certain moral blindness in journalism. When a moral violation is egregious and the absence of a legal violation or legal threat is clear, the press and the public often recognize the importance of the distinction between morality and law. For example, when Janet Cooke fabricated a story about juvenile drug abuse that wound up costing the city of Washington thousands of dollars in resources and even more emotional anguish, her action was not illegal, nor was the negligence of her editors. But few argued at the time that her action was not seriously irresponsible or that her editors' actions were not negligent merely because they did not fit legal categories of responsibility and negligence. This case—one of the most publicized examples of irresponsible journalism in recent years—was never cast in legal terms, but the lack of an applicable criminal statute did not deter a judgment that some form of punishment was appropriate. To this breach of trust we can add dozens of other categories, some more subtle than others, where the legalities are trivial and the moral problems significant. At one time or another, most of them have been addressed thoughtfully in the press, but they are not the subject of sufficient attention, and much of the attention they attract is not sufficiently thoughtful.

We have noted that legal innocence does not presuppose moral innocence, but it also deserves notice that guilt under the law does not presuppose moral guilt. A single example will illustrate both points. For a long time before the Foreign Corrupt Practices Act was signed by President Jimmy Carter (on December 20, 1977), slush funds, bribes, and so on, had not been illegal for American corporations dealing with foreign governments. Such conduct had often been examined by journalists, however, because it seemed morally problematic.[26] Journalists, like almost everyone else, recognized that bribery was not morally right simply because it was legally permissible. However, long after this very stringently worded legislation was enacted (some say as an overreaction to Watergate), an intense debate continues to surround the act's implications because of the way it has limited American business's ability to compete in countries where paying bribes to win contracts is considered acceptable. Many today believe there is nothing unethical or corrupt in these now illegal acts.[27]

We do not mean to dismiss legal considerations as trivial in the affairs of journalists. *The Alton* (Illinois) *Telegraph* had to file for bankruptcy to pay legal fees and a settlement in a libel case just before the 1982 jury decision in Tavoulareas.[28] In the end, however, we believe that moral evaluations of the press are no less significant than legal evaluations and that moral problems are far more pervasive in journalism, with a greater impact on the conduct of the press's daily affairs. Every encounter and story in journalism has a moral dimension: reporter–source relations, editing a tape, securing consent to publish sensitive material, and deciding whom to or whom not to interview are moral matters, which—perhaps because they are so pervasive—are easy to neglect.

## Morality: Its Virtues and Its Rules

This book is about morality, but we have not yet said what we mean by *morality*. This word denotes culturally transmitted rules of right and wrong conduct that establish the basic terms of social life. Because the rules are pervasively acknowledged and shared in a culture, morality is not merely a matter of what a person subjectively believes. That is, individuals do not create their morality by making their own rules, and "a morality" cannot be purely a personal policy or code. Sometimes morality is cynically or frivolously dismissed, as if it were no more significant than superstition, but this claim is untenable. Morality is absolutely essential to social stability and the preservation of human decency, and the fact that it is sometimes ignored serves only to emphasize its significance.

Morality in this sense is different from *ethical theory* and *moral philosophy,* which are synonymous terms referring to systematic reflection on morality. Moral philosophers reflect on social practices in order to bring them into a unified, clear, and consistent package of action guides.

*Rules as Specifications of Duties and Rights.* Moral philosophy also formulates principles to help develop and evaluate moral beliefs and arguments. All rights, duties, and obligations are based on these principles, most of which are already present in public discourse, but usually in an imprecise form. Fairness is an example. Any reader of editorials and op-ed articles will frequently encounter appeals to fairness—for example, in considering the fairness of the tax system. Editorial writers and columnists are not expected to analyze the concept of fairness and the rules of fairness with philosophical depth and precision. Their claims and conclusions are usually left at an intuitive or common-sense level. The reason is that in the brief analyses typical of journalism, basic claims can only be presupposed rather than defended by lengthy, well-developed theories.

Consider as an example a comment by CBS Chairman Thomas Wyman about cable TV network owner and entrepreneur Ted Turner, who at the time was considering a hostile financial bid for ownership of CBS: "He [Turner] is not qualified because he doesn't have the conscience. When what you are broadcasting goes out to 70 million people, you better be thinking about something broader than the things I think occupy his thinking, and that includes money."[29] This comment typifies the moral criticism found in journalism. Wyman is, in effect, saying that Turner does not have either the character or the sense of responsibility required to run a network. Such comments are generally made without providing any supporting analysis or, as in this case, any idea of what conscience, character, or responsibility mean to Wyman.

This brevity or lack of analysis and supporting argument also typifies government in its dealings with the press. Wyman's comment about Turner derived from a context in which CBS sought to thwart Turner's hostile takeover bid by questioning whether Turner was fit to receive a transfer of CBS's broadcast license from the Federal Communications Commission. The FCC had routinely denied license applications in the past on grounds of deficiencies in moral character.[30] A criminal record, for example, generally was sufficient as a test of moral unfitness, but broader sets of criteria would be used as well. The underlying idea was that people who cheat, perjure themselves, and so on, are not likely to be responsible station owners and should therefore be disqualified. However, over the years it became clear that the FCC had no well-informed, systematic criteria or tests, and the role of these character judgments diminished. Now the agency is more narrowly concerned about whether a candidate would lie to the commission or otherwise violate its rules. But even under the narrower conception, the FCC still has no carefully drawn criteria or tests that inform its moral judgments.

The job of moral philosophy is to transcend moral intuition and purely contextual judgments by defining with precision such notions as conscience, responsibility, and fairness, without oversimplification or excessive abstraction. One objective of an ethics for journalism is proper interpretation of rules of conduct directed at the amelioration of specific professional problems. These rules are generally—although not necessarily—rules of duty, and they are often accompanied by correlative rights. Problems often arise over the demands made by rules about freedom, respect for privacy, fairness, avoidance of harm, and the like, and over how to handle situations in which the rules are vague. Because abstract rules cannot anticipate all possible situations, they must leave appropriate latitude for judgment and thus potentially for disagreement. Like many matters in life, sound judgment in applying rules is as vital as the rules themselves. (*Rules,* as we use the term, are statements either of duties or of rights that may or may not be formally recognized in a code of professional ethics; *responsibilities* are generally established by the rules of duty.)

Imagine, for example, a newspaper attempting to frame rules that specify when it will and will not publish confidential information obtained from sources. The bare fact that the information is confidential is not a sufficient reason to rule out publication. Publication is sometimes warranted by reasons that outweigh the standard reasons for protection. Conversely, there is no warrant for rules declaring that it is fair to publish all the confidential information a reporter can unearth. *The Washington Post* in 1971 briefly followed the so-called Bradlee rule (named for Benjamin C. Bradlee, the editor who devised it). This rule decreed that a maximal effort be made to identify all sources by name in one-on-one interviews and that press briefings be for direct attribution (or the *Post* reporter would leave). The rule was a stab at one aspect of source confidentiality. It was quickly dropped, however, because it was too confining and because other newspapers did not adopt it. The Bradlee rule tried to cover too much and demanded too much, although it was appropriate for many journalist–source relationships. A subtler, more selective rule of confidentiality was needed.

Newspapers should have a policy—neither too specific nor too vague—governing matters such as permissible use of confidential information, and they probably should also have procedural rules or guidelines that specify how editors and reporters should decide whether and how to use confidential information. We will explore various guidelines as we proceed, but first we will explore the concept of virtue, which some moral philosophers see as substantially different from and more important than rules.

*Virtues and Character.* In the midst of the 1984 presidential campaign, columnist Richard Cohen wrote that Vice-President George Bush "has consistently shown a lack of character," something "reprehensible in a politician, frightening in a president."[31] Cohen wrote that Bush was arrogant and untruthful, confusing "truth and political expediency" and in various ways "stretching the truth." "To Bush," Cohen said, "truth is the sum of the votes on Election Day." We are not concerned with whether Cohen was right about the vice-president, but we are interested in character traits such as truthfulness and arrogance. Cohen is correct when he says we should expect good character in our national leaders, and the same expectations are justified for anyone in whom we regularly place trust.

One ironic example of a failure of character involved a writer who submitted a book manuscript to a publisher titled *Telling Right from Wrong*.[32] Along with the manuscript he also submitted a letter by the respected philosopher Robert Nozick endorsing the book. Although the publisher received rave reviews from those who read the manuscript, it turned out that the letter from Nozick was forged by the author in an attempt to get his book accepted. There is something more than faintly odd about a man who writes a book about how to tell right from wrong but lacks the character to act according to his own prescription. Even if we admire his intellect, he seems untrustworthy and dishonest. In this case knowledge has failed to enrich character.

The language of both *character* and *virtue* sometimes sounds ridiculously prim, as journalists occasionally delight in pointing out. Thus, Henry Allen writes that " 'Character' is one of those horrible Victorian virtues that makes you think of cold baths, savings accounts, the Protestant work ethic, self-sacrifice, manhood, duty and so on in a list of everything we though we'd ripped out of American culture like a weed."[33] However, despite their prissy connotations, *character* and *virtue* are accurate and appropriate terms for discussing moral behavior. Moreover, whether or not they recognize the nature of the appeal, editorial writers often use these concepts in stating their cases. For example, in an editorial on news credibility, *USA Today* said that the "so-called crisis of [news] credibility has been self-inflicted. With accuracy, balance, sensitivity, humility, and humor, those who bring the news to the nation can heal themselves."[34] Here we have an overt appeal to a list of virtues, and for sound reasons. Even journalists who are repelled by virtue language would probably agree that the public is better served when journalists perform well because of good character than because of sanctions, threats, rules, laws, regulations, and the like.

There is nothing novel about a virtue-based approach to professional responsibility, as the following example of virtue-based advice for physicians illustrates. In 1959 a Harvard anesthesiologist named Henry Beecher was deeply troubled by numerous experiments that physicians had performed on human subjects. Beecher was convinced that rules, regulations, and threats, if used to restrict experimentation in medicine, were "more likely to do harm than good." He argued that physicians needed to be more sensitive to sound training in scientific methodology and to the abiding importance of cultivating a virtuous character.[35] The most reliable safeguard against abuses in research involving human subjects, he proposed, is "the presence of an intelligent, informed, conscientious, compassionate, responsible researcher."[36] Accordingly, Beecher recommended educating physicians through a virtue-based rather than a rule- or duty-based ethic—an approach that may prove to be as sound for journalists as for doctors.

But what do we mean by virtue and character, and how do these concepts play an important role in our arguments about morality and virtue? A virtue, as we use the term, is a beneficial disposition, habit, sentiment, or trait, and a moral virtue is a fixed disposition to do what is morally commendable, which entails a desire to act according to moral principle. Almost all professions have virtues that are keys to success in the profession but are not moral virtues. Philip Dougherty, in his advertising column in *The New York Times*, quoted a member of Beber Silverstein and Partners to the effect that the key to their success in advertising is found in the virtues of "tenacity, talent, and perseverance."[37] These dispositions no doubt are virtues in business, but they are different from moral virtues such as respectfulness, kindness, gratitude, and benevolence. These latter virtues are fundamental to moral behavior, while the first set is fundamental to success in business.

Nora Boustany, who reports from Lebanon for *The Washington Post*, provided a striking account of how different people respond when moral and business virtues like those quoted by Dougherty come into conflict. She wrote as follows:

Television cameras that had been set up outside the hotel to film [Anglican envoy Terry] Waite crossing the street from a news agency office caught the attention of a militiaman standing by an earth mound nearby. He fired a shot at nothing in particular. The driver of a yellow-and-black Austin happened to be driving down the street. He was killed instantly.

Meanwhile, the fighting got worse—preventing rescue workers from getting near the car. Goskun Aral, a Turkish photographer working for the French Sipa agency, joined Visnews soundman Ali Moussa, a Lebanese, in a rescue effort. They dragged [an] injured man, Raja Fuleihan, an administrator at the American University Hospital, from the car under a hail of machinegun fire. *Other photographers displayed a different kind of courage. They braved the shooting and clicked away at their colleagues.*[38]

Aral and Moussa, whose good character provided their guide to action, did not need to stop and think. They acted to save a life at considerable risk to themselves. The other photographers displayed courage (which may be a moral virtue as well as a professional virtue) solely in the service of their professional goals. Saving a life meant less to them than getting the pictures.

Virtuous traits of all kinds are especially significant in crises and in environments such as journalism that are often too pressured to permit prolonged and careful reflection. By cultivating moral virtues, doing what is right in these situations can become a matter of course rather than a conflicted debate over how to interpret rules whose meaning and application may be less than clear. No one can be expected to possess all the moral virtues or to behave virtuously with complete consistency, but some virtues such as honesty and trustworthiness are fundamental to the notion of a morally virtuous character. If a single incident of moral failure were all we had to go on, we could not say that a person lacks character, because we need a pattern of action to justify such a judgment. At most we can say that a person made an error, which is an assessment of an action rather than character. Even several blameworthy errors do not necessarily indicate a failure of character.

Our arguments suggest that a person's character is good or bad, virtuous or vicious, praiseworthy or blameworthy, depending on the particular virtues or vices he or she possesses. But which virtues should journalists cultivate? To answer this question, contrast for a moment journalists with St. Francis, who was admired for the tenderness and compassion exhibited in his spontaneous displays of affection for others—such as embracing a leper or giving away his only blanket on a cold night. These virtues may be appropriate for a saint, but they are not the ones that leap to mind when deciding which virtues should be exhibited by reporters and editors. Rather, virtues like fairness, truthfulness, trustworthiness, and nonmalevolence (avoiding harm) come to mind. We should not look, however, for some finite list expressing the traits of virtuous journalists. Whereas our table of contents provides a list of the major virtues that we believe are essential for journalists, this list should not be considered exhaustive.

As we hinted earlier, many writers in contemporary moral theory are undecided about whether their arguments are best expressed in terms of virtues or in terms of duties or rights. Although our book is titled *The Virtuous Journalist*, and the chapter titles are cast in virtue language, we do not mean to imply that virtues can or should replace rights and duties. The virtuous journalist acknowledges the execution of duties and respect for the rights of others as fundamental matters in moral conduct. These categories can all be used profitably in discussions of journalism ethics.

Whichever category is used, however, the standard of moral scrutiny must not be so high that the expectations for conduct are that the journalist be heroic or saintly. The rather heroic (even if flawed) character of *New York Times* reporter Sydney Schanberg and his even more extraordinary assistant, Dith Pran—as depicted in the film *The Killing Fields*, based on their wartime experiences in Cambodia—is certainly praiseworthy, but such character, while admirable, is not morally required. A virtue-based or duty-based ethics for journalism must be within reach of ordinary persons. It is not always easy to divide the moral life into the ordinary and the extraordinary, but if we were to forgo this distinction entirely, we would either set impossibly high standards or give up on the possibility of setting any standards at all.

A further word of caution is in order at this point. No system of ethics can provide full, ready-made solutions to all the perplexing moral problems that confront us, in life or in journalism. A reasoned and systematic approach to these issues is all that can be asked, while appreciating that practical wisdom and sound judgment are indispensable components of the moral life. The absence of neat solutions may seem to prop up the views of those who are skeptical or cynical about the possibility of journalism ethics, but such views are based on the false premise that the world is a tidy place of truth and falsity, right and wrong, without the ragged edges of uncertainty and risk. The converse is the case: Making moral judgments and handling moral dilemmas require the balancing of often ill-defined competing claims, usually in untidy circumstances.

## Fairness

Moral concepts like fairness exist to handle situations in which claims are pressed by parties with conflicting interests. As the eighteenth-century philosopher David Hume argued, there would be no point to having rules of fairness if society were not composed of persons in competition and conflict. These rules of fairness—or justice—serve to strike a balance between conflicting interests and claims that repeatedly occur in society.[39] Like moral rules generally, rules of fairness function to ameliorate or counteract the tendency for things to go wrong in human relationships.

Although this pragmatic vision is well suited to our examination of journalistic fairness, the concept of fairness is so general as to be almost worthless for balancing conflicting interests unless specific criteria of fairness and unfairness are presented for specific contexts. A person, group, or institution has been treated fairly when accorded what is due or owed under specific rules, such as those governing food stamp allocation, medicare coverage, plagiarism, allocation of exotic medical resources, or admission procedures for universities. The problem is that these specific rules themselves rely on, and may be evaluated in terms of, more abstract moral principles such as equality of persons, nondiscriminatory treatment, compensatory justice, and retributive justice. Without both the general and the more specific rules, we could not adequately evaluate alleged violations of fairness or justice in contexts of professional ethics.

As one would expect, the many general and specific rules of fairness applicable to journalism are often ill defined. One example is the so-called Fairness Doctrine (see pp. 221–24), which invokes federal authority in the United States to ensure that broadcasters make editorial decisions that allow equal time to opposing political candidates and to ensure that coverage of controversial issues is balanced. Here *equal time* and *balance* are terms of fairness, and they need conceptual and moral analysis for us to grasp the nature of the Fairness Doctrine and the moral controversy that surrounds it. This (legal) doctrine has often been criticized as (morally) unfair, because—however noble its intent—it may have the practical effects of penalizing the broadcast media for good investigative reporting and of giving free air time to politicians and public figures who do not deserve it.[40] Words like *penalizing* and *deserve* are also terms of fairness that need careful analysis.

Issues of fairness in journalism encompass impartial treatment, bias, incompleteness, imbalance, and numerous similar subjects. Israeli journalist Ze'ev Chafets has accused the American press of unfairness in virtually all of these forms in its reporting on the Middle East, especially regarding the 1982 Israeli invasion of southern Lebanon. In an unusually detailed fashion he argues both that the reporting does not place events in their historical context and that it suffers from various political biases.[41] Chafets's allegations are typical of a larger set of concerns about unfairness that have long troubled thoughtful journalists and their critics. But, unlike Chafets, many who criticize the press for being unfair and who proclaim the need for fairness in media, tend to be vague about the nature of the unfair bias and subjectivity that they claim to detect.

We do not mean either to dismiss critics or to excuse journalists. An unfortunate fact about contemporary journalism is that readers or viewers are often left with too little information either to judge the fairness of a story or to evaluate a charge of unfairness contained in the story. Consider the following example. In late 1984, Marlys Harris wrote an exposé in *Money* magazine on the broker–client relationship at Merrill Lynch, titled "The Stumbling Herd." Harris developed the thesis that Merrill Lynch engages in systematic unfairness in fiduciary relationships with its clients. In particular, she charged, that "Commissions and other incentives encourage Merrill Lynch brokers to push what the company needs to sell—not necessarily what the client needs to buy. And the firm's phenomenal growth has come at the cost of deteriorating customer service and increased back-office botches."[42] The story met with a predictably hostile reaction from Merrill Lynch, which labeled it unfair for a variety of reasons.[43]

Irrespective of its truth or falsity, balance or bias, Harris's story will seem persuasive to almost any reader of *Money* who lacks detailed inside information about Merrill Lynch. Harris adroitly surveys the conflicts of interest that can occur in brokerage houses, quotes Merrill Lynch analysts, and claims to have documented numerous problems. But the ordinary reader has no realistic way of knowing whether Harris's presentation—beneath its convincing surface—reflects the facts in a fair way. It is far from evident that all of the relevant facts are presented so that any evidence that might conflict with Harris's general thesis is adequately treated or that the article is balanced in presenting the views of all the parties involved. Our own assessment is that although much of the article is accurate, it is not balanced or adequately disposed to giving the brokerage house's side of the story.

Problems of this kind that turn on completeness are common in journalism. Even "Doonesbury" cartoonist Garry Trudeau once found himself embroiled in controversy over a sequence of strips in which he depicted Frank Sinatra as a foul-mouthed friend of mobsters undeserving of the honorary degree that he had received from an institute of technology. Trudeau had placed a picture of Sinatra and a friend in the strip with the following caption under it: "Dr. Francis Sinatra uplifting the spirits of alleged human Aniello Dellacroce, later charged with the murder of Gambino family member Charley Calise." Trudeau did not mention, however, that Dellacroce had been acquitted of the criminal charge. Editors at several papers, including *The New York Daily News, The San Francisco Chronicle, The Philadelphia Inquirer, The Chicago Tribune,* and *The*

*Washington Post,* either refused to run the strip, altered it, or ran simultaneous stories to distance themselves from Trudeau's characterization. Editors who deleted the reference to Dellacroce invoked a criterion of fairness that turned on the concept of completeness of statement. As the managing editor of *The New York Daily News,* James Willse, put it, "If you say someone is charged with a crime in the past and don't give the disposition of the case, that's not complete reporting."[44] There were additional complaints about the use of stereotypes and the inappropriateness of comic strips as a means of making editorial comment.[45]

Questions of fairness may arise about virtually any form or piece of journalism. Setting aside specific questions of fairness or unfairness of the Harris article or the Trudeau strip, our intent is to call attention to a range of questions about fairness to sources, fairness to the facts, fairness to the general public, fairness to special publics, fairness to subjects of stories, fairness to employers, and so on. These questions and others raised above indicate the sweeping, morally generic character of fairness. To answer them requires analysis of concepts such as truth, facts, balanced coverage, bias, understanding, impartiality, privacy, harm, and public benefit. Much of the rest of this book treats these problems of fairness, although the umbrella word *fairness* itself seldom appears. The same is true of *competence,* another umbrella notion that we group in this first chapter with freedom, virtue, rights, and duties as the abstract foundations of our moral structure.

## Competence in the Craft

Former CBS News President Richard Salant once said, "No two people, if they took 25 minutes [of videotape] and edited it down, would get the same two minutes."[46] Salant was probably right, but it does not follow that any two-minute segment is as fair, representative, or competently edited as any other two-minute segment. Tape can be edited accurately, fairly, and objectively, or it can fail to meet these criteria. The editing cannot justifiably be called competent unless they are satisfied, which suggests that moral criteria are embedded in our very conception of competent journalistic practice. That is, standards such as fairness and accuracy are moral dimensions of competence.

Many professional standards and codes of ethics make an open appeal to the concept of competence, even if the word *competence* is not specifically used in the code. "Be competent" may seem such an obvious rule that it scarcely deserves attention, but it is also among the more frequently violated norms of journalistic practice. Lying, conflict of interest, malevolence, unfairness, and lack of respect for persons are, quantitatively, minor moral problems compared to incompetence. For example, one criterion of competence that reporters often fail to satisfy is the ability to place a distance between personal beliefs and what is being reported.

A different but related problem of competence arises when reporters fail to keep their notes and writing or phrasing sufficiently distant from source materials. Roy Peter Clark reported the story of a *Miami News* reporter who wrote an article on stock car racing that was reprinted in an anthology Clark edited titled "Best Newspaper Writing 1982." The reporter, Tom Archdeacon, borrowed about a hundred words almost verbatim from a book written by Jerry Bledsoe of *The Greensboro Daily News and Record*. Bledsoe called the apparent plagiarism to Clark's attention. Clark responded that "Archdeacon told his editors that he admired Bledsoe's book, that he had used it for background on Linda Vaughn [a beauty queen], and that under deadline he had confused Bledsoe's words for his own in more than 100 pages of sloppily taken notes."[47]

The American Society of Newspaper Editors (ASNE) sponsored the competition in which Archdeacon's article was selected for publication. Its board, as quoted by Clark, issued a statement that said: "While what happened is a journalistic misdemeanor and not a felony—and appears to be a mistake rather than plagiarism—the board deplores that such gross carelessness and sloppiness could be part of the working procedure of such a talented writer."[48] Assuming that the ASNE board is right that there was no intentional plagiarism, when they accuse Archdeacon of gross carelessness and sloppiness they are describing incompetence with a moral dimension.

There is, of course, no single criterion of competence in journalism, moral or otherwise. If someone says, "Peter Jennings is incompetent," one might ask, "Incompetent to do what?" To make intelligent news judgments? To convince viewers? To write unbiased copy? Here we need to distinguish between general competence as a journalist and a specific competence in journalism. General competence refers to the ability to perform the myriad tasks that are basic to any journalist's responsibilities. Specific competence requires a specific context and a defined task. Although criteria of general competence are not well established in journalism, some criteria can be listed with assurance. Any generally competent journalist must be able to recognize a story (the intrinsic importance of an event, its inherent human interest, its novelty, its consequences, etc.), must be able to use language well enough to convey the story adequately to readers or television viewers, must be able to organize and edit copy so that a story can fit into a limited space in a newspaper or a limited time slot on television or radio, must be able to check facts quickly and accurately, and must be able to weigh the various elements of a story so that they are fairly represented in the final product.

Copy editors—who cut news stories to size; evaluate their coherence; check facts; correct grammar, syntax, errors of style, and organization; and write headlines—must have the same qualities to do their jobs competently. So must reporters, columnists, and editors with broader responsibility. But these criteria must be supplemented by others to describe competence in specific cases. Investigative reporters, for example, must be able to gain access to persons and information that are not easily available. Columnists must have insights and sources that make their analyses and opinions worthwhile. Editors with responsibility for planning coverage and making judgments about how stories are played in the paper or on the air must have a sure grasp of where stories fit in the broad sweep of events and what they are worth in the context of history and the day's news. This list is not meant to be a comprehensive set of criteria for competence. It merely suggests what is entailed by the notion of general and specific competence in journalism.

We indicated earlier that moral qualities are intrinsic to journalistic competence, an idea that apparently conflicts with the common assumption that simply possessing the required professional skills makes a professional competent. To emphasize that competence is not limited to these skills, consider how a reporter should answer the following questions: How many credible sources does a journalist need before reporting something as factual? Is one very reliable source sufficient? Must a reporter have at least two? Three? Must they be independent? Adversarial? During a televised symposium on national security and the press, Lyle Denniston of *The Baltimore Sun* took the position that one reliable source would be enough to publish secret government information on a CIA-sponsored covert operation.[49] Dan Rather of CBS, Jack Nelson of *The Los Angeles Times,* and others disagreed, arguing for at least two and generally three reliable sources for that kind of story. Despite the unavailability of a simple or definitive answer to these questions, any answer depends on taking a view about what constitutes a responsible use of sources. Moral criteria of responsibility are clearly linked in this example to general considerations of journalistic competence.

Incompetence in journalism therefore often results from moral failure, not merely a lack of professional rigor or experience. Here is an example involving an incompetent use of sources. When UPI reported on Israel's use of a "vacuum bomb" on August 7, 1982, it attributed its information to a U.S. congressional delegation. But *The New Republic* reported a few weeks later that "the official Congressional delegation turned out to be neither official, nor Congressional, nor a delegation."[50] The group was fraudulent, and so was the bomb; there was no such thing as a vacuum bomb. Nevertheless, UPI's hundreds of clients received a story on August 7 describing how such a weapon flattened an eight-story building in West Beirut.[51]

*The New Republic* offered this version of how the bomb story got on the wire: "[Brenda] Pillars [a member of the self-styled delegation] says the UPI dispatch stemmed from a conversation at Beirut's Commodore Hotel as a few members of the 'delegation' chatted with a few members of the press. Susan Hedges, who said she was doing research for [Sen. James] McClure (she was not), was discussing a bomb she claimed to have seen the previous day. Pillars says the report resulted from a misperception of a reporter."[52] A little checking into the nature of the "delegation," the credentials of Susan Hedges, or those of the leader of the group, Franklin Lamb, who had a record of fraud and deceit, would have saved UPI the considerable embarrassment of sending out corrections that never caught up with the original story. The failure to investigate Lamb and his group adequately is an unambiguous example of incompetence on the part of the reporter, and possibly the editors as well. It is no less an example of a moral than a professional failure.

A standard approach to this kind of problem is to say that a newspaper should have a policy to deal with such situations. However, the implication of this recommendation often seems to be that any among a wide range of possible policies will suffice, as long as there is some consistent policy to follow. We agree that policies may justifiably vary, but to adopt a policy just to have guidelines may provide more of an excuse than a morally satisfactory response. A policy can be a moral instrument, because it can be a means of expressing what counts as responsible conduct—in this instance, responsible use of sources and responsible corroboration of claims—and it is possible to argue in a morally principled way about the kinds of policies that are acceptable.

Because of its critical public-service function, the level of acceptable performance should be set fairly high for journalism. But it is equally important that it not be set too high. When CBS Cable went out of business in September 1982, a Wall Street analyst said, "CBS designed a solid-gold Cadillac when what might have worked was a Chevrolet."[53] Among CBS's mistakes was a nightly interview series and a series on modern history by Bill Moyers of a quality so high that advertising revenues could not be raised to support the enterprise.

This book is not designed to provide criteria for general levels of professional competence in journalism. Its purpose is to examine, analyze, and illuminate moral problems that arise in reporting and editing news.

The chapters that follow are conceived partly to serve that end, partly to give substance to the idea of fairness in journalism, and partly to put before the profession and the public a set of virtues that we think are essential to the ethical practice of journalism.

NOTES

1. David Broder, "Newsmen Work for the Reader," *The International Herald Tribune,* July 21, 1983, op-ed page.

2. George Crile, private correspondence, January 28, 1985.

3. Meg Greenfield, "The Morality of Bitburg," *The Washington Post,* April 29, 1985, p. A11.

4. Leonard W. Levy, *Emergence of a Free Press* (New York: Oxford University Press, 1985), p. 290.

5. Quoted in ibid., p. 110.

6. Ibid., p. 112.

7. Daniel Schorr, *The New York Times,* January 16, 1979, p. A15.

8. See Levy, *Emergence of a Free Press,* pp. 212–13.

9. Patrick Tyler, "Mobil Chief Sets Up Son in Venture," *The Washington Post,* November 30, 1979, p. A1.

10. Oliver Gasch, *Tavoulareas* v. *Washington Post,* U.S.D.C. District of Columbia (80-3032), 9 *Media Law Reporter,* 1554–55.

11. George E. MacKinnon, *Tavoulareas* v. *Washington Post,* U.S. Court of Appeals for the District of Columbia (83-1605), p. 4. See also William P. Tavoulareas, *Fighting Back* (New York: Simon and Schuster, 1986).

12. J. Skelly Wright, *Tavoulareas* v. *Washington Post,* U.S. Court of Appeals for the District of Columbia (83-1605), Dissent, pp. 48–49.

13. See Al Kamen and Eleanor Randolph, "Court Urged to Reinstate Libel Verdict," *The Washington Post,* October 4, 1985, p. A7.

14. Ibid. See also, for interpretation, Stuart Taylor, Jr., "New Ruling on Libel," *The New York Times,* April 11, 1985, p. 10.

15. See Stephen Wermiel, "Attention Shifts to How Washington Post Should Fight Libel Ruling Reinstatement," *The Wall Street Journal,* April 12, 1985, p. 10; and Earl M. Maltz, "Press Should Put Its House in Order," *The Philadelphia Inquirer,* May 4, 1985, p. 9-A.

16. Alex S. Jones, "Editors Voice Dismay at Libel Ruling," *The New York Times,* April 10, 1985, p. 9; and Editorial, "Freelance Libel Law," *The New York Times,* April 13, 1985, p. 16. See also Eleanor Randolph, "Editors, Lawyers Say Libel Award Against Post May Alter Journalism," *The Washington Post,* April 11, 1985, p. A3.

17. Editorial, "Free Speech," *The Wall Street Journal,* June 19, 1985, p. 6 (European edition).

18. Theodore Roosevelt, Address on the Laying of the Cornerstone of the House Office Building, Washington, D.C., April 14, 1906.

19. As quoted by Eleanor Randolph, "Ex-CBS Official Assails TV's Role in TWA Crisis," *International Herald Tribune,* August 2, 1985, p. 3.

20. John Stuart Mill, *On Liberty* (Chicago: Henry Regnery, 1955), Chapter 2.

21. See "Reporter Ordered to Testify in Rockland Trust Trial," *The Boston Globe*, May 17, 1985, p. 83.

22. ABC advertisement, "What You *Won't* See on Television," *USA Today*, April 9, 1985, sec. D, p. 2; *The New York Times*, April 10, 1985, p. 27; *The Washington Post*, April 16, 1985, p. A12; and *The Wall Street Journal*, April 18, 1985, p. 28.

23. Scott Wood, in "Free for All," *The Washington Post*, April 20, 1985, p. A21. See the original article by Sam Zagoria, "The Ethics of Printing Point Spreads," *The Washington Post*, April 10, 1985, p. A22.

24. Anthony Lewis, "Getting Even," *The New York Times*, April 11, 1985, p. A23. Emphasis added.

25. Haynes Johnson, "A Ruling the Muckrakers Would Decry," *The Washington Post*, April 14, 1985, p. A3 (paraphrase and quotation of Judge J. Skelly Wright, in part).

26. See 1975 stories and editorials, for example, in *The Wall Street Journal*, May 19 and July 14, 1975; *Newsweek* (International Edition), May 26, 1975; *Business Week*, June 23, 1975; *International Herald Tribune*, May 19 and 23, 1975; and *The New York Times*, August 24, 1975.

27. Mark Pastin and Michael Hooker, "Ethics and the Foreign Corrupt Practices Act," *Business Horizons* (December 1980), pp. 43–47.

28. *Time*, August 9, 1982, p. 43.

29. *USA Today*, March 14, 1985, Money section, p. 1.

30. See Elizabeth Tucker, "FCC Weighs 'Character' Issue," *The Washington Post*, May 22, 1985, p. D3.

31. Richard Cohen, "A Question of Character," *The Washington Post*, October 27, 1984, p. A19.

32. Timothy J. Cooney, *Telling Right from Wrong* (Buffalo: Prometheus, 1985), with an afterword by the author on the subject of the falsified letter.

33. Henry Allen, "Character Takes on Personality: A Victorian Virtue Is Trying to 'Find Itself' in the '80s," *The Washington Post*, January 5, 1986, p. D5.

34. Editorial, "Media Can Improve, but Laws Won't Do It," *USA Today*, April 12, 1984, sec. A, p. 12.

35. Henry K. Beecher, *Experimentation in Man* (Springfield, Ill.: Charles C. Thomas, 1959), pp. 15–17, 43–44, 50.

36. Henry K. Beecher, "Ethics and Clinical Research," *New England Journal of Medicine* 274 (June 1966): 1354–60, esp. 1354–55.

37. Philip H. Dougherty, "Beber Silverstein on Move," *The New York Times*, April 11, 1985, p. 45.

38. Nora Boustany, "A Lebanon Diary: Gathering News in the Heart of Darkness," *The Washington Post*, March 30, 1986, p. D3. Emphasis added.

39. David Hume, *A Treatise of Human Nature*, ed. by L. A. Selby-Bigge, rev. by P. H. Nidditch (Oxford: Clarendon Press, 1978), pp. 497ff.

40. See Milton Mueller, "Repeal of Fairness Doctrine by Enforcing It," *The Wall Street Journal*, April 2, 1985, p. 28.

41. Ze'ev Chafets, *Double Vision: How the Press Distorts America's View of the Middle East* (New York: William Morrow, 1985).

42. Marlys Harris, "The Stumbling Herd," *Money*, December 1984, p. 258.

43. See Letters to the Editor, *Money*, December 1984, p. 224.

44. See James Kelly, *Time*, June 24, 1985, p. 42.

45. See Sam Zagoria, "When Funnies Aren't Funny," *The Washington Post,* October 16, 1985, p. A22.

46. Eleanor Randolph, "Libel Jury Sees TV Outtakes," *The Washington Post,* October 24, 1984, p. A12.

47. Roy Peter Clark, "The Unoriginal Sin—How Plagiarism Poisons the Press," *Washington Journalism Review,* March 1983, 42–47.

48. Ibid.

49. "National Security and Freedom of the Press," from "The Constitution— That Delicate Balance," PBS, November 6, 1984.

50. Laurence Graftstein, "The Implosion Plot," *The New Republic,* September 6, 1982, pp. 8, 9.

51. UPI wire story on vacuum bomb in Beirut, August 7, 1982.

52. Graftstein, "Implosion Plot," p. 8.

53. As quoted in "The Cadillac Runs Out of Gas," *Time,* September 27, 1982, p. 65.

# Chapter 2

# Reaching for
# Truth

"Eyewitness News 7," a local program in New York, took out a full-page advertisement in *The New York Times* to present the following message:

> The truth is, there's nothing on television more important, more entertaining, more thrilling than the true human drama of the news. And because it's the most important part of your day, we're here to tell you the *truth*.[1]

This advertisement presumes, correctly, that reporting the truth is at the heart of the journalistic enterprise. Just as physicians and lawyers are morally required to be truthful with their patients and clients, journalists are morally obliged to deliver the truth to the public. But what does it mean for a news story to be true, and how demanding is the obligation to be truthful? Is it enough to report selected facts accurately, while omitting others that may be crucial to many viewers or readers? Is it enough to marshal facts to support a thesis that a more objective or a more balanced account would weaken? If a reporter's reconstruction of the facts conflicts with alternative versions that have a reasonable claim to reliability, is omitting all reference to those versions justified?

We think the answer to each of these questions is no, but our judgment does not entail that in reporting complicated stories journalists need to meet unrealistic criteria of accuracy, objectivity, completeness, and balance. Journalism cannot be entirely complete, always accurate, perfectly balanced, or totally objective. Moreover, the same standards of completeness, accuracy, balance, and objectivity do not apply to all stories or to all forms of journalism. But for a news report, feature, or opinion piece to be truthful, it must satisfy a reasonable standard under each of these categories.

Although the belief that readers have a right to truthful information from journalists is rarely challenged, and is mentioned in virtually all codes of journalism ethics, there is no clear consensus—and hardly any commentary—about the scope of that right. Often the focus is on the use of deception or the intrusion of bias, but there are many other problems related to truthfulness. There are, for example, questions about completeness. When a reporter writes a news story about health risks, how much should be reported about these risks? From another perspective, how much information can a reader or viewer absorb, and at what level of sophistication? There are also questions about the quality of information published or broadcast. For example, how much responsibility do journalists have for making sure the information is not unduly alarmist? And there are questions of knowledge. What does it entail for an article to be written in a sufficiently informed manner?

In the many right-to-know laws passed in recent years in the United States (e.g., the Freedom of Information Act; the Federal Insecticide, Fungicide, and Rodenticide Amendments and Regulations; the Truth-in-Lending Act; the Pension Reform Act; the Real Estate Settlement Procedures Act; the Federal Food, Drug, and Cosmetic Act; the Consumer Product Safety Act; and the Toxic Substances Control Act), provisions commonly require guidebooks, detailed explanations of what products are and how they work, and clearly worded warranties. The implicit and sometimes explicit message is that businesses and fiduciary agents have a moral and in some cases a legal obligation to disclose to the public information without which individuals could not adequately make decisions about matters such as their health, employment, and retirement.

A standard set this high, of course, is unattainable in journalism because of constraints, not the least of which are time and space. The obligations of journalists in reporting on important events fall somewhere between the poles of full disclosure capable of promoting an in-depth understanding and a cursory account of the bare facts. Just as a dentist cannot be held accountable for providing each patient with a course in dentistry before pulling a tooth, journalists cannot be expected to provide a graduate-level seminar through a newspaper article or a television documentary. But just as dentists and physicians are obliged to make sure that patients understand the implications of what is about to happen to them so that they have adequate grounds for consent or refusal, journalists are morally responsible for helping people adequately understand events and issues, especially those of substantial public interest.

We argue below that in covering issues and events about which the public has a need to know, stories should be *substantially complete,* should be presented so as to encourage an *objective understanding,* and should be as *balanced and accurate* as possible under the circumstances. Even major newspapers and networks have limited resources to commit to a story, and limited space and time. But as long as we take into consideration the constraints that contribute to setting those limits we can still inquire into the scope of the press's obligations.

## The Reasonable Reader Standard

What the press has a duty to report is roughly correlated with what the public has a need to know. To express this obligation concretely, we draw on a legal model known as "the reasonable person," which we have renamed "the reasonable reader." We assume this person to be equally reasonable when watching television.

This standard is designed to incorporate the common body of assumptions that the members of a society make about their fellow citizens in order to cooperate efficiently. For example, the reasonable-person standard provides a basis on which parties to contracts can avoid hidden misunderstandings. The reasonable person is never to be understood as a specific person or as the average person. As William Prosser has put it, "The courts have gone to unusual pains to emphasize the abstract and hypothetical character of this mythical person. He is not to be identified with any ordinary individual, who might occasionally do unreasonable things; he is a prudent and careful man who is always up to standard. . . . He is a personification of the community ideal of reasonable behavior, determined [e.g.] by the jury's social judgment."[2]

The legal litmus test under this standard for determining, for example, the extent of disclosure between a professional and a client is the "materiality"—that is, significance—of information to the decision-making process of the client.[3] The volume and type of information that should be provided are not matters of the professional's judgment, nor is there any need for expert testimony. The jury, using the reasonable-person standard, determines the reasonableness of the disclosure. A professional can be found negligent according to this standard, even if the disclosure was well within the established bounds of professional practice.[4]

We take a similar approach throughout this chapter in applying the reasonable-reader standard. The reasonable reader is to be understood from the point of view of a reader's needs rather than from the point of view of the routine practices or policies found in the media. The reasonable reader is a constructed composite of reasonable news consumers, as we collectively know them. This mythical person does not do unreasonable things or have unreasonable expectations and in this respect is the personification of the community ideal of an informed person—one who has certain informational needs of the sort that quality general-news media are designed to serve. The reasonable reader, then, is a person with needs for information about matters such as the risks, alternatives, and consequences of what is being reported. Using this general model, we argue for standards of completeness, accuracy, understanding, and objectivity that are designed to yield fair and responsible journalism that is, within attainable limits, impartial and objective.

Although we cannot provide an account of every category under which the reasonable reader seeks information, we can offer some guidance. We set aside the specialized reasonable reader of sections such as Sports, Business, and Science, because the reasonable reader with whom we are concerned here has no special expertise or sophistication. Our reasonable reader is a generalist and may be a Republican or a Democrat, a smoker or a nonsmoker, a sports lover or a sports hater.

To help make the concept more concrete, consider this example. In a first story about the nuclear accident at Three Mile Island in Pennsylvania, what would the reasonable reader living in California need to know and have a right to expect from a local newspaper? Initially there is a need to know what happened and what is known about the implications of what happened. The reasonable reader is not interested in the press's irrelevant comparisons to a film (The China Syndrome) that treats the subject of a nuclear accident in fictional form and was coincidentally released almost simultaneously with the Three Mile Island accident. The reasonable reader needs to know about the range of risk and whether there are similar nuclear plants in his or her local region where a similar event might occur. As the story develops more information will be needed about how the utility and the government are handling the aftermath of the accident, new information about the accident itself and its implications, how it affects the physical and mental health of people in the area, and the implications for the nuclear power industry in general.

In a story as complex as Three Mile Island, the reasonable reader's thirst for information could not be satisfied by a single story, except possibly in a major takeout when enough is known to write about it comprehensively. But if the press provides a regular flow of accurate and objective coverage, written understandably and with enough information to permit evaluations of the events or issues, then the reasonable-reader standard will be satisfied. Much the same standard could be applied to reporting for the specialized reasonable reader, except that more depth and sophistication are demanded. But the requirements of accuracy and objectivity are identical to those for the general reasonable reader.

The sections that follow elaborate on the reasonable reader's need for journalism that is accurate, objective, balanced, understandable, and substantially complete. These concepts are designed to be flexible because of the futility of trying to put an enterprise as broadly encompassing as journalism into a straitjacket of philosophical abstraction and prescription.

## Completeness

Given the constraints of publishing and broadcasting, it is futile to try to impose an inflexible standard of completeness that exceeds realistic demands of journalistic responsibility. We agree, however, with Alan Barth, a *Washington Post* editorial writer and civil libertarian, who wrote:

> Many a time in traveling around the country, I have picked up a strange newspaper in a strange city—and found myself almost completely cut off from news I wanted and needed to know of the larger world. It is disconcerting, for example, to read a wire story from Washington telling that the Supreme Court has decided a major case by a five-to-four division and then discover that this is *all* the story is going to tell about the decision; there is nothing to let one know which Justices were in the majority, nor what they said in their opinion, nor what views are expressed by the dissenters. How can readers form for themselves any intelligent judgment about the decision on the basis of such incomplete and inadequate reporting?[5]

To put in focus what we mean by a reasonable standard of journalistic completeness, consider the reporting on the 1977 debate in the United States over whether to build and deploy so-called neutron bombs—nuclear shells that kill by prompt radiation rather than blast, heat, and fallout. The national and international debate was needlessly confused by incomplete and misleading press reports that labeled the weapon a death ray that killed people while preserving property. *The Los Angeles Times* took note of the problem created by the press coverage in an editorial titled "Dr. Strangelove Is *Not* Loose":

There is a clear danger that [President Carter] will make a [deployment] *decision against a background of public confusion and misunderstanding* as to what the controversy is all about. The basic responsibility for this confusion lies at the door of the press and the broadcast media. . . . For the past month, stories describing the neutron bomb have almost universally described it as a weapon that will kill people through enhanced radiation while doing the least possible damage to surrounding real estate. *This is the truth, but not the whole truth.* It is misleading unless accompanied by the additional information that the new weapon would kill fewer people than would existing warheads, which it would replace in NATO's arsenal. As a result, there is a widespread public impression that the weapon is the brainchild of cold-blooded Pentagon planners who value the preservation of property above human life.[6]

We are not competent to evaluate conflicting technical claims about the respective kill radii of fusion and fission warheads of various sizes. (The neutron warhead is a fusion-type device, and the older ones stored in Western Europe are of the fission variety.) We also would not expect journalists to report such detailed evaluations in most stories. But in this case, by failing to explain the consequences of factors such as relative kill radii, much of the press coverage obscured rather than illuminated the issues. Reporters could easily have used straightforward language like that found in the *Los Angeles Times* editorial to explore the issues needing discussion and to satisfy a threshold criterion of completeness, thereby eliminating a bias from the coverage.

If we view the concept of completeness as a continuum with "no truth" at one end and "the whole truth"[7] at the other, the threshold standard that journalists should satisfy is *substantial completeness,* the point at which a reasonable reader's requirements for information are satisfied. A decision about precisely where to situate the threshold of substantial completeness on the continuum depends on practical, institutional, moral, political, and policy considerations. By providing substantially complete coverage, we mean that within the constraints of these competing values, as well as the availability of space, staff, and other resources, and the accessibility of sources and documents (we presume a professional level of resourcefulness in uncovering information that is not readily accessible), a news organization would, over the course of its coverage, publish enough information to satisfy the needs of an intelligent nonspecialist who wants to evaluate the situation.

Because each case of reporting and each institutional commitment to report is so different, we cannot give more precise content to this criterion without making it excessively demanding for many cases. Although it would be foolish to try to pinpoint a threshold line of substantial completeness, it is wrong to infer from the need to leave some latitude for informed disagreement that a standard of substantial completeness is arbitrary or entirely subjective. The concept of substantial completeness can be given substance and situated on our continuum by reference to specific goals, policies, and responsibilities. Once these considerations are specified, substantial completeness becomes a reasonable and achievable objective.

However, general moral requirements of substantial completeness in providing information do not arise in a social vacuum: We have a good idea of what salespersons, physicians, or professors should tell us about products, procedures, or scholarly research. We do not demand all the information such persons may have, but we need enough for the purpose at hand. Reasonably well-informed persons are qualified to judge when a responsible threshold of information has been provided (although sometimes they will not know enough to do so until after the fact). If a salesperson deceives customers by disclosing too little about a hazardous product, or a physician leaves a patient more panicked than enlightened by an abbreviated diagnosis and explanation of its implications, or a professor rambles and excludes important ideas or information, any reasonably well-informed person will recognize that a minimum threshold level of responsibility has not been met.

Journalists have analogous responsibilities. Consider two examples, one critical of the press and the other laudatory. Eleanor Holmes Norton gave an address to the American Society of Newspaper Editors in which she argued that American newspapers are doing a poor job of reporting on civil rights and related race and policy issues, despite a history of thorough and comprehensive reporting in the early days of the civil rights movement. A key element in her criticism was that the press has failed to keep up with the increasing complexities of the issues.[8] In general, this criticism seems justified. The press often looks at narrow policy questions, motivations and executive-branch officials, or spectacular cases involving affirmative action and comparable worth (such as *Bakke* and *Weber*), while losing sight of broader historical and cultural patterns of discrimination and hiring, which form the context for the policy debate. The consequence is that the public is not as well informed as it should be about issues concerning minorities, civil rights, and the relevant government policies.

By contrast, Alan Otten, a member of the Washington bureau of *The Wall Street Journal,* successfully handled one of the most complex, emotional, and perplexing moral problems of our day: the clash between women's rights and fetal rights in the controversy over abortion.[9] This is an issue with which we have considerable familiarity, and in our judgment Otten wrote a comprehensive, accurate, and pertinent summary in twenty-five column inches. He interviewed the right people, got their positions straight, placed the issue in the larger context of ethics and law, and in general wrote a piece that refutes the view that a complex issue cannot be treated well in relatively few column inches.

The problem in journalism is generally not space restrictions but rather how well complexity is handled in reducing a confusing mass of material to a comprehensible form. We will illustrate this point by considering in detail the press's coverage of the story of Baby Jane Doe, an infant born October 11, 1985, with spina bifida and additional defects in Port Jefferson, New York. The parents of this child initially rejected life-prolonging corrective surgery, based on evaluations provided by a neurologist at University Hospital, Stony Brook. Subsequently, right-to-life advocates and the U.S. government entered the case, intending to force corrective surgery and to gain access to Baby Jane Doe's medical records.[10]

Much of the coverage of this story demonstrates why it is inadequate for the general press to present complex issues of legitimate public interest without sufficient reference to a broader context. This happened in Baby Jane Doe's case because reporters often emphasized only those elements that were compelling in their human or political drama, while committing few resources to exploring the long-term social, philosophical, and medical implications of the situation. We can see how this occurred by examining the case from five different perspectives, each of which would be relevant to the concerns of the reasonable reader: (1) practical or decision-making, (2) political, (3) policy, (4) human interest, and (5) moral.

From a practical perspective, what could have been more important to the parents of Baby Jane Doe, or to parents who might face similar choices involving their own newborns, than the range of prognoses and available medical options in this and similar cases? In spina bifida infants, the prognosis after surgery can vary dramatically. Yet, with the exception of the Long Island daily *Newsday*, the many publications and television news programs we reviewed did not provide this basic information.[11] In their early coverage they printed only the judgment of the neurologist who advised the parents against surgery. By contrast, *Newsday* interviewed a neurosurgeon who had seen the child and who favored surgery (although he believed the parents were entitled to make the choice). Even in *Newsday*'s generally excellent coverage,[12] it never clearly emerged that the medical community was deeply divided about appropriate decisions and actions in cases of this kind. As it turned out, the baby, whose real name is Keri-Lynn, lived. As of this writing she is not a vegetable as the neurologist had predicted. Moreover, she might well have benefited substantially from early surgery, although what counts as a benefit is contestable in such cases.

The Baby Jane Doe story also had significant political implications. It became a cause célèbre both for the right-to-life movement, which provided substantial support for Ronald Reagan in both of his campaigns for the presidency, and for the Reagan administration, which sued to obtain access to Baby Jane Doe's medical records. The coverage of these political dimensions—which we reviewed by examining a wide range of media presentations—satisfactorily noted the broad political implications of the Reagan administration involvement but was missing critically important details. None of the newpapers and news magazines and none of the television news broadcasts, for example, quoted or adequately paraphrased the brief but relevant language of the Rehabilitation Act of 1973, the legislation on which the government based its case. The relevant sections of this act and their interpretation were the key considerations in assessing the legal merits of the government's case.

The Baby Jane Doe story also had major policy—as distinct from political—implications. Whether intimate family matters are appropriate subjects for public policy debate was then, and still is, a topic of considerable importance. By law and tradition, such therapy decisions are covered by rights of privacy, unless a legal challenge is mounted by a directly interested party, such as a parent or a physician. Should this view be revised? What role, if any, should the government play in decisions involving the life and death of defective newborns? Does the government have more of a right to participate if it provides funding for the hospital? This case raised these and other questions of broad public interest. Reporters are not responsible for answering such questions, but they should present the current state of the debate to the public better than they did in this case. With the exception of a "symposium" carried in *The New York Times*'s Week in Review,[13] such questions were barely addressed.

With respect to human concerns, the press did well in its reporting of the Baby Jane Doe story, as it often does with the human-interest elements of a story. The human dimensions were not only presented fully, but in a tasteful, fair, and compassionate manner. Among other things, the press was sensitive to the privacy concerns of the infant and her parents. At this writing, more than two years after the birth of the baby, the family's name has yet to be published or broadcast.

By contrast, the moral issues illustrated or sparked by the case were cast in highly simplistic terms, as if the tension were simply between absolutist right-to-life advocates and those who contend that parents have an absolute right to decide whether a defective newborn should live or die. The coverage failed to convey that perhaps the majority of philosophers and physicians who have reflected seriously on this issue are arrayed in the vast middle ground, according—among other things—to individual views about the status of rights, fair treatment of the handicapped, and what constitutes an acceptable quality of life.[14] Very little of the complexity of this debate and the breadth and depth of the moral divisions within the philosophical, religious, medical, and legal communities was adequately covered by the news organizations we reviewed.

Our assessments of the media's performance in reporting on Baby Jane Doe have been reached by reference to our reasonable-reader standard of substantial completeness. We did not expect disclosure of the "whole truth" or anything close to it. The medical facts alone regarding spina bifida (and the accompanying hydrocephalus and microcephalus) would have been difficult to convey even through the most comprehensive coverage. And if it were possible to report the whole truth and space were available to publish every detail, it would not always be desirable to do so. In some cases it is even uncertain what the whole truth entails. For example, what would it mean in the context of reporting on risk and uncertainty to tell the whole truth? Must every potentially relevant item be mentioned? Every unknown and every scientific doubt?

Although journalists, like academics and scientists, are devoted to the disclosure of truth, journalists are not obligated to tell the truth no matter whom or how much it hurts. Journalists routinely, and properly, suppress certain kinds of relevant information when they publish stories. The desire to avoid harming others (see Chapter 4) and to maintain a relationship of trust with sources (see Chapter 6) often provides the justification for suppressing useful information. For example, journalists covering national security affairs will sometimes justifiably withhold information so as not to disclose state secrets, and also to protect lives.

On other occasions, however, new sources try to persuade journalists not to publish less sensitive information in which the public has a legitimate interest. And if persuasion fails they sometimes try in other ways to prevent publication, usually by withholding information. An example of the latter is the control on news about the artificial heart program and its patients exercised by Dr. William C. DeVries, who heads the program at the Humana Hospital in Louisville. A few weeks after he had allowed unusually free access to information about his program and its patients, DeVries abruptly announced that he would thereafter sharply limit access. At the time, and some weeks later in an address to the American Society of Newspaper Editors, he gave the following reasons: He needed to ensure the accuracy of information that he intended to obtain from experimental procedures; the press had been "overzealous" in a few instances, putting out false information; "new" news was now likely to be simply old news in new clothes; and there was a need to protect the welfare of patients and their families. Several prospective patients had indicated to him that they and their families could not accept the attendant publicity and lack of privacy typical of previous cases. Although the press was still eagerly in pursuit of additional information at the time, DeVries maintained that "You just don't need to know as much as you did before."[15] We question DeVries's judgment, although we would certainly give some weight to the argument that prospective patients might be deterred from seeking help by excessive publicity. Nonetheless, it is the kind of judgment that the press should at least consider and not reject out of hand.

The virtue of truthfulness and the goal of completeness, then, should be interpreted neither as unyielding standards that are incapable of being overridden nor as licenses to publish or broadcast every piece of information that might be gathered. Valid exceptions exist to the obligation of substantially complete disclosure, but in the absence of an overriding value it should be honored.

## Understanding

The reasonable reader is rarely in a position to grasp every detail that would contribute to an understanding of a situation that is being reported. But not every detail is necessary. In some cases it takes only a single fact or set of facts to provide what is needed to sufficiently understand the reported events. Part of good reporting is to be able to distinguish information and events that are irrelevant or trivial from those that are relevant and vital. A story meets the reasonable-reader standard by communicating clearly and accurately information a person needs to possess a substantial understanding. The story is not a gateway to omniscience, but rather to becoming informed.

But what does it mean to have a substantial understanding of events? A definitive answer would require a comprehensive theory of understanding that far surpasses the ambitions of this book, but a brief discussion is essential to developing our account of truth in journalism. We begin with the ideal of complete understanding. A person would fully understand a situation or event if the person were to apprehend all relevant propositions or statements that accurately describe the nature of what is reported, as well as their possible outcomes or consequences. To the extent that this ideal for understanding is less than satisfied, an action is based on less than full understanding. What journalism can be expected to produce is, of course, something considerably less than this ideal.

Not all the relevant descriptions of an event or situation are equally important, and we would hardly expect or want all such descriptions. Substantial understanding involves apprehension of all the material or important descriptions—not all the relevant, and certainly not all possible, descriptions. Thus, a person could be wholly ignorant of relatively unimportant but nevertheless relevant propositions about an event and still understand it adequately. Reporting every relevant proposition would result in absurdly long and largely useless stories that might not serve anyone's interests and needs. Too much information is likely, under many circumstances, to overwhelm and confuse readers and inhibit rather than enhance understanding.

Given these problems, can practical and realistic guides be developed for structuring reports that produce substantial understanding? The answer is yes, but not by using abstract standards for disclosure of information. A different approach to understanding is needed—one that focuses broadly on serving the diverse needs of the full spectrum of readers. The question should not merely be "What facts should be provided?"—as important as that is. But we should also ask questions like "What should the journalist admit to not knowing?" "How much background is necessary?" and "How elementary must the starting point be?"

Matters that need special attention are tone, context, and background information. Sometimes, for example, it is important to explain the cultural assumptions underlying even the simplest report. Ruth SoRelle, a reporter for *The Houston Chronicle*, tells of having once written about the aforementioned Dr. DeVries that after implanting an artificial heart he slept on the floor near his patient. Many of her readers, unfamiliar with the hospital terminology (the culture of medicine), inferred that he literally slept on the linoleum alongside the patient's bed.

The press also often reports on social institutions such as medicine without conveying adequately the assumptions, rules, and conventions of those institutions. For example, routine patterns of decision making and authority in hospitals may be essential to understanding a report about "extraordinary" or emergency care being denied to a patient. From an outsider's point of view the denial of treatment may seem inscrutable unless these patterns are explained. Another criticism of American journalism, frequently expressed by foreigners who read American reports of activities in their home countries, is a failure to include enough historical background so that untutored readers can understand not only why events occur but also the underlying rationale for actions by leaders and governments.

The more dissimilar in background an audience is, or the more persons are strangers to a context, the greater the likelihood that readers will make mistaken assumptions or inferences, and therefore the more elementary the presentations must be. Journalists often omit information that may be central to their intended message but which they presume—sometimes mistakenly—can be inferred by the reader or listener. The more the speaker and listener or writer and reader deviate from a shared language and set of background assumptions, the less the reader or listener can be counted on to supply the missing information.

While these generalizations may seem obvious, they are worth noting because this process of inference is so central to human communication.[16] Communicating parties are constantly hypothesizing, often in unnoticed ways, about what the other party is reporting. These hypotheses represent attempts to infer what is meant by the other person. Consider, once again, reporting on medicine. Recent research indicates that laypersons' ideas about disease and the meanings they give to specific illnesses are often surprisingly different from standard medical definitions and conceptions in dimensions such as symptomology and etiology, consequences for patients, and whether the illness is acute or chronic.[17] Journalists and even doctors have difficulty in cutting through medical and scientific jargon to give untutored persons a basically accurate conception of medical events and developments. Even basic medical language like "work-up," "myocardial infarction," "taking a history," and "the patient presented" may be meaningless to the typical reader. In the jargon of the cognitive sciences, if hearers do not have the conceptual database, cognitive constructs, or categories from which to make appropriate inferences and interpretations, then they have to be provided with clear explanations to take account of such limitations.

At this point, the objection may be raised that journalists are not, cannot, and ought not be teachers who provide an elementary education to their audience. The mission of journalism cannot be to eradicate illiteracy—especially scientific illiteracy, which is pervasive in American society. The reasonable reader has to be able to read. But this objection is beside the main point, which has been made compellingly by contemporary cognitive psychologists. These psychologists are not examining ignorance but rather psychological processes through which persons respond, and how these processes can lead to distortions and misunderstandings. Sometimes the problem is one of not possessing the cognitive ability to adequately evaluate a message, as when young children cannot distinguish the bias in advertising or place indiscriminate trust in televised fiction and advertising messages. But more typically, and more relevantly, the problem concerns distortions, fear responses, and exaggerations to which virtually all of us are subject.

There is often a need to anticipate and avoid mistaken and misleading inferences that many readers or viewers are likely to make. For example, ample evidence indicates that experts, journalists, and laypersons alike can easily distort their assessments of the riskiness of certain events. Some biases are so ubiquitous in the human experience that—as Amos Tversky and Daniel Kahneman suggest—it may be "psychologically unfeasible" to expect persons to resist acting in accord with them.[18] One of the more troublesome of these biases for journalism is the so-called framing or formulation effect, in which persons' choices between risky alternatives can be predictably influenced by the way the information about risk is presented or framed.[19] A frame of reference against which risky outcomes and contingencies are viewed as either losses or gains, fearsome or encouraging, and so on, will be established by whether the proverbial glass is described as half empty or half full, or whether disease is depicted in terms of survival statistics or mortality statistics.

Here is an example from two polls conducted almost simultaneously by the *New York Times*/CBS polling organization and the *Washington Post*/ABC polling organization. They asked the same question in different ways and received strikingly different results. The *Times*/CBS poll put the question this way: "Here are some ways people say you can get AIDS. For each of them, tell me whether you think it is possible to get AIDS that way. Can you get AIDS by drinking from a glass just used by a person with AIDS?" The responses were 47 percent "Yes," 34 percent "No," and 20 percent "Don't know or no answer." The *Post*/ABC poll asked the question this way: "I'm going to read you a list. For each item please tell me if you think that it is or is not a way for someone to catch AIDS from someone who has it. If you are not sure, please tell me. Can you catch AIDS from using the same drinking glass?" The responses were 28 percent "Yes," 55 percent "No," 16 percent "Don't know or have no opinion." The difference is substantial, apparently because of the way the information in the question was framed.[20]

The *Times*/CBS poll phrased the question assertively (and perhaps tendentiously) as "Here are some ways *people say you can get* AIDS." The *Post*/ABC poll framed it less assertively and both positively and negatively: "For each item please tell me whether you think it *is or is not* a way for someone to catch AIDS. . . ." The *Times*/CBS construction is also active and immediate ("just used by") compared to the Post/ABC construction, which is passive ("using"). Even though the difference may appear relatively small, it apparently had a major effect on the perceptions of many respondents.

These dangers of misunderstanding are serious and not always appreciated by journalists, yet there are techniques for reducing confusion and erroneous inference that should be routine matters of journalistic practice. As the polling example indicates, rather than framing a statement in either positive or negative language, it can be presented in both positive and negative language. That is, the prudent if slightly more space-consuming course would be to provide readers with both sides of the story—the half-full and the half-empty presentations, both mortality statistics and survival statistics, both failure rates and success rates—in the hope of avoiding gaps in understanding that may simply be the result of the way the information is framed.

It would be a mistake to conclude from these cognitive problems that most persons cannot reach substantial understanding through journalism because of the space or time constraints. Educational and psychological literatures strongly suggest that it is possible to communicate even novel, alien, and specialized information to laypersons in a brief space or time.

## Objectivity

According to the *American Heritage Dictionary of the English Language,* objectivity entails being "uninfluenced by emotion or personal prejudice." It is, of course, unrealistic to expect even the most objective persons to be totally uninfluenced by these sources. People are often motivated jointly by emotion and reason, and in many cases it is difficult to distinguish one from the other. A reporter may be motivated to pursue a story from just such a tangle of emotion and reason. Nevertheless, we can still distinguish personal attitudes, religious dogmas, and the like from facts and justified beliefs. This does not mean that there cannot be controversy and disagreement surrounding facts, beliefs, and the evidence supporting them, only that journalists should strive to remain as distanced from the disputed domain as circumstances permit. The essence of some professional commitments is engagement, but in contrast to adherents of the so-called new journalism, we believe, with the mainstream journalistic community, that journalists are obligated to maintain a professional distance.

To analyze what this statement implies, we need to distinguish between the motivation, goal, or reason for reporting a story and the content of the story. The press often covers some types of events while excluding others for reasons that turn on evaluative judgments of relative social importance. Splitting large-city newspapers, for example, into sections such as Business, Sports, International, and Style suggests a commitment to report regularly on important events in these areas. These newspapers do not generally have comparable sections on Australian News, Gambling, Scientific Research, or Professional Ethics. Of course, some aspects of the press's commitments and priorities may change dramatically, sometimes overnight. Since the accident at Three Mile Island, for example, the press has paid closer attention to the financing, hazards, and construction of nuclear power plants by electric utilities. Decisions that such issues are of major social importance and merit unusual amounts of space are made every day in journalism, often on the basis of what best serves the public interest.

Once a high value has been placed on the importance of reporting particular events, it is vital to present the material facts even if they conflict with the goal that motivated increased reporting on these facts. If the motive in reporting on nuclear power plants, for example, is to warn the public about possible danger, reports should reflect the possibility that there may be good reasons for believing that the danger is less than has often been alleged. Before Three Mile Island almost all the journalistic reporting on the facility had been positive (e.g., reports on its good rating from the Nuclear Regulatory Commission), but afterward the reporting was almost entirely negative.[21] If a reporter were to write a series on such a plant or on the nuclear power industry suggesting only that it was running up unjustifiable costs and represented a significant public health danger, the reporter would have taken up a cause and used the story as a means of advancing it, rather than as a means of providing a fair, objective, and balanced account.

A subtle version of this problem appeared in an extensive cover story in *Time* magazine headlined "Pulling the Nuclear Plug." This story ran in February 1984, near the peak of public concern about the destiny of nuclear plants in the electric power industry. *Time* put an almost entirely negative cast on the situation, describing some abandoned plants as "nuclear white elephants" and suggesting that the entire industry was vulnerable to the same fate. The goal of informing the public about the dangers of nuclear power was commendable, but the *Time* account lacked objectivity and balance. The magazine became so caught up in the problems suffered by the industry that it failed to adequately cover a range of informed but conflicting perspectives.[22]

"60 Minutes," the most watched news-magazine program in the history of television, is often subjected to criticism for this kind of reporting, and it too had a troubled episode with nuclear power. One subject, the Illinois Power Company, was so wary of the show that the company made its own videotape of Harry Reasoner and the CBS crew while "60 Minutes" was taping its story. The result was instructive. Like *Time*, CBS put a negative construction on the story, focusing on cost overruns and other problems encountered in the building of Illinois Power's Clinton nuclear energy plant. (Unit 2 at the Clinton Power Station was canceled on October 14, 1983, at a cost of $34.8 million, but Unit 1 was constructed. The company has never had serious financial or regulatory problems.) The Illinois Power tape ("60 Minutes/Our Reply") suggests that "60 Minutes" went out of its way to portray the Clinton project as a disaster and used unfair techniques to do so, including a failure to air the company's rebuttals to and explanations of many of the charges made by Reasoner.[23] There may have been more than an antinuclear bias at work, but it is not implausible that such a bias played some part in determining how the segment was shaped. "60 Minutes" was not merely reporting on the construction of the Clinton plant; it was evaluating it (as, of course, "60 Minutes" and similar programs such as "20/20" regularly and properly do).

The distinction between a journalist's evaluative commitment to a goal and objectivity in content is illustrated by an encounter between Attorney General Edwin Meese and Spencer Claw, editor of the *Columbia Journalism Review*. Meese gave an address to the Washington Press Club in which he suggested that the press drop its traditional sense of detachment and assist the Justice Department in mobilizing public opinion against dangerous street-marketed drugs. He maintained that the department and the press had a "mutual interest" in getting out the message and in fighting crime. Meese proposed stories, for example, that showed how narcotics users who "bought for pleasure" were in fact supporting dealers in "terror, torture, and death." Claw objected that government officials step outside their bounds by trying to get reporters to push a particular point of view. He drew a sharp distinction between "suggesting story ideas" and collaborating to get a message across.[24]

The underlying question, however, is not whether government officials and reporters should collaborate to push a point of view. It is whether news reporters should be pushing a point of view at all—whether commitment to a message rather than simply to coverage (of subjects deserving investigation) is a perversion of journalistic objectivity. A commitment to describing "terror, torture, and death," for example, would appear to be tantamount to a loss of objectivity before the investigation is underway.

This observation raises questions about just what objectivity—including balance—does involve. To present a story objectively entails writing and organizing the material so as not to express or suggest a preference for one set of values over another (even though, of course, there are reasons for covering the story that are themselves evaluative judgments of what is newsworthy). In news stories about Baby Jane Doe, for example, reporting objectively would require, among other things, presenting divergent views of qualified experts on the various aspects of the so-called right-to-life issue. But fairness does not always entail giving equal weight to the views of those on either side of an issue; some views might be absurd, uninformed, framed and calculated to political ends, and so on. If the preponderance of thoroughly assembled evidence overwhelmingly supports the conclusion that the earth is an oblate spheroid, this view deserves more weight than the tenuously supported opinion that the earth is flat.

The ideal of objectivity therefore includes a notion of balance that is more complex than the common-sense conception of the term. Balance entails more than a mechanistic measuring of words so that each partisan position is given an equal number of inches, minutes, or representation. Moreover, in most cases issues are susceptible to multiple interpretations; a reporter cannot simply report both sides. Baby Jane Doe's prospective quality of life, for example, was probably unpredictable with any real accuracy at the time of her birth, and the expression "quality of life" was subject to competing and inconsistent interpretations. These problems did not stop physicians, including some who had seen neither the child nor her medical records, from predicting a likely course of events, or ethicists from stating a position on the nature and relevance of quality-of-life judgments. Nonphysician reporters covering complex stories like Baby Jane Doe, Baby Fae (which involved the implantation of a baboon's heart in an infant), and mechanical heart implant cases cannot be expected to be more expert than highly specialized physicians or ethicists. So how should they present the range of views to provide readers with the most objective account possible? Should they include every viewpoint and let readers make their own diagnoses, prognoses, and evaluations?

One difficulty with an approach that puts the burden of evaluation on readers or viewers is that most readers or viewers, like most journalists, are ill equipped to make such judgments. A possible solution is to report flatly that there was no consensus about the prognosis among the medical sources interviewed or agreement about the nature and relevance of quality-of-life judgments by experts in ethics. Physicians' predictions, for example, ranged from "vegetative" existence (the neurologist who recommended no surgery), through a handicapped but functional life (the neurosurgeon who favored surgery), to the possibility of a well-adjusted and happy life, with some mobility and negligible, if any, mental disability (a right-to-life advocate who did not see the baby or her records, but who has treated such cases in his medical practice).

How does the plural-opinion approach to the requirement of objectivity and balance serve readers in this case? Presumably it makes them aware of what was, here and elsewhere, the central knowable truth of the situation: uncertainty and a range of informed to uninformed speculation by the experts. Similarly, reporting on the level of risk associated with exposure to a particular chemical like dioxin, kepone, or benzene may be best accomplished by impressing on readers that only the range of risk reported has any warrant as "accurate"—not some particular reported risk—because so much uncertainty underlies any single judgment. As we discussed above in the section on "Understanding," such information must be not only nuanced but carefully phrased to avoid distorted inferences.

These cases still do not fully capture the essence of balance in reporting. The "balance of reason" in thinking and reporting is the use of a fair process to compare different sides of an account or issue, often weighing the different considerations against each other. A part of the balancing may be to ascertain the differences between competing accounts, but a set of balanced quotations should not serve as a substitute for trying to place the situation being reported in proper perspective.

An article in *Barron's* titled "Big Black and Blue: Is All the Bad News Out on IBM?" illustrates the nature and importance of balanced reporting. The article was filled with "glum projections" and negative quotes from portfolio managers. These bearish viewpoints were not balanced by a single bullish viewpoint, despite the fact that IBM was at the time the most highly recommended stock on the New York Stock Exchange by leading brokerage houses and investment periodicals. The bearish assessment might have turned out to be correct (it did not, however, as the stock rose dramatically in subsequent weeks), but that possibility is irrelevant. *Barron's* is a source of financial news, not an investment advisory service. The article was written "By the staff of Barron's" and purported to be on "The IBM Record" and the company's prospects. Even if the *Barron's* staff had collected voluminous evidence about problems at IBM (it had not), this article would nonetheless have been imbalanced because there was voluminous and credible evidence to the contrary that had been collected elsewhere and went unreported.[25]

In a well-publicized case involving a question of balance of a different type, *The New York Times* published the following editor's note:

> An article . . . about Mortimer B. Zuckerman, the real-estate developer and magazine publisher, described his career, which reached a high point last month when his company was chosen to develop the Coliseum site at Columbus Circle. Through opinionated phrases and unattributed characterizations, the article established a tone that cast its subject in an unfavorable light. . . . The pejorative phrases and anonymous criticism created an unbalanced portrait. They should not have appeared.[26]

The editor's note makes the valid point that balance in a news or feature article depends on how ideas are framed. The article characterizes Zuckerman as "plotting" real-estate deals; it say his latest purchase "does not sate him"; it says he befriended people "to win a place in their world." Even if all these pejorative characterizations were true, they were presented without any suggestion that Zuckerman might have positive personal qualities to balance them. The Zuckerman article[27] was much discussed because A. M. Rosenthal, executive editor of the *Times* and a friend of Zuckerman, implicitly criticized the reporter, even though the article itself was tailored to meet the requirements of the *Times* editors who approved it for publication. That fact aside, the criticism in the editor's note is justified: the feature article on Zuckerman simply lacked balance.

A similar example from the *Times* that did not stimulate an editor's note was a story by Charlotte Curtis on John De Lorean.[28] In virtually every paragraph Curtis used pejorative phrases to characterize the auto manufacturer, who had been charged with trafficking in cocaine in an effort to save his failing sportscar company. Curtis wrote a three-column article that repeated a range of criminal and other charges against De Lorean. With supercilious innuendo, she wrote: "He worked [in California] in the late 1960s and early '70s, promoting Chevrolets and cutting something of a big-spender's swath among Los Angeles's lesser luminaries and starlets." This sentence is typical of the tone of the article, which contains no effort to balance the portrait of De Lorean, who was subsequently acquitted of the drug-trafficking charges.

It is not difficult to imagine other cases in which a strongly stated view may seem so authoritative that it alone appears to deserve lengthy coverage. In such a case, conflicting views of significantly less authority may not seem worthy of more than passing mention. But extreme caution—indeed, outright skepticism—may be the best attitude for journalists and editors to adopt in many such instances. When *The Times of London* was trying to decide whether the alleged Hitler diaries being offered for syndication by the West German magazine *Der Stern* were genuine, the editors called on the distinguished historian Hugh Trevor-Roper (Lord Dacre) to independently verify the diaries' authenticity. The *Times*'s parent company purchased the rights largely on Trevor-Roper's recommendation. He also wrote a lengthy article describing how the diaries were acquired and evaluating their significance.[29] What reasonable reader would question this "verification" by the author of *The Last Days of Hitler* and *Hitler's Table Talk?* Was he not a distinguished scholar who had been at the Nuremberg trials? However, a troubled Trevor-Roper, deciding that his judgment had been made in too much haste and on the basis of too little evidence, did a quick turnabout. At that point the scheme rapidly began to unravel, revealing a fraud of massive proportions.[30]

The lesson would seem to be that providing an objective account may involve making judgments about the authoritativeness of an ostensibly authoritative source. Even when the authority is a distinguished historian, objectivity may require a clear-eyed assessment of the circumstances in addition to the authority's reputation and skills. (Trevor-Roper had only brief and extremely limited access to the purported diaries.) In the case of the Hitler diaries, the editors and owners of the *Times* newspapers and *Der Stern* (as well as *Paris Match* and Italy's *Panorama*) appear to have

had their vision clouded by the prospects of a story of sensational proportions and perhaps by an opportunity to earn significant profits from syndication rights.

## Accuracy

According to a lead editorial on "News Credibility" in *USA Today*, "Journalists must always make accuracy their *first* priority."[31] It may be correct
to assign a top priority to accuracy, but the nature of this commitment is
far from clear. In this context, accuracy implies both exactitude and meticulousness. Exactitude does not mean correctness, but rather proceeding
from sound evidence. To be as accurate as possible requires reporting as
facts only information for which there is good and sufficient evidence, and
no reasonable doubt about the preponderance of the evidence. If doubt
remains about the accuracy of a purported fact, the doubt should be in-
corporated into the story. Here is one example in which remaining doubts
went unreported: Hamilton Jordan, chief of staff in the Carter White House,
described an experience he had as a cancer patient witnessing a report on
his own illness.

> I turn on the television. I am startled to see a picture of myself and catch
> the line . . . "CBS News had just learned that former Presidential aide
> Hamilton Jordan is in Emory Hospital and has been diagnosed as having
> inoperable lung cancer." Panic grips me, then rational thought returns. If
> my doctor doesn't know what I have, how in the hell can CBS News
> know?[32]

CBS News had neither good nor sufficient evidence to report that Jordan
had inoperable lung cancer. He had not even been diagnosed at the time,
and when he was diagnosed he was found to have a form of lymphoma
for which cure rates are highly promising.

Meticulousness also refers to such matters as precision in quotation,
paraphrasing, and description. In proposing criteria of this kind, we are
not demanding perfection or a major revolution in journalism's self-
understanding. As with the whole truth, we appreciate that standards can
be set too high as well as too low. Standards of accuracy in the gathering
of data used by rigorous social scientists, for example, would be too high
for most journalism. But it is possible to set standards of accuracy for
journalism that are both desirable and attainable.

One traditional standard of accurate reporting is proper attribution.
Reporters should usually only describe without attribution that which they
have witnessed, that which can be properly called general knowledge, and

information that has been properly verified. Anything that is not general knowledge or that the reporter has not experienced directly or verified personally should be attributed to the source of the information. (One among a narrow range of possible exceptions might be the reporting of an event witnessed by a trusted colleague.) The attribution should also give some indication of the reliability of the source, especially if the source cannot be identified by name or position.

However, even these minimal standards are sometimes extremely difficult to satisfy. A reporter at a scene obscured by chaos or confusion, such as a battlefield, may be overwhelmed by the sensory evidence and the myriad opportunities for inference and instant judgment. Such instances demand checking and double-checking, where possible, of even those events occurring within the reporter's earshot and field of vision. If particularly difficult conditions prevail, news reports should be appropriately qualified.

Concern for accuracy also may require enough restraint to withhold information until it can be verified. The "election" of Governor Thomas E. Dewey to the presidency in 1948, for example, or the "death" of President Reagan's press secretary, James Brady, in 1981 were both reported as fact, although neither occurred.[33] An especially telling example of this problem of premature rushes to judgment involved reports of the number of civilians killed and left homeless in the first weeks of the Israeli invasion of southern Lebanon in 1982. Israeli writer Ze'ev Chafets reconstructed these events as follows in his book *Double Vision:*[34]

> On June 10, the Palestine Red Crescent floated the figure of 10,000 killed during the first four days of the war, and at about the same time Francesco Noseda, the representative of the International Committee of the Red Cross (ICRC) in Beirut, said that there were an estimated 600,000 refugees.
>
> The figures were first reported (and accurately attributed) by the BBC, and then picked up and repeated throughout the West. Israel claimed that both were wildly inaccurate. It had no exact figures of its own (indeed, such figures during the midst of battle are impossible to calculate), but it appealed to the common sense of the press corps. It pointed out that the Palestine Red Crescent, far from being "the Lebanese equivalent of the Red Cross," as it was often called, was in fact an adjunct of the PLO run by Yasser Arafat's brother, Dr. Fathi Arafat, and that its assessments were, at the very least, suspect. Moreover, the casualty figures related to south Lebanon, but the PLO was no longer in the area, and thus had no means of arriving at any accurate figure. Finally, Israel reminded the Beirut press corps that even during the relatively less frenzied period of the Lebanese civil war, the journalists in Beirut themselves had often written about the unreliability of "official" casualty figures and the impossibility of getting accurate statistics.
>
> The prima facie evidence against the ICRC refugee figure was, if any-

thing, more obvious. Simply put, there hadn't been 600,000 civilians—Lebanese and Palestinians—in the entire area before the war.

Despite the improbability of both the 10,000 and 600,000 figures, they were given wide currency in the American press. On June 10, NBC's Roger Mudd stated, "Neither side has even estimated its loss of life, but the Red Crescent, which is Lebanon's Red Cross, is quoted as estimating that ten thousand civilians have been killed or wounded since Friday"[35]—as if the Red Crescent were not a side in the dispute. The casualty figure was echoed, without qualification, by ABC's Barrie Dunsmore and NBC's Steve Mallory (who spoke of 9,000 killed) on June 14.[36] They attributed these estimates to the "Lebanese police" or the "Lebanese government," although they must have known that neither existed, nor had they existed in south Lebanon since the PLO had taken over that part of the country in the mid-1970s.

As for the refugee figure, it was so absurdly high that the Red Cross took the almost unprecedented step of recalling its representative, Francesco Noseda, after Noseda himself repudiated his earlier exaggerated estimate on June 15. Despite this, NBC's Jessica Savitch said, four days later, "It is now estimated that 600,000 refugees in south Lebanon are without sufficient food and medical supplies."[37]

Print journalists were somewhat more careful than the television reporters, but they too made use of the exaggerated and obviously politically motivated statistics without sufficient explanation or caution. The New York Times, The Washington Post, and other major American newspapers used the Red Crescent number without properly explaining that it was in fact a PLO statistic, and quoted the Red Cross refugee assessment without wondering how so many refugees could have come from a region with so few people.

Israel later published official casualty figures for south Lebanon—265 dead in Sidon, 50 to 60 in Tyre, and 10 in Nabatiyah. These figures were flawed by the fact that they included only Lebanese civilians and not Palestinians in the camps, a piece of intellectual dishonesty that cost Israel considerable credibility. Despite this, however, the Israeli figures were much closer to reality than the PLO and Red Cross inventions of early June 1982. As David Shipler of The New York Times later put it, "It is clear to anyone who has traveled in southern Lebanon, as have many journalists and relief workers, that the original figures of 10,000 dead and 600,000 homeless reported by correspondents quoting the representatives of the International Committee of the Red Cross during the first week of the war were extreme exaggerations."[38]

If the news is less fast-breaking than in a war situation, newspapers, news magazines, and television news programs sometimes rely on time-tested but less than scientific systems of determining the accuracy of stories such as checking clipping files or calling additional sources. As we will see in Chapter 6, these systems sometimes break down entirely, as in the case of "Jimmy's World," Janet Cooke's fraudulent account of the life of an eight-year-old heroin addict, which won a subsequently withdrawn Pu-

litzer Prize. Despite considerable suspicion among her editors and reporters about the accuracy of the story, it was published anyway.

Another example of how news organizations try to guarantee accuracy
but sometimes fail was described by *Time* magazine writer William E. Smith
during Ariel Sharon's $50 million libel suit against *Time*. According to a
*New York Times* report of the trial, Smith said:

> A writer is assigned to write in New York. A great many specialists work
> on it (a cover story). Files begin to come in from the bureaus. The writer
> sits down with all this material that has been collected. By this time there
> is a snowstorm of paper. . . . The writer organizes the material and writes
> the story, researchers check it for accuracy, and an editor checks it for
> content and balance as well as accuracy. The article is sent to all the
> bureaus that were involved in the preparation to ask them to check it for
> accuracy, and *Time*'s managing editor edits it again."[39]

Despite such precautions, the system failed to catch the fact that *Time*
included a key paragraph in its February 21, 1983, cover story titled "The
Verdict Is Guilty" that was not supported by the explicit testimony of any
of correspondent David Halevy's sources.[40] Halevy wrote that a secret appendix of an official Israeli report into allegations of Israeli responsibility
for the massacre of Palestinian refugees by Christian Phalangists in Lebanon's Sabra and Shatila refugee camps contained the charge that General
Sharon had given Phalangist leaders the "feeling" that "he understood their
need to take revenge." Halevy testified at the trial that he drew the inference that this kind of language was present in the appendix from conversations with high-level military and intelligence sources, but that none of
them had specifically said it was there.

The problem was compounded in New York. Smith said he interpreted
phrases and additional language in Halevy's memorandum "to mean words,
words."[41] Therefore, he wrote, and *Time* published, the following:

> One section of the report, known as Appendix B, was not published at
> all, mainly for security reasons. That section contains the names of several
> intelligence agents referred to elsewhere in this report. *Time* has learned
> that it also contains further details about Sharon's visit to the Gemayel
> family on the day after Bashir Gemayel's assassination. Sharon reportedly
> told the Gemayels that the Israeli army would be moving into West Beirut
> and that he expected the Christian forces to go into the Palestinian refu-
> gee camps. Sharon also reportedly *discussed* with the Gemayels the need
> for the Phalangists to take revenge for the assassination of Bashir, but the
> details of the conversation are not known.[42]

The following is the relevant part of the text of the Halevy memo, which
Smith used as the basis for the sentence in which the controversial word
"discussed" is found (as italicized above):

Sharon indicated in advance to the Gemayels that the Israeli Army was moving into West Beirut and that he expected them, the Force Lebanese, to go into all the Palestinian refugee camps. He also gave them the feeling after the Gemayels' questioning, that he understood their need to take revenge for the assassination of Bashir and assured them that the Israeli Army would neither hinder them nor try to stop them.[43]

Smith subsequently contended that the phrases "after the Gemayels' questioning" and "assured them," taken together with "he also gave them the feeling," "conveyed the meaning that a discussion had taken place."[44] It is possible to draw such a conclusion, but there is insufficient justification to report, without further questioning, that he had "*discussed* with the Gemayels the need for the Phalangists to take revenge. . . .'' Smith, knowing that his version would be sent to the Jerusalem bureau for approval, said he did not see a need to flag the change, even though the words "assured them that the Israeli Army would neither hinder them nor try to stop them" could refer to going "into all the Palestinian refugee camps" and not "their need to take revenge." The same is true of the phrase "after the Gemayels' questioning." The questions might have referred only to a legitimate military operation in the camps and no more.

The first lapse in accuracy was Halevy's failure to make clear in his memorandum that he was reporting an inference about the contents of Appendix B, not a fact documented through a credible source. The memorandum, after approval by *Time*'s Jerusalem bureau chief, Harry Kelly, was then sent to New York where Halevy's inaccuracy was compounded by Smith's rewriting. Finally, when the copy was sent back to Jerusalem for checking, neither Halevy nor Kelly objected to Smith's insertion of the word "discussed." It is hard to conceive of a more thorough procedural system for checking accuracy that would still be practical. Nevertheless, significant and preventable inaccuracies still appeared. As in the case of Janet Cooke, more than a slip was involved. The inaccuracies in the paragraph in question—whether or not they reflect a poetic truth or even the real truth about what took place between Sharon and the Gemayels, as opposed to what was in the appendix—result from one or more of the following causes: bias (Halevy, an Israeli national, was known to detest Sharon), negligence, or incompetence. Few editors would defend such reporting and writing (except perhaps in a courtroom in a libel trial), yet it is an everyday occurrence in journalism. The *Time* example subsequently came to light only because it was made public in a major libel trial.

*Time* ultimately conceded in court that it had been mistaken about the contents of the appendix.[45] The magazine then printed a partial retraction,[46] but the statement reasserted that *Time* "stands by the substance" of the paragraph. *Time* called its account "substantially true" and said it stood by the paragraph because it still believed that Sharon discussed the need for revenge with the Gemayels. Even if *Time* were correct on the latter point, for which it has provided no better substantiation than for its original claim, it stretches both logic and credulity to suppose that a substantially false paragraph can also be substantially true. *Time* seems to have had grounds for saying only that it had made a serious error in an otherwise substantially correct news story, considered as a whole. But *Time* specifically cited the disputed paragraph as substantially true. Sharon's lawyer, Milton Gould, was quick to label *Time*'s "retraction" both "arrogant" and "outrageous."[47] We agree.

Still another problem of inaccuracy arises from the uncritical repetition of an initially inaccurate report that is not subsequently checked, as happened in the case of a New Bedford, Massachusetts, barroom rape that was reported to have been witnessed by a crowd of cheering onlookers. Jonathan Friendly of *The New York Times* later reported, correctly, that only one man had cheered, jeered, or otherwise egged on the rapists in Big Dan's Tavern.[48] The incorrect report had relied uncritically on a version the victim gave the police; the press en masse picked up and repeated the incorrect depiction. But reporters later could not locate the men who purportedly had done the cheering, and testimony in the trial subsequently made it clear that they did not exist. Nonetheless, news organizations around the country picked up the original report and kept repeating it, which left the false impression that this disturbing element of the story was true.

According to Friendly, "Journalists and academics interviewed said they could not recall another case in which such a crucially newsworthy element of a story, one that strongly influenced public opinion, was subsequently found to be so misleading."[49] Nevertheless, a few months later, in *The Washington Post* of October 13, Charles Fishman reported that despite initial police reports of cheering and jeering during a rape in the bathroom of a northern Virginia high school, no evidence could be found that anyone had encouraged the rapist in any way.[50] The press error in New Bedford had by then been given wide coverage, but it was virtually repeated in the Virginia case—not only in the *Post* itself but also on the AP and UPI news wires.

## Conclusion

Although it is axiomatic that journalists are duty bound to report truthfully, the nature and scope of that duty have not been well understood. The legitimate needs for information of a reasonable reader or viewer have played an especially prominent role in our analysis, and we have argued that journalists are responsible for satisfying those needs to the extent that normal constraints of journalism permit. The elements of truthfulness on which we have concentrated are completeness, understanding, objectivity, and accuracy. However, one important dimension of truthfulness in journalism has scarcely been mentioned in this chapter: the need to avoid bias. This subject is so broad and pervasive that the entire next chapter is devoted to its analysis.

NOTES

1. Advertisement, *The New York Times,* April 26, 1985, p. C32.

2. William L. Prosser, *The Law of Torts,* 4th ed. (St. Paul: West Publishing, 1971), p. 151.

3. See Ruth R. Faden and Tom L. Beauchamp, *A History and Theory of Informed Consent* (New York: Oxford University Press, 1986), Chapters 2, 4.

4. See, for example, Alan Meisel, "The Expansion of Liability for Medical Accidents: From Negligence to Strict Liability by Way of Informed Consent," *Nebraska Law Review* 56 (1977): 51–152.

5. Alan Barth, *The Rights of Free Men,* (New York: Knopf, 1984), p. 294. Emphasis in original.

6. Editorial, "Dr. Strangelove Is *Not* Loose," *The Los Angeles Times,* July 11, 1977, part II, p. 6. Emphasis added.

7. As we use the term, *the whole truth* is unobtainable in actual practice, but the concept is useful, just as infinity is useful in mathematics. The whole truth is that for which scholars and scientists strive, and against which journalists measure their performance. While it can never be reached, it can be approximated. We use it to help us situate on a continuum a practical yet morally well-defined standard of substantial completeness that journalists might realistically attain and for which they are morally bound to strive.

8. See Jacqueline Trescott, "Minority Coverage Faulted," *The Washington Post,* April 12, 1985, p. C2.

9. Alan L. Otten, "Women's Rights vs. Fetal Rights Looms as Thorny and Divisive Issue," *The Wall Street Journal,* April 12, 1985, p. 31.

10. See *Weber* v. *Stony Brook Hospital et al.,* 95 A.D. 587 (1983), 60 N.Y.2d 208 (1983).

11. ABC, "20/20," June 7, 1984; CBS, "CBS Evening News," November 2, 1983, and April 6, 1984; CBS, "60 Minutes," October 9, 1983, and March 11, 1984; *The Los Angeles Times,* coverage from October 21, 1983, to June 30, 1984; *The New York Times,* coverage from October 20, 1983, to July 9, 1984; Eloise Salholz, "Baby Doe's Legal Fate," *Newsweek,* November 14, 1983, p. 84; Aric Press, "The Case of Baby Jane Doe," *Newsweek,* November 28, 1983, pp. 45–46; Tom Morganthau, "The Case of Baby Jane Doe, Continued," *Newsweek,* December 12, 1983, p. 47; "Whose Lives Are They Anyway?" *Time,* November 14, 1983, p. 107; "Death Agonies," *Time,* January 9, 1984, p. 44; "No to the Feds," *Time,* November 28, 1983, p. 69; "Baby Jane Doe," *The Wall Street Journal,*

November 21, 1983, p. 24; "Baby Doe Rules," *The Wall Street Journal,* January 6, 1984, p. 1; Burt Schorr, "Rules to Protect Infants with Defects Revised by Reagan," *Wall Street Journal,* January 10, 1984, p. 19; "Doctors and Paradox," *The Wall Street Journal,* May 14, 1984, p. 26; *The Washington Post,* coverage from October 23, 1983 to June 24, 1984.

12. See *Newsday* Special Reprint, *The Baby Jane Doe Story* (Long Island, N.Y.: Newsday, 1984): B. D. Colen, "A Life of Love—and Endless Pain," *Newsday,* October 26, 1983, pp. R4–R6, and "Prognosis of One Doctor for a Spina Bifida Baby," *Newsday,* November 9, 1983, p. R10; Joye Brown, "A Legal Battle and a Hope . . . ," *Newsday,* November 13, 1983, p. R15; Irene Virag, ". . . And a Life at Death's Door," *Newsday,* November 13, 1983, p. R15. See also Kathleen Kerr, "Reporting on the Case of Baby Jane Doe," *Hastings Center Report* 14 (August 1984): 7–9.

13. "A Roundtable: Morality, Ethics and 'Baby Doe' Cases," *The New York Times,* November 13, 1983, sec. 4, pp. 56–57.

14. For a representative sample, see President's Commission for the Study of Ethical Problems in Medicine and Biomedical Research, *Deciding to Forego Life-Sustaining Treatment* (Washington: Government Printing Office, 1983), Chapters 4, 6; Essays 17, 18, and 22 by Richard A. McCormick in *How Brave a New World?* (Washington: Georgetown University Press, 1981); and Anthony Gallo and Bonnie Steinbock, "The Case of Baby Jane Doe," *Hastings Center Report* 14 (February 1984): 10–19.

15. Lawrence K. Altman, "Doctor Seeks to Limit News on Artificial Heart Program," *The New York Times,* February 23, 1985, p. 6; Leslie Phillips, "DeVries: Press Hurts Experiment," *USA Today,* April 11, 1985, sec. A, p. 3.

16. See Richard J. Harris and Gregory E. Monaco, "Psychology of Pragmatic Implication: Information Processing Between the Lines," *Journal of Experimental Psychology: General* 107 (1978): 1–22.

17. See, for example, H. Levanthal, D. Nerenz, and A. Strauss, "Self-regulation and the Mechanisms for Symptom Appraisal," in D. Mechanic, ed., *Psychological Epidemiology* (New York: Neale Watson, 1980), and "The Common Sense Representation of Illness Danger," in S. Rachman, ed., *Medical Psychology,* Vol. 2 (New York: Pergamon, 1980).

18. Amos Tversky and Daniel Kahneman, "Choices, Values, and Frames," *American Psychologist* 39 (1984): 341–50; "Judgment Under Uncertainty: Heuristics and Biases," *Science* 185 (1974): 1124–31; "The Framing of Decisions and the Psychology of Choice," *Science* 211 (1981): 453–58; and Daniel Kahneman and Amos Tversky, "Prospect Theory," *Econometrica* 47 (1979): 263–92.

19. Kahneman and Tversky, "Choices, Values, and Frames," pp. 344, 346; and "The Framing of Decisions," passim.

20. "ABC News/Washington Post September 1985 Poll," conducted September 19–23, 1985; "The New York Times/CBS News AIDS Survey," conducted September 9, 1985.

21. See Sharon M. Friedman, "Environmental Reporting: Before and After TMI," *Environment* 26 (December 1984): 4.

22. See Peter Stoler, "Pulling the Nuclear Plug," *Time,* February 13, 1984, pp. 34–42.

23. CBS, "60 Minutes," "Who Pays? . . . You Do!" (November 25, 1979); Illinois Power Co., "60 Minutes/Our Reply," (December 3, 1979).

24. Loretta Tofani, "Meese Seeks Press Help in Drug Fight," *The Washington Post,* March 21, 1985, p. A4.

25. "Big Black and Blue: Is All the Bad News Out on IBM?" *Barron's,* June 17, 1985, pp. 15, 24–28.

26. "Editor's Note," *The New York Times,* August 7, 1985, sec. B, p. 1.

27. Jane Perlez, "Mortimer Zuckerman: A Developer Who Thrives on High-Stakes Dealing," *The New York Times,* August 5, 1985, sec. B, p. 1.

28. Charlotte Curtis, "De Lorean: A Life of Extravagance," *The New York Times,* November 9, 1982, p. A20.

29. Hugh Trevor-Roper, "Secrets That Survived the Bunker," *The London Sunday Times,* April 23, 1983, p. 1.

30. Michael Binyon, "Historians Call for Deeper Scrutiny of Hitler Diaries," *The London Times,* April 26, 1983, p. 1. For the failures at *Der Stern,* see Janice Castro, "Judging the Hoax That Failed," *Time,* February 25, 1985, p. 60.

31. Editorial, "News Credibility," *USA Today,* April 12, 1985, sec. A, p. 12.

32. Hamilton Jordan, "Hamilton Jordan's Journal: Winning over Cancer," *The Washington Post,* January 26, 1986, p. B1.

33. See "Dewey Wins!" *Chicago Tribune,* November 4, 1948, p. 1; and CBS News Special Bulletin, March 30, 1981.

34. Ze'ev Chafets, *Double Vision: How the Press Distorts America's View of the Middle East* (New York: William Morrow, 1985), pp. 300–302.

35. NBC "Nightly News," June 10, 1982. Cited in ibid., p. 301.

36. ABC "World News," June 14, 1982; and NBC "Nightly News," June 14, 1982. Both cited in ibid., p. 301.

37. NBC "Nightly News," June 19, 1982. Cited in ibid., p. 302.

38. *The New York Times,* July 14, 1982. Cited in ibid., p. 302.

39. Arnold H. Lubasch, "Time Employee Tells How He Wrote Sharon Article," *The New York Times,* December 11, 1984, p. 10.

40. William E. Smith, "The Verdict Is Guilty," *Time,* February 21, 1983, pp. 26–34.

41. Lubasch, "*Time* Employee Tells," p. 10.

42. Smith, "The Verdict Is Guilty," p. 29.

43. Memo from David Halevy to *Time,* December 6, 1982. Emphasis added.

44. Lubasch, "*Time* Employee Tells."

45. See Herbert H. Denton, "Key Detail in Article False, *Time* Concedes," *The Washington Post,* January 10, 1985, p. A4.

46. "Appendix B Retraction," *Time,* January 21, 1985, p. 59.

47. Robert Friedman, "Judge Sends Sharon Libel Suit to Jury; *Time* Magazine Prints Partial Retraction," *The Wall Street Journal,* January 15, 1985, p. 7.

48. Jonathan Friendly, "Press Somehow Failed to Clarify Reports of Cheering in New Bedford Rape," *The New York Times,* April 11, 1984, p. A19.

49. Ibid.

50. Charles Fishman, "Prosecutor Can't Find Evidence of Jeering," *The Washington Post,* October 13, 1984, p. C4.

# Chapter 3

# Avoiding Bias

The problem of the intrusion of personal beliefs and values into news coverage was addressed in a March 1985 *Wall Street Journal* editorial that brought a charge against former CBS News anchorman Walter Cronkite. The editorial said that he "more than anyone else can take credit for a style of TV news reporting that persists to this day—a hybrid of straight facts, analysis and editorializing done simultaneously by the same reporter." Cronkite responded that this hybrid was precisely what he had stood against throughout his career: "I made every attempt to keep any hint of prejudice or bias, analysis or commentary, out of the news reports. . . . I believed that the straight presentation of news and a commentary by the same reporter would only confuse the public, although we in the profession know that it is possible for the same person to write a front-page, factual, unbiased report and a strong editorial on the same subject."[1] This juxtaposition of views crystallizes perhaps the single most intractable problem in journalism.

Although the debate has a long history, few issues in journalism are as poorly understood as *bias,* a term that is often used so broadly as to encompass any form of evaluation or appraisal. In this chapter we attempt to distinguish bias from legitimate forms of opinion and appraisal.

## The Concept of Bias

Bias entails a value-directed departure from accuracy, objectivity, and balance—not just a distorted presentation of facts. If, for example, a reporter fails to notice that the computer has swallowed a crucial paragraph in a news story, and the story is published without the paragraph, the inevitable distortion results from error, not bias. For a story to be biased, the distorted information it contains must be causally connected to the writer's or editor's values. Charges of bias are also frequently leveled incorrectly in response to a superficial presentation of facts. As columnist Robert J. Samuelson has pointed out, much of what is called political bias in the media is more often traceable to the fact that journalists are "a profession of outsiders; superficiality is often the best we can do."[2]

It is sometimes assumed that being biased requires holding a narrow-minded opinion. As an example of why this is not so, consider someone given to wishful thinking about his or her family's social status. This wishful thinking could produce a bias (if it satisfies other conditions listed below), but one born more of family loyalty than of narrow-mindedness. Biases also may or may not be ideological. Although ideology can produce bias, not all bias is ideological. Bias may derive from various sources, including irrationality, illusion, prejudice, greed, ambition, and religious fervor. And the distortions introduced may be intentional or unintentional.

In journalism, charges of bias often stem from the belief that a reporter or news organization holds partisan views and therefore reports issues and events in a partisan fashion. The disposition to partisanship and the need to eliminate it have been the focus of considerable criticism of the press. Certainly partisanship can be a cause of bias, but being partisan is not equivalent to being biased. A partisan reporter may restrain his or her partisan beliefs in writing a story, and a reformist reporter may write a story that is biased but not partisan. Moreover, a news or opinion piece is not biased merely because it represents a partisan viewpoint—no more, say, than a Democrat or Republican necessarily displays bias by representing a partisan position in Congress. A partisan position may be thoroughly justified by evidence or reasoned argument. To be biased, the partisan position taken must involve a distortion caused by the underlying partisan values. For example, when James Whelan resigned as editor of *The Washington Times,* he said he did so because the Unification Church, owner of the publication, distorted news coverage by imposing political beliefs on reports in the paper.[3] If Whelan is correct in his charge, the conservative political reporting of the *Times* results directly from the management's partisan political views and therefore represents a bias.

The most widely discussed form of bias in journalism is manifest when personal beliefs or values intrude into news coverage. These personal views often blend with and thereby distort factual accounts in news or opinion pieces. This is the basis for the charge of a "liberal bias," persistently leveled by some American politicians at various journalists and news organizations. It implies that a predominantly liberal political perspective on the part of reporters, editors, news executives, and publishers in the national media distorts the news that most Americans see on television or read in their newspapers—especially through the national networks and the news services of the major newspapers.

Some have argued that to qualify as a bias a distorting slant must have occurred over an extended period of time.[4] This view is understandable, but it is misleading without distinguishing between persons (or groups) and their actions. It would not be correct to say that a person or an institution is biased unless the bias is part of the person's character, habits, or ingrained approach, which can only be manifest over time. A biased action or an instance of bias might occur only once. Because we are interested more in instances of bias (in news reports and opinion pieces, in particular), the time factor will play no role in our definition of bias.

Another important question is whether a distortion must be unfair to count as bias. We are not asking whether a bias in any context where the word *bias* is correctly used must be unfair. That is not the case. For example, Canada recently passed a gas exploration bill that was intended to end what it acknowledged to be an existing bias against foreign companies. The Canadian policy had been intentionally discriminatory to promote the welfare of Canadian companies.[5] The fact that the policy was discriminatory, and thus biased, did not make it unfair. Similarly, a U.S. policy is biased in favor of rescuing large banks and savings and loan institutions that are in danger of going under, while leaving smaller banks to their own resources. Finally, to take an example from a different sphere, the award-winning play and movie *Amadeus* took extreme liberty with the facts of a person's life and times, and yet it is a matter of conjecture whether the bias introduced was either unfair or condemnable. In art, distortion is a tool of the trade and may be commendable. But we are not concerned here with bias in the arts, or in public policy for that matter. In journalism, as in science and history, reports have to be objectively and fairly presented to qualify as unbiased.

A bias in journalism, then, is a distorted and unfair judgment or disposition caused by the values of a reporter, editor, or institution. Bias is not necessarily ideological, partisan, or manifest over an extended period; and it need not be introduced intentionally.

## Distortion and Objectivity in the Use
## of Evaluative Language

There is a tendency to treat bias as a mortal sin in journalism on the ground that news reporting should be value-free. As a result, insufficient attention has been paid to bias that may be equally or more egregious in news analyses, columns, and editorials, where overt evaluation is not only acceptable but desirable. Moreover, it is a mistake to think that news reporting should be limited to a purely factual approach any more than editorials, columns, and news analyses should be entirely evaluative. Sophisticated news reporting often requires a perspective on events that may be heavily value-laden, and evaluative perspectives in opinion pieces often rest on factual reporting. We do not suggest that there is no distinction between news and opinion pieces, but it is a difficult distinction to apply.

In simplest terms, a factual statement is a statement of *what is,* whereas a value statement (at least a moral, political, or legal one) presents a view of what is good or virtuous, or *what ought to be.* A factual statement is generally assumed to be an empirically confirmable or falsifiable statement that describes some event or object. Factual statements are therefore either true or false. By contrast, value statements are not confirmable or falsifiable, because they assess and appraise rather than describe. These two kinds of statements are distinct and cannot logically be derived from each other. For example, there is no way logically to derive the statement *"The New York Times* covers sports" from *"The New York Times* ought to cover sports," nor can the latter be derived from the former.

However, not everyone subscribes to the theory that statements of fact and value can be kept neatly separate, as if there were no relation of dependence, or any similarity whatever. Many values are supported by facts, and the evaluations are likely to change if the facts supporting them change. The noble ideal of neutral facts uninfluenced by values often dissipates in the real world of human judgments. In criminal trials, for example, credible eyewitnesses frequently report the facts differently. Similarly, journalists sometimes report the same events in starkly contrasting factual terms. Moreover, factual statements are often presented as if they were values, or sometimes they are embedded in evaluative statements. To report, for example, that "an assistant secretary of defense is a zealous opponent of any budget cuts that would endanger the retirement plans of servicemen" may be an assessment of the motives and conduct of the official, a factual statement regarding the official's conduct, or some combination of the two. Criticism of the press as one-sided, provincial, biased, or prejudiced often centers on this problem of reporting as fact what "in fact" may be evaluative.

But might not an evaluation also be a fact? Might not description and evaluation overlap? By distinguishing between value distortion and value objectivity we can show that value-laden and value-driven stories do not necessarily amount to biased stories, and may in a reasonable sense be termed descriptive. Consider the following *Wall Street Journal* headline: "Philippines' Marcos and Political Cronies Resist IMF Plan to End Sugar Monopoly."[6] The word *cronies* may be indicative of a political bias. Certainly a word like *associates* could have been substituted (or *allies* if *associates* would not fit in the headline). The first sentence of the story discusses a "political boss" in the Philippines. Again, the word *leader* or *figure* might have been substituted. But perhaps the individuals referred to *are* cronies and bosses. Would it not then be a descriptive statement while at the same time evaluative? Surely there are cronies and bosses in the world, just as there are brutal massacres, vicious murders, and slanderous statements. Even as pejorative-sounding a headline as "The Shadowy World of Financial Planning Is Swarming with Slick Operators" can be justified and reasonably called descriptive if it describes a shadowy world of slick operators.[7] The real problem is that such claims too often are metaphorical, hyperbolical, poorly supported by evidence, and indeed biased.

Should journalists shy away from such value-based language if it provides the most accurate description of what is being reported? We think not, even though the uncritical use of evaluative words makes it easy for bias to emerge, as in this example of reporting following the accident at Three Mile Island nuclear power plant. Jane Wallace of CBS News introduced her piece this way: "The farmers in this valley call it 'radiation alley.' Almost four years after the nation's worst nuclear accident the towers stand before them as monuments to their mistrust. Jeremiah Fisher suspects Three Mile Island killed some of his cows. . . . Emmy Whitehall lost four goats, a cow, 52 ducks and some rabbits shortly after the plant lost control." This report contains highly evaluative language: "radiation alley," "mistrust," "the plant lost control," and so on. Yet there is no scientifically sustainable evidence that any human or animal was physically affected by the accident, and the total radiation dose received by the population in the area surrounding the plant was far below their annual exposure to natural and medical radiation.[8] The plant also did not "lose control." There was an accident involving a malfunction in the cooling system, which may have done more to prove the workability of backup safety systems than anything else. The key dispute surrounding the accident at Three Mile Island had to do with the competence of the manager,

GPU Nuclear Corporation. It is not self-evident from these reports that Wallace had a personal bias against the nuclear power industry, but the use of evaluative language weighted her story toward a pro-environment, anti-industry view of the events.

Less problematic, and certainly more subtle as a problem of bias, is the financial press's ubiquitous use of the expression *junk bonds* to describe high-yielding but riskier-than-usual issues. There are problems with many of these bonds, but this overused and generally inappropriate metaphor has taken hold in every quarter of financial news, to the detriment of some sound corporations and financial plans. *Newsweek,* in a single page, described corporate takeovers as "junk parties," high-yielding bonds as "junk issues," and the reputable firm of Drexel Burnham Lambert as "junk peddlers" and "junk addicts."[9] This frequent and unfair mislabeling of high-yielding bonds and their exponents has taken a toll: the bonds are now widely perceived as, literally, junk, and to be avoided at all cost.[10]

While acknowledging the danger of using evaluative language in a biased fashion, we nonetheless believe that evaluative terms can be used in an objective report without introducing a distortion. The careful use of evaluative language is not an automatic indication that objectivity has been lost or that a story is a perspective on the news and not the news itself. The pertinent point is that evaluative language should be used in news stories only when there is a substantial factual base to support it. And reporters and editors should resist the temptation to use it unless they are certain it contributes to the reader's understanding of what actually happened.

In a dispatch from Moscow jointly bylined by *Washington Post* Moscow correspondent Gary Lee and the *Post*'s experienced diplomatic reporter, Don Oberdorfer, the second paragraph said: "In a *somber* report at the end of 14 hours of intensive discussion, including nearly four hours with [Soviet leader Mikhail] Gorbachev . . . today, [U.S. Secretary of State George] Shultz said there had been 'no narrowing' of the positions between the two sides on nuclear and space arms, the topic of current negotiations in Geneva."[11] Two paragraphs later the story said, "Shultz's assessment was *almost startling* in its *bleakness* and its *bluntness*." In covering the same story, Bernard Gwertzman of *The New York Times* took a different approach. He avoided strongly evaluative works such as *somber* and *bleakness,* relying instead on formulations such as, "Shultz . . . seemed to hold out little expectation of any major breakthrough." This formulation was followed by a supporting quote from the secretary of state, which said, "I can't say anything definitive was settled. Basically, we have a lot of work to do."[12]

In the world of diplomacy the real meaning of statements by officials often can be best captured by evaluative language (journalists tend to prefer the term *interpretative* language) like that used in the Lee–Oberdorfer story. The language might be not only justified but genuinely useful. But is the Lee–Oberdorfer language sufficiently grounded in fact to justify its use in a news story? Is it based on a realistic idea of what could have been expected from the meeting? If one opts for the Lee–Oberdorfer approach, it would help to identify more clearly the evaluative material by setting it off in interpretive paragraphs rather than weaving it into paragraphs containing news. In other words, interpretation or evaluation is perfectly acceptable in a diplomatic story, but it is a service to readers to differentiate the news from the reporter's evaluation.

Sometimes an evaluative analysis is presented as a factual report, although the underlying evaluation is forcefully present and never intended to be hidden. For example, *Money* magazine ran a brief article on the statistical claims made in advertising by mutual funds such as Fidelity Magellan, Dreyfus Fund, and United Services Gold Shares.[13] *Money* reported that these funds advertised that they had returned several hundred or even several thousand percent on shareholders' money over some period of years ranging from five to thirty-three. *Money* pointed out that the "dazzling" figures they quote can mask other facts, such as that the average annual return over the period was 11.8 percent or that the performance of the funds in the most recent six months had reduced the value of the shares or percentages well below the advertised level. *Money*'s concluding paragraph read as follows: "Neither Dreyfus' nor United Services Gold Shares' performance figures are false. Both funds did exactly what they say they did. But the numbers they flaunt tell only part of the story."[14]

The same conclusion may be reached about the article in *Money*: nothing it says is false, but the true statements tell only part of the story. The underlying aim of the article is to say that the advertising can be misleading and even seductive, so watch out. The form of the sentences in the story is that of factual statements, but the content of the sentences taken collectively is at least as evaluative as factual. If readers are to be well served, stories of this kind should be clearly identified as what they are, especially when they appear in general-interest publications such as daily newspapers where readers may not expect news articles to be evaluative.

In an article in *The New York Times,* Midge Decter addressed the question of separating bias from the justified introduction of value-influenced judgments or opinions. Although Decter was writing about bias in teaching, her point is equally valid for journalism: "Bias is something that anyone with opinions can be accused of. How can a person without opinions be qualified to teach? The question is, will he be honorable in the way he permits his opinions to stand against the facts, or the texts or the opinions of others?"[15] Her use of *honorable* is one way of expressing the necessity of fairness as a condition of unbiased reporting.

Journalists write about human conflicts, and when they try to balance competing perspectives they must select what is important. Each act of selection is evaluative, but that does not prevent the selection from being objective, balanced, and fair. Evaluative analysis is desirable in journalism, as long as it is properly identified and executed. One of the press's potential contributions is to help us grasp what news and views mean and to help us sort through them. In this respect, merely presenting the unevaluated views of "interested" parties may be a disservice rather than a service to the public. It is appropriate, for example, for journalists to seek out the "disinterested" views of knowledgeable observers to help readers understand and evaluate the event or issue being reported on.

## Do Selectivity, Subjectivity, and News Judgment Entail Bias?

It is commonly claimed that the mere selection of certain events as news while omitting other events regularly introduces bias into reporting. There are even those who contend that all news reporting, because it is selective, is biased. At its core, this argument proceeds as follows. The news is presented to the public through some conception of news judgment, taste, and balance. From a virtual infinity of events in a given day, for example, the nightly national news on network television is condensed to twenty-two or twenty-three minutes. Even if the selection is an intelligent and revealing structuring of this massive array of events and issues, there is still, these critics say, a distorting bias because the editor or producer must take a point of view, one that can be subtly or even dramatically different from another editor's or producer's point of view—or from the president's point of view, or the corporation chairman's point of view, or the consumer advocate's point of view.

The force of this argument can be illustrated by a theory and an example provided by philosopher R. G. Collingwood, who contends that reports on the causes of events vary in accordance with the perspective taken on those events. Collingwood holds that different persons who are differently situated will give different answers to the question, "What is the cause of the event?" Relativity of judgment occurs, he argues, because the cause for any given person is that condition from among the set of relevant causal conditions that the person is capable of controlling or preventing. He offers this example:

A car skids while cornering at a certain point, strikes the kerb, and turns turtle. From the car-driver's point of view the cause of the accident was cornering too fast, and the lesson is that one must drive more carefully. From the county surveyor's point of view the cause was a defect in the surface or camber of the road, and the lesson is that greater care must be taken to make roads skid-proof. From the motor-manufacturer's point of view the cause was defective design in the car, and the lesson is that one must place the center of gravity lower.[16]

Whether one fully agrees with Collingwood or not, the same point has often been made about relativity of perspective in news reporting, which necessarily involves selection and taking a point of view. For example, reporting in American newspapers on complex events abroad, such as in Lebanon or South Africa, is almost invariably condensed and reflects an American perspective on what is important. The result, many Lebanese and South Africans contend, is a distorted picture of events in their countries that fails to capture the situations' complexity. News stories whose material is selected and structured according to a point of view communicate what C. Richard Hofstetter has called a "second-hand reality."[17] This selective description of reality is the reader's or viewer's substitute for a first-hand witnessing of reality.

It is undeniable that the technical demands of television—which include everything from getting an unwieldy camera crew to a fast-breaking news event hundreds of miles away to producing the tape in time to beam it up to an orbiting communications satellite—contribute significantly to shaping what will go on the air. Also many dimensions of news judgment are based on conventions about what constitutes news. For example, wars are news, at least in the beginning; the president and other prominent personalities are news; disasters are news, especially if they involve large numbers of people or if they happen close to home; and stories involving large sums of money are news, irrespective of whether the money is in a new tax bill or has been robbed from a bank. Dramatic content, pictorial opportunities, and program balance are also factors in decisions about what to air. News producers must select from among the vast number of competing stories already being promoted by dozens of the network's television correspondents, stringers, wire services, public relations firms, government public affairs officers, and so on. To make this kind of selection daily, in a way that brings order out of chaos, requires guiding principles and quick reflexes.

How can such a process possibly be free of bias? In the first place, if distortion is to have any meaning, then some things must be undistorted, and there must be criteria of nondistortion, evidence, and objectivity. In the second place, even if the premises in the argument about selectivity and relativity were entirely correct, they still would not be sufficient to prove a bias, because there is no necessity for unfairness, imbalance, or lack of objectivity. All judgments are value-driven in the sense that it is necessary to select from a myriad of detail in order to report what is important. The key question is what values inform the selection process, which is like a set of filtering devices through which some items pass successfully and others do not. A standard of balance, for example, would be a journalistic filtering device; so would a standard of accuracy. Similar criteria are used as filtering devices in every discipline. So, if selectivity alone causes bias in journalism, inevitably it does so in every discipline.

Relativity of perspective, in Collingwood's sense, need not introduce bias if the filters are functioning properly. Collingwood himself points out that the judgments of cause made by the parties in his example can all be correct and undistorted judgments. There is an engineering perspective, a highway safety perspective, a driver's perspective, and so on. Each of those perspectives is controlled by what Collingwood calls principles that determine what can legitimately count as a cause. Each of the causal judgments reached by the various parties is correct because each conforms to these standards of objective judgment. A reporter is in a similar situation: As long as proper standards of objective judgment are used, selectivity and relativity will not introduce bias.

Some commentators on media bias have focused not so much on selectivity and news judgment as on a particular kind of selecting and judging, which they contend is not subject to any controlling principles of objectivity because a reporter necessarily sees things from a purely subjective and therefore biased point of view. Columnist and television commentator James J. Kilpatrick, for example, has often expressed the view that all media reports are subjective and therefore biased.[18] Kilpatrick refers to those of us who believe in "neutral reporting" as "old fashioned." However, Kilpatrick's view suffers from a crippling bias of its own: His account of bias is by its own logic subjective (in the eye of the analyst) and necessarily biased. Kilpatrick's view is roughly like asserting the contradiction that "X [one's own account] is true and free of bias," while denying that any account like X could be true and free of bias. If Kilpatrick were correct, the term *bias* would have no meaning or critical use, and there would also be no meaningful account of fairness and truthfulness.

All such views of bias in the end reduce to the thesis that there is no such thing as truth, justified belief, or sound evidence; there is simply belief. But as the previous chapter demonstrates, objectivity, accuracy, balance, and the like are not purely subjective concepts; they are intersubjectively recognized. While criteria of truth claims and judgments of fairness vary depending on the context (for example, criteria for fair conduct in sports are different from those for fair conduct in the courtroom), terms like *truth* and *fairness* have applications apart from any subjective evaluation or bias on the part of the journalist.

Other analysts of media bias push the debate in the opposite direction from Kilpatrick. They assert that a quest for criteria of bias and objectivity is a search for the holy grail, because they view bias as largely in the eye not of the journalistic beholder of events but rather the consumer beholder of media presentations. Robert L. Stevenson and Mark T. Green have argued: "What news consumers see as biased news is often material which is discrepant with the information already in their heads, material which evokes an evaluative response. If so, news bias is *less a function of reporters' accuracy or fairness* and more a function of what readers and viewers think the situation is or ought to be."[19] Advocates of this position note that many polls have shown that most readers and viewers who see a conservative bias are Democrats, and most of those who see a liberal bias are Republicans.[20] Research by William Schneider and I. A. Lewis, which does not take account of party affiliation, indicates, however, that despite the fact that a large number of journalists hold liberal views, the public does not consider the media to be overwhelmingly biased. In this research, 25 percent of the respondents thought the newspaper they read regularly had a liberal bias, and 24 percent thought their regular newspaper had a conservative bias. Of those surveyed, 26 percent thought their newspaper was middle-of-the-road, and 25 percent were not sure. But, when asked to compare the fairness and impartiality of various major institutions in American society, the press was rated in this poll as the fairest and most impartial institution, with 44 percent of the sample placing it first. Government was second at 17 percent, business third at 13 percent, and organized labor fourth with 11 percent. Schneider and Lewis concluded, "The public gives the news media high marks for professionalism, fairness, accuracy, and reliability, and people perceive no serious left-wing bias in the material they see and read."[21]

Some try to use such polls, and arguments and data such as those provided by Stevenson and Green, as a defense against charges of media bias. They argue that bias inevitably flows from human conflict and controversy. However, this argument is self-serving, narrow, and inadequate. No doubt it is correct that many allegations of biased journalism result from what readers and viewers interpret as biased reporting or editing as opposed to its actual accuracy or fairness, but this fact illustrates only that some readers and viewers express judgments without adequate evidence. It tells us nothing about media bias.

It could, of course, be plausibly argued that our filtering mechanisms for avoiding bias do not work because the standards of objectivity, balance, accuracy, evidence, and the like are defective or imperfectly implemented. There might also be alternative and rival standards or filtering devices, and no objective way to choose among them. Someone who took this point of view would argue that we are presupposing standards of objectivity, evidence, and truth of such near perfection that a report would qualify as unbiased only if it served as "the mirror of nature" (in Richard Rorty's felicitous phrase). Yet, according to the critic, there is no mirror of nature, only perspectives on nature; and this explains why liberals find a conservative bias in the American press, conservatives a liberal bias, and Marxists a traditionalism fostered by the bourgeois control of the media. There is no neutral standpoint, such a critic will insist; there is only a viewpoint that accepts or rejects certain proposed standards governing the proper filtering of information. Because there can be many such viewpoints—each with its own rival set of standards of objectivity, balance, accuracy, comprehensiveness, fairness, competence, and so on—there is no viewpoint independent of the many viewpoints.

These are important arguments that raise legitimate questions for which we cannot here supply comprehensive answers. We would agree that there is no mirror of nature and that there are rival and incompatible sets of standards governing what will count as bias. We would also agree that Chapter 2 of this book does not refute all opposing views about evidence and that our views rest on traditional and deeply embedded cultural perspectives about the proper role and functioning of the press.

The difference between us and those whose views we reject is that we see nothing wrong with having a perspective; nor do we think that the fact that both journalists and consumers of news have perspectives prohibits developing standards of bias that are relevant for journalism. Of course, we assume a cultural and historical perspective. What other perspective could we reasonably take? But do journalists or the general public find fault with the standards that we contend underlie our tradition of a free and responsible press? The big questions about the standards we analyzed in Chapter 2 all turn on how to give substance and detail to these standards—not whether they should be the standards. In short, we admit that our standards contain vital cultural assumptions, but, far from disqualifying our claims, this background helps give them legitimacy. We are, after all, writing about journalists in this tradition of journalism, not about all possible journalists in all possible worlds.

As an example of the standards in this tradition, Sidney Hook once offered the following concrete case of objective criteria for describing a news report as fair or biased:

> The "MacNeil-Lehrer Report" on PBS is often cited as being "fairer" than the newscasts on CBS, NBC and ABC. One of the chief reasons for

this belief is that on "MacNeil-Lehrer," both sides of controversial issues are heard, and roughly *equal time is allocated* between them. Further, the program is shown *live and unedited*, whereas when opposing views are presented on other networks, what we hear are snippets of tape that can be *artfully arranged* to give the advantage or the last word to the side *the reporter favors*.[22]

Hook does not say—nor do we—either that the "MacNeil-Lehrer Report" is fairer than other network news programs or that the other programs are biased. He is making a conceptual point about the structure of such judgments, that is, (1) that judgments of fairness and bias require objective standards of balance and truthfulness, (2) that there can be degrees of deviation from these standards and therefore degrees of bias, and (3) that these standards are not so ethereal that they cannot be readily applied to the news broadcasts we see every evening. As Hook points out, these standards (roughly the standards we discussed in Chapter 2) are independent of our abilities to know the truth and to discern that a report is biased. The implementation of these standards so that we can know what is right or true has its pitfalls. Nevertheless, there are objective ways of distinguishing good evidence from poor or biased evidence, and these ways can generally be called on to distinguish biased journalism from unbiased journalism.

This argument rests on an analysis provided in Chapter 2 that went as follows (see pp. 33–42). We should not look for certain truth in assessing a journalist's performance Rather, we should ask whether journalists are justified in believing what they assert to be true. There is, of course, more than one standard of evidence. All evidence—in science, history, journalism, and everywhere—must be evaluated in the context of some theory that determines what counts as the facts or as evidence, even if the criteria for assessing the theory are in dispute.

This is a knotty problem in modern epistemology and philosophy of science, but not in journalism, where the dispute should rather be over whether the press lives up to available standards that are generally recognized to be appropriate. There are degrees of objectivity and fairness, and virtually no one is able always to be entirely accurate or as fair as possible, but this problem holds for most standards in most settings. We reject the relativistic approach to media bias because its acceptance leads to the conclusion that all claims to truth and fairness, no matter how sloppily or even dishonestly arrived at, have equal claims to acceptability. And this, as best we can tell, no one really believes.

## Factors Distorting Media Presentations

On April 1, 1984, *The New York Times* published an article under the headline, "Chief U.S. Rights Official Says Press Is Painting Distorted Picture." The story depicted a series of charges made by then Assistant Secretary of State for Human Rights Elliott Abrams. The *Times* article said in part:

> Mr. Abrams said coverage was inevitably affected by "systemic" factors. Reporters cannot get much information about abuses in the countries with the worst records, such as Cuba, North Vietnam or the Soviet Union, he said. But they can find dissidents and protestors in "partially open" nations like South Korea or El Salvador, he noted.
>
> "The media are business," Mr. Abrams said, and editors "tilt toward the visually interesting and exciting stories."
>
> "They will choose the Philippine protest over the Rumanian practice," he said.
>
> But the reporting is also tainted by ideological bias, he asserted. He cited a 1983 survey for *Public Opinion* that indicated that Washington reporters for leading news organizations were substantially more liberal politically than those in the rest of the country.
>
> He said that many reporters had a preconceived belief that the [Reagan] Administration was indifferent to abuses generally and that it preferred corrupt dictatorships to genuinely nationalistic revolutionary movements. He said such bias was evident in the cant of many articles; the Philippines are said to have "a dictator," the Soviet Union "a leader," he said.[23]

Abrams somewhat misleadingly suggests that systemic factors and ideological biases are similar forms of distortion. Although what he calls systemic factors—which he suggests are inherent in either the situations being reported on or structural factors peculiar to the medium—are different in kind from what we have identified as bias, such distorting factors are significant and merit discussion because they are similar to bias and often produce the same effect as bias—that is, distortion because of value priorities. Abrams's systemic factors and related forms of distortion therefore deserve at least brief attention.

*Situational Factors.* Distortions caused by situational factors arise from a condition inherent in the nature or circumstances of the subject of a news story. Skewing might occur, as Abrams suggests, as the result of constraints on reporting imposed by repressive governments, or it might occur, for example, in an American political campaign. The 1984 contest for the Democratic presidential nomination provides an example. William Keyserling saw the campaign shaping up as follows on Christmas Day, 1983 (Keyserling was national director of Sen. Ernest F. Hollings's campaign from June 1982 through October 1983): "The trial heats for the 1984 Democratic Presidential nomination are over. Oh, yes, it's still 1983, but that doesn't matter. The principal arbiters at this stage of the contest—the news media—have made their fundamental decisions. They'll be concentrating on the three candidates whom they consider most newsworthy—Walter F. Mondale, John Glenn and Jesse Jackson."[24]

Assuming that Keyserling is right, what is he describing? Newspapers and networks, after all, do not have unlimited resources. If there is a large field of candidates, they must decide who will get the heaviest coverage in the early stages of a campaign, even if there is something self-fulfilling about the process. But on what basis can such decisions be made without introducing an unwarranted distortion? Can editors and reporters legitimately decide to cover particular candidates, for example, because they like those politicians' views on arms control and taxes? Or should they cover someone because he is black or she is female? Or should the substantial resources involved in following a presidential candidate around the country be reserved for someone the editors think has a good chance to win?

If decisions were made strictly on grounds of the candidates' political positions on issues, bias would likely be at work. However, substantial commitment to cover a black candidate for the presidential nomination of a major party was justified in 1984 on other grounds. Not only had it never happened before, but the events reflected a significant shift on the American political scene. If journalists expended more of their limited resources on covering Jackson than on covering Hollings or Reubin Askew, that selectivity is certainly justifiable for reasons other than the political positions defended by the candidate. At least in the case of coverage of Jackson, Keyserling might just be describing news judgment, and not necessarily biased judgment.

*Structural Factors.* Marshall McLuhan had structural factors in mind when he argued that "the medium is the message." There are distinct characteristics in each medium that determine the way in which information conveyed by that medium will be understood. Television obviously conveys images better than arguments, and print does the reverse. We use the term *structural,* however, to encompass anything specific to the medium that distorts the choice of information presented and the way information is presented. For example, the fact that prime time on television can be worth $10,000 a second influences the amount of news that is shown in prime time (almost none), and the economic value of all television time influences the way in which news is packaged to attract the largest audience.

The need for action and pictures to hold the attention of a viewing audience also plays an important role in determining what television covers and how it covers the events selected for inclusion. For example, as Hodding Carter has observed, television packages information in a form that is well suited to a key goal of all campaign managers: polishing the images of candidates.[25] Press coverage of the struggle over apartheid in South Africa provides another example. The priority for television has generally been street violence. It does not matter whether whites are attacking blacks or vice versa; and it does not matter if 99 percent of South Africa is free of street violence. What matters are pictures, action, and the interests of the American public in one set of events rather than another. The street violence may be a symptom of a serious illness (which, in turn, may be why the South African government effectively banned this kind of coverage in the fall of 1985 and again in the spring and summer of 1986), but to focus on it as intensely as television does may be to confuse the symptom with the disease.

Another area in which structural factors have emerged significantly is in television coverage of terrorism and such tragedies as the explosion of the space shuttle *Challenger*. Here a judgment about what most viewers want to watch, and how much of it they want, more often determines what news will be broadcast—or at least the length at which it will be broadcast—than judgments about the intrinsic importance of the events or data. Television needs to find ways to make the drama of hostage-taking explicit, a fact that makes it relatively easy for terrorists to capture air time and manipulate the media through, for example, a press conference that provides selective access to the hostages. Reporters usually complain that distortions occur when their complex, sophisticated stories are cut to a minute and twenty seconds, but the opposite often happens in covering terrorism and profound tragedies. Distortion results from expanding the news—for structural reasons—to fill an excessive amount of allotted time during which there is little to say.

*Cultural Factors.* A distortion and imbalance resting on cultural assumptions can result from gaps in historical knowledge, reliable cultural information, or personal experience. These deficiencies may lead to false stereotypes, romanticizing cultures that are considered exotic, and the like. For example, a survey published by *The New York Times Magazine* indicates that most Americans have a lamentably distorted view—gained from press reports, presumably—of what Russians are like, what they think about authoritarian government, and what choices they would make if they were given the opportunity to have more freedom or more creature comforts.[26] Reporters who have not worked in the Soviet Union, who have not carefully followed the consistently excellent reports by Moscow correspondents of *The New York Times, The Washington Post, The Los Angeles Times,* and others—or who have not followed the specialized literature—may fall prey to these cultural misconceptions.

Similarly, a letter to *The Washington Post* criticized an article about customs in rural Liberia for what the letter writer considered distortion resulting from a misconception of cultural factors or preconceptions tainted by stereotypes:

> Blaine Harden's "Magic Rules Rural Life in Liberia" [December 7] unnecessarily reinforced many uncomplimentary stereotypes that Americans have about Africa and Africans. In the first paragraphs we learn that Gbonwea, Liberia, is a "devil-worshiping region," with a witch doctor dispensing superstitious-sounding dictums. . . .
> My problem with the article is that it does not attempt to go behind the superstition to examine the belief structure on which it is based.[27]

Another letter to the *Post* the same day said: "A subject as complex as the religious practices of a culture requires more thorough research than that carried out by Harden. . . . Far from offering valuable insight, this article sadly contributes to a misunderstanding of Africa by fueling misconceptions and stereotypes."[28] Both letters, in effect, charge Harden with distortion based on cultural misconceptions or preconceptions. We lack the credentials to judge whether the Harden article contributes to such misunderstanding, but if the critics are correct, they are describing an instance in which a lack of historical knowledge, reliable information, or personal experience led to distorted information about another culture.

Journalists sometimes pick up the cultural viewpoints of public officials and transmit them uncritically to the public. This has often happened in coverage of Japan, a subtle and complex society that differs substantially from Western societies. Japanese "protectionism," for example, was long characterized in the press as nothing but predatory trade practice, until it emerged that deeply ingrained patterns in Japanese society make it almost as difficult for a Japanese company to break into the closed network of manufacturers and suppliers (a system known as *keiretsu*) in Japan as it is for a foreign company.[29]

## A Study in Multiple Forms of Bias and Distortion: CBS's "The Uncounted Enemy"

The "CBS Reports" documentary "The Uncounted Enemy: A Vietnam Deception" illustrates several of the problems of bias and other distorting factors that we have discussed. This documentary is only one of many cases in electronic or print journalism that might be chosen for an extensive examination, but it contains particularly instructive examples.

The months leading up to the major North Vietnamese and Vietcong assault known as the Tet offensive at the end of January 1968 were intensely political in the United States. It was a presidential election year, and the predominant campaign issue was the Vietnam War. A consensus was building in the press that the war was unwinnable. President Lyndon B. Johnson was increasingly identified as the chief hawk, and Democrats with presidential aspirations were beginning to attack him. Official reports from the war zone were more encouraging from the president's perspective. In November 1967, the Johnson administration launched a high-powered campaign to spread the word that the tide was turning. Ambassador Ellsworth Bunker, the U.S. envoy in Saigon, Ambassador Robert Komer, the president's special representative for Vietnam, and Gen. William Westmoreland, commander of U.S. forces in Vietnam, all declared publicly that progress was being made.

Meanwhile, a seemingly less cosmic but closely related contest was being fought. It concerned the size of the enemy in Vietnam, and it centered on a judgment about the political and military weight that should be given to irregular enemy forces facing U.S. and South Vietnamese troops. A key question was whether partially trained and poorly armed irregular units should be lumped together with fully trained and well-armed local and main-force units and included in the running total of enemy strength. This total was the central figure in the overall evaluation of enemy forces and was known as the order of battle. It was treated by the press as an important indicator of the Vietcong and the North Vietnamese army's capacities to continue fighting. The order of battle had considerable political importance. If President Johnson were to be reelected, the American people had to be convinced that the war was going well, which meant that some attrition in enemy force levels had to be shown.

Westmoreland argued then, as he still does today, that new, significantly higher numbers of self-defense militia, secret self-defense militia, and other irregulars being reported by some U.S. civilian and military intelligence analysts should never have been included in the order of battle. He maintained that the units to which those forces belonged lacked offensive capabilities and that their counterparts on the South Vietnamese side had never been counted in the order of battle. He said there was a danger that the press and some officials would misinterpret the higher numbers and mistakenly assume that the United States was losing the war. Such an assumption by the press could affect the upcoming elections.

Sam Adams of the CIA was one of the order-of-battle analysts who had concluded, mainly from captured documents, that more enemy forces existed than had been previously estimated. These forces were usually farmers by day and soldiers by night. Adams discovered that some military intelligence analysts had made estimates lower than his but significantly higher than those carried on the official books. He concluded on the basis of conversations—principally with Col. Gains Hawkins, who was in charge of providing order-of-battle estimates in Saigon—that these estimates were being suppressed for political reasons. After a series of negotiations between intelligence officers of the Military Assistance Command—Vietnam (MACV), headed by Westmoreland, the CIA, and other intelligence units, a compromise on how to calculate the numbers was reached, but it did not satisfy Adams. The key number to be used, the central order-of-battle total, was Westmoreland's figure of less than 300,000, not Adams's figure of 600,000 or more. The estimated increase in irregular forces was included as a textual note.

A magazine journalist, George Crile, became aware of the controversy in the mid-1970s while working as Washington editor of *Harper's*. He met Adams and encouraged him to write an article expressing his viewpoint. Crile later edited the article, which was published in May 1975.[30] It was based on research Adams had done after failing to get his 600,000-man estimate accepted as the official enemy strength figure. The article was instrumental in the establishment of the House Select Committee on Intelligence (the Pike Committee), which examined the issues raised by Adams.

Four years later Adams contacted Crile, then a CBS producer, to share the results of his continuing research. Crile found Adams's new evidence compelling and agreed to propose a documentary to his CBS superiors that would demonstrate that Westmoreland had "cooked the books." On November 24, 1980, Crile submitted a blue sheet, the document CBS producers use to sell a program to network decision makers. The blue sheet is usually one page long, but in this case it ran sixteen single-spaced pages. "It was all overwhelmingly clear to Adams," the blue sheet said. "He had come across the most significant intelligence discovery since World War II. The captured enemy documents [he was analyzing] *proved* that we were fighting a far larger war than anyone in authority had imagined. Now the President, the congress, the American people would have to make a choice: Either escalate dramatically or get out."[31]

After winning executive approval to make the documentary, Crile spent months interviewing about eighty sources. His primary list had been supplied by Adams. It consisted mainly of persons who could be expected to contribute to proving the thesis that Westmoreland had conspired to falsify the order of battle. Not everyone interviewed was of the same mind, but none of those who challenged the Adams thesis, with one twenty-one-second exception, got on the air. Of those who supported it, nine—including Adams himself, as the documentary's paid consultant—were used on the program. Mike Wallace, who had the title of chief correspondent, was there not only because of his skill as an interviewer but to give the show star quality. Wallace handled the toughest interviews, including the one with Westmoreland. Finally, on January 23, 1982, fourteen months after Crile delivered his blue sheet (a week short of the fourteenth anniversary of the Tet offensive), "The Uncounted Enemy: A Vietnam Deception" was aired. Almost eight months later, on September 13, 1982, Westmoreland sued CBS for libel. After many emotionally draining weeks in court, Westmoreland dropped his suit, convinced that he was unlikely to prevail under the existing legal standards for libeling a public figure.[32]

The trial's outcome, however, has no bearing on whether "The Uncounted Enemy" was a biased documentary. It was. The bias in "The Uncounted Enemy" was manifested mainly in Crile's skillful selection and marshaling of information to make his case as convincingly as possible, even though a fair and distanced reading of all the available evidence would not necessarily have yielded the same conclusion. Our assessment is not intended to suggest that Crile was dishonest. On the contrary, he apparently believed that what he put on the air was as close as he could get to what he called "the essence of truth." The problem is that he chose a method of inquiry that, together with his personal convictions, was predestined to yield biased or otherwise distorted results. He formed a hypothesis—or, rather, adopted Adams's hypothesis—and carefully gathered evidence to support it, rejecting almost every conflicting piece of evidence. Even the interview segments with Westmoreland and Lieut. Gen. (then Col.) Daniel O. Graham that were used on the air looked as if they had been chosen because they made the two officers appear either foolish or guilty.

Crile was following fairly common procedures in documentary production, and he had arguments for breaking a few more rules than usual. For example, he was forced to condense an extremely complicated story into a relatively tight time frame, an instance of a structural constraint. The program, exclusive of commercials and station breaks, ran about an hour. The printed transcript runs just over twenty-six single-spaced pages. Of the eighteen military officers, diplomats, and intelligence analysts who were central to the dispute, most were interviewed, and many appeared on the program. Some did not appear, and at least six potentially important sources were not interviewed at all. If all eighteen had been interviewed and all of the interviews had been aired—and the entire show had been devoted to them—each interview would have had to be reduced in the cutting room to barely three minutes in length. If a minute and a half had been allowed for questions and a minute and a half for answers, the interview subjects would have been allocated about 250 words each. There were simply too many sources to pack into a single documentary.

To portray such a complex story effectively on television, a medium that for the most part is not used in a nuanced fashion, required an uncomplicated story line that most viewers could follow with a minimum of mental exertion. Television requires movement, a parade of pictures across the screen that holds the viewer's attention. It demands clarity, simplicity, and repetition to reach the largest possible audience with maximum impact. It must capture complex ideas in simple images to drive home its message effectively. Therefore, if Crile believed he had the goods on Westmoreland and that his basic obligation as a journalist was to make the most compelling case possible, he had little choice but to produce the program in the language and images of certainty, not ambiguity. These are the terms of television. Thus, Crile was, at least in part, a captive of structural distortion.

This kind of technically distorted presentation is not without justification, however. Assuming that the preponderance of evidence supported Crile's case, both justice and the public interest arguably might be served by marshaling the considerable power of an incisive television documentary. Just as a segment on "60 Minutes" had contributed to overturning the robbery conviction of Lenell Geter, an engineer sent to prison in an apparently blatant example of racism,[33] so "The Uncounted Enemy" might have corrected the historical record and contributed to a proper apportioning of credit and blame in one of the most politically and socially wrenching of America's wars.

Crile and his colleagues did seem convinced that they were investigating "one of the major national security scandals of our recent past,"[34] and the evidence gathered by Adams in highly detailed chronologies warranted a vigorous examination of the thesis that high-ranking military officers were coerced by Westmoreland into suppressing evidence of a larger enemy. Moreover, one military officer and CIA officer after another gave persuasive testimony supporting the Adams–CBS thesis. After the program was aired, several key CBS witnesses were asked by Westmoreland to make statements that their words were taken out of context. They refused.[35] None of these "friendly" witnesses complained to CBS about bias, misrepresentation, or out-of-context editing. Furthermore, Westmoreland was briefed in advance about the subject matter of his interview, and the nature of the program was discussed with him before he was interviewed.[36] His denials that his command was "cooking the books" were aired on the broadcast.

*TV Guide* charged, in an article titled "Anatomy of a Smear," that the supervisory work at CBS was sloppy and that the standards for safeguards against bias, unfairness, and inaccuracy were loose.[37] However, the magazine provided no hard evidence to support those charges, and at least some evidence supports the contrary view. For example, a CBS News vice-president, Roger Colloff, appears to have been more extensively involved than is usually the case. According to CBS's internal review of the broadcast, usually referred to as the Benjamin report because it was prepared by senior producer Burton Benjamin, "Roger Colloff went far beyond what a vice president with extensive managerial functions normally does on a broadcast—reading some transcripts and meeting with the producer." Benjamin also wrote that Mike Wallace, who was not as fully engaged as he is in the average "60 Minutes" segment, "was hardly uninvolved in the Vietnam broadcast. He attended some screenings, adjudicated some creative disputes and conducted four interviews."[38] CBS also had a veteran staff working on the program. The show did not suffer from a lack of testimony supporting its central thesis. Moreover, to persuade the high-ranking military officers and former CIA officials to make the confessions on camera that they did, and to marshal so much statistical and historical evidence, was a considerable achievement. It is therefore far from obvious that CBS produced a biased documentary or that a charge of personal bias against Crile can be sustained.

Yet a biased program is exactly what CBS did produce, although there was no way in which the average viewer could discern it. Even someone reasonably knowledgeable about the history of the war would almost certainly find the documentary persuasive—unless, of course, that person had at some point focused on the highly specialized question of pre-Tet enemy force levels and knew more than a little about the art of intelligence gathering and interpretation—or unless he or she had been permitted to see the outtakes or read the transcripts of the interviews conducted for the program, which provide potent circumstantial evidence of bias.

Crile stated his central thesis as follows:

> That in 1967, American military and civilian intelligence discovered evidence indicating the existence of a dramatically larger enemy than previously reported [and] that instead of alerting the country, U.S. military intelligence under General Westmoreland commenced to suppress and alter its intelligence reports, in order to conceal the discovery from the American public, the Congress, and perhaps even the President.[39]

Later, in response to the controversy ignited by the TV Guide article, Crile said that only a minor modification of this statement was required. He wrote, "Now that I look at it I would put a period after the words 'intelligence reports,' "[40] thereby eliminating the phrase "in order to conceal the discovery from the American public, the Congress, and perhaps even the President." But Crile's comment is unsatisfactory. Even if there were no objection to his contention that military intelligence was suppressed, it would be journalistically unacceptable to produce a documentary without at least offering defensible hypotheses regarding why it was suppressed.

The Benjamin study was ordered by the president of CBS News, Van Gordon Sauter. Benjamin found that "The premise [of the program] was obviously and historically controversial. There was an imbalance in presenting the two sides of the issue. . . . Even today military historians cannot tell you whether or not MACV 'cooked the books' as the broadcast states. The flow of definitive information is painfully slow and may never be conclusive."[41] Benjamin's judgment is correct, but was the imbalance he cited sufficient evidence of bias to be termed immoral? Did "The Uncounted Enemy" significantly overstate its case? Or, worse still, did it present a case that was not sustainable through an unbiased use of the available evidence?

The answer to all these questions is affirmative. Deletion of views opposed to the Adams–Crile thesis was at times egregious. Crile seemed resistant to virtually all evidence at odds with his fundamental premise, although material exists in the deleted portions of "The Uncounted Enemy" to produce an equally sound documentary that would support precisely the opposite thesis from the one Crile was promoting. It would demonstrate, mainly through the use of quotations cut from interviews used on the program, that Westmoreland acted to present the most militarily valid view of enemy force levels in Vietnam just before the Tet offensive.

Had it been produced, the excerpts from such a program—drawn from CBS's own interview transcripts—would have appeared as follows:

> *Wallace:* The people we're talking about here, the self-defense militia, these very people that sharpen the pungy stakes . . . ?
> *Westmoreland:* In order to include a lot of teenagers and old men, village defenders who could prepare pungy stakes, in the enemy order of battle, we had to also include the counterpart in the order of battle of the South Vietnamese. The fact is that these village defenders had a minimum to do with the outcome of the war.[42]

Westmoreland made substantially the same point nine times in his interview with Wallace. Why include irregulars of this sort in the enemy order of battle, he asked, if we do not include them in our own? The question is never raised or discussed in "The Uncounted Enemy," yet it is Westmoreland's firm position, and it directly challenges Crile's thesis.

Two other excerpts from the outtakes read as follows:

> *Crile:* What did you think of Mr. Adams' argument, of his figures?
> *Col. Gains Hawkins:* I disagreed with Sam on the magnitude of the strength. And we just . . . . I just disagreed with him on the methodology. My figures were . . . . I believe, at all times generally lower than Sam's figures.

> *Crile:* You had some concerns about the—the reliability of the overall estimate, didn't you?
>
> *Comdr. James Meacham:* Oh, we always have concerns about—sure.
>
> *Crile:* Did you think they should have been considerably higher?
>
> *Meacham:* No, I don't recall having thought they should be considerably higher; I thought they should've been more accurate, but I think we just couldn't make them any more accurate.[43]

These were Crile's witnesses—the people who made his case on the air unequivocally. They were able to do so because all the equivocation—all of the contradictions, qualifications, and ambivalence—was edited out before the airing.

The same interviews that Crile and Wallace conducted could have been mined to produce a program that would discredit the Crile–Adams thesis no less convincingly than Crile discredited Westmoreland's. However, it too would be biased in much the same ways that "The Uncounted Enemy" was biased. No strong thesis either way can, without bias, be sustained, because the record, including thousands of pages of unused interview transcripts, is replete with ambiguity and conflicting testimony. The editing of the interviews demonstrates that Crile and Wallace were not interested in getting the answers to hard questions that might weaken their thesis, such as: Is the task of collecting order-of-battle intelligence as General Westmoreland has suggested more like estimating roaches than counting beans? Are disputes of the kind described unusual between intelligence agencies? Is it uncommon to negotiate an order of battle total in the way it was done by CIA, DIA (Defense Intelligence Agency), and MACV? Was General Westmoreland wrong in wanting to keep irregular forces out of the order of battle? Did the analysts who were making order-of-battle estimates—Hawkins, Meacham, and McArthur—have sufficient information to make accurate estimates? Did Westmoreland believe he was reporting the best possible estimates of enemy capabilities?

These are tough questions, especially considering the structural constraints of television documentary and the situational constraint of reporting on an event that had occurred years before. It would have been extremely difficult for Crile to have simultaneously used the medium effectively and to have accurately characterized the uncertainty of the situation. Those interviewed repeatedly qualified their statements and offered exceptions to facile generalizations. Many interview sequences would have left audiences confused about what conclusion to draw. For example, what would viewers have made of the following exchange between Crile and Gen. Joseph McChristian, Westmoreland's chief of intelligence, had it been aired:

> *Crile:* How should I put this—so that I can best express it? Maybe just this question: Did—did you ever, while in command of MACV Intelligence, have pressures put on you to keep enemy estimates down?

> *McChristian:* I had pressures put on me from time to time, George; not exactly that bluntly to keep any estimates down. Never. But I did have pressures put upon me to review my criteria: maybe my criteria wasn't (sic.) just right. . . .
>
> *Crile:* Were there any other [instances or] incidents?
>
> *McChristian:* There were other instance[s] when my intelligence was questioned. At one time, the chairman of the Joint Chiefs of Staff considered that what information he had been furnished in Washington that he used to brief the President, was not agreeable to the intelligence that was coming from my office, so he sent a team of officers from his—from the Joint Chiefs of Staff to Saigon to investigate. And they found out that what they had been using back in Washington was not my intelligence to brief the President, but it was operational reports, which is raw information and not intelligence. I was completely vindicated in that case; and in every case where my reporting was questioned, every single case I was vindicated, and in no case was there the slightest change made in any of my reporting or any of my criteria.[44]

McChristian here acknowledges that whereas he was pressured to review his criteria, neither his reporting nor his criteria were ever changed. This contention does not definitively falsify the Adams–Crile conspiracy thesis, but it dilutes the thesis and directly calls it into question.

The structural constraints of a television documentary may have left Crile with little choice but to scrap the program, at substantial cost to CBS and possibly his career, or to proceed as he did despite the testimony that conflicted with his findings. But, if so, he made the wrong choice. By purging the documentary of ambiguity, by avoiding the hard questions, by using loaded language, and by compromising the integrity of the evidence to a kind of dramatic intensity, Crile produced a biased program that deceived viewers into thinking that the case against Westmoreland was solidly grounded. He also damaged the general's reputation in a way that, if not legally libelous, certainly carries moral liability.

Even if Crile is given the benefit of the doubt by assuming that he was entirely persuaded by Adams's thesis, he failed to fulfill his obligation to the public to avoid presenting an unfair and one-sided version of a delicate and complicated subject. Consider how Westmoreland is presented and how a viewer who is unfamiliar with the background of the controversy almost inevitably must react. First, the general's defense is confined to five minutes and thirty-eight seconds of personal testimony. CBS argued that General Graham also testified on Westmoreland's behalf, but this claim is misleading. Graham was on the air for twenty-one seconds and testified in defense of himself, not Westmoreland. By contrast, eight interview subjects pilloried Westmoreland at length—nine if Adams is included. Yet, as the Benjamin report correctly noted, "For every McChristian there was a Davidson; for every Hawkins, a Morris; for every Allen, a Carver."[45]

General Philip Davidson, who succeeded McChristian as chief of mili-

tary intelligence in Vietnam, supported Westmoreland. CBS said they believed he was dying of cancer and therefore did not make a serious effort
to interview him for the program. Although Davidson did have cancer of
the prostate in 1974, his personal physician reported that the retired officer was in good health at the time the broadcast was being prepared. Crile
assigned his secretary to contact Davidson. She tried only during working
hours at his home number. Two other equally qualified observers, who
held views that were dramatically different from the views of those who
appeared on the program, were not heard on the air. One was George
Carver, George Allen's boss at the CIA. He personally negotiated the final
order-of-battle compromise with Westmoreland. His view of the events
depicted on "The Uncounted Enemy" was closer to Westmoreland's than
to Allen's. Col. Charles Morris was Davidson's deputy. He, too, disputed
the Adams thesis. Moreover, Walt W. Rostow, President Johnson's national security advisor, was interviewed and disputed the conspiracy thesis,
but did not appear on the program. Ambassador Bunker, the U.S. envoy
in Vietnam at the time, and Robert Komer, Johnson's special representative for Vietnam, were not even interviewed.

There were equally compelling examples of biased interviewing and
editing, such as a critical omission in the following cable sent by Gen.
Creighton Abrams to the Joint Chiefs of Staff on August 20, 1967, and
misattributed by CBS to Westmoreland (who "signed off" on it, but was
not its author). Wallace read it on the air, in modified form, and it appeared in large type on the screen, as follows (with the phrase in brackets
deleted by CBS): "We have been projecting an image of success over the
recent months, [and properly so]." Wallace then added, "The self-defense
militia must be removed," words that do not appear in the cable at all,
and concluded, "[or] the newsmen will immediately seize on the point that
the enemy force has increased. No explanation could then prevent the press
from drawing an erroneous and gloomy conclusion."[46] The deletion of
"and rightly so" has the effect of making the preceding language, "We
have been projecting an image of success over recent months," sound like
a fabrication because of the ill-chosen words "projecting" and "image."

When Westmoreland was quizzed on "Meet the Press" in November
1967 about the number of North Vietnamese infiltrating into South Vietnam in the months leading up to the Tet offensive, he gave this answer: "I
would estimate between 5,500 and 6,000 a month, but they do have the
capability of stepping this up."[47] Asked the same question fourteen years
later when interviewed for "The Uncounted Enemy," he answered with a
figure of 20,000. The Tet offensive began more than two months after the
"Meet the Press" interview, and therefore the phrase in brackets, which
was deleted from Westmoreland's answers by CBS, was highly relevant.

Furthermore, on June 9, 1981, seven months before the broadcast, West-moreland sent Crile and Wallace an official MACV document that put the infiltration total for January 1968 at 21,100 and the highest monthly total for September through December at 6,300 (in September). This document was accompanied by a letter acknowledging that he had misspoken about the infiltration rate (during the fall of 1967) when he was interviewed by CBS in 1981. Neither the letter nor the document was mentioned on the air. The program contains numerous similar examples of selective and mis-leading editing and use of materials, and in virtually every case the presen-tation serves, without adequate justification, to undermine Westmoreland's credibility.

To understand what Crile says he was trying to accomplish, it helps to know his conception of the art of interviewing for a television documen-tary. He expressed his views on this subject in a conversation with Benja-min on June 22, 1982:

> The documentary interview is so different from live news, hard news or print interview. It is not supposed to be timeless, but you are supposed to get certain truths. It is a producer's nightmare. You are out on a limb. In print it doesn't matter if you get it over 12 hours. In a documentary the producer can only deal with what is on film. I need to find a way to get in the clear that person's perceptions of what we are dealing with. If a person is only saying lies or speaking uncharacteristically, you have a different truth than what you know him to be. You're in a pickle. . . . To get to that right moment you go another route to get it out. . . . It's like a dance, an art form. You're moving toward a moment. You're trying to get the essence of truth on film.[48]

Crile's description of the interview process goes directly to the heart of the problem with "The Uncounted Enemy." The war footage, the menacing helicopters, and the driving, table-thumping speeches of Lyndon Johnson are dazzling and add drama to the program, but in the end the premise of the show can only be sustained by the spoken words of the interview sub-jects and the documentation of events of which few, if any, pictures are available. Furthermore, if this kind of documentary is to be lively enough to meet the dramatic requirements of the medium, the interviews must generate drama independent of the file footage that supports them. Care-fully hedged answers are undesirable because they lack clarity, sound pe-dantic, and will quickly drive viewers to another channel. To hold an au-dience, the remarks of those interviewed must be hard-hitting and unambiguous. But editing for that effect produces a warped result. The distortion of television technique replaces the objectivity of sound report-ing. The search for "truth" fades and becomes a search for a preconceived "moment," a biased hypothesis that captures the "essence of truth" in the mind of the documentary maker.

When Crile described the technique as "a dance, an art form," his metaphor was apt. Questions were asked, rephrased, and asked again, approaching the subject from various angles, until the desired response was elicited. If the interview subject seemed about to say too much, Crile or Wallace often cut him off by asking the next question. If that maneuver failed, the quotation could easily be—and often was—edited or used out of context to fit the interviewer's apparently preconceived requirement. For example, Crile's interview with Meacham shows the process at work. Almost nothing of what Meacham said was aired, and what was used failed to reflect the essence of what he was saying—that is, his general viewpoint. No matter how hard Crile tried, he could not induce Meacham to support the documentary's central thesis that intelligence had been falsified. Nor could Crile get Meacham to agree that Graham was seeking to change the computer database without proper justification. Instead, Meacham says that no intelligence was falsified, "all of the numbers were soft," and "at the end of each month, we didn't have much faith in that [enemy strength] figure anyway."

Graham had access to data to which Meacham did not have access, and Meacham did not question that Graham believed he was justified in changing the computer database. Meacham said he thought "we could have lost an argument before an objective jury" about this matter of changing the database. None of this appeared on the air. Here is what Crile chose to use from the Meacham interview:

> *Wallace:* According to Colonel Cooley, there was a general agreement at this time that something had to be done. Cooley and another senior intelligence officer, Commander James Meacham, have told CBS REPORTS that several weeks after Tet, Col. Daniel Graham, General Westmoreland's chief of estimates, asked them to alter MACV's historical record. In effect, they then accused Graham of personally engineering a cover-up. First, Commander Meacham:
> *Crile:* There comes a time when Colonel Graham asked you and Colonel Weiler to tamper with the computer's memory, to change the data base in some way.
> *Comdr. James Meacham (Retired):* Yes, that's it.
> *Crile:* You said no.
> *Commander Meacham:* Well we—we didn't say no. I mean, this thing wasn't our private property. It belonged to the intelligence directorate. We were the custodians of it. We didn't like what Danny Graham proposed to do. We didn't want him to do it. At the end of the day, we lost the fight, and he did it.
> *Crile:* What was so wrong about going back into the memory? What got Meacham so distressed about it?
> *Colonel Cooley:* I would—a little bit of the 1984 syndrome here, you know, where you—you can obliterate something or you, you know, can—can alter it to the point where it never existed type of logic.

*Commander Meacham:* Up to that time, even though some of the current estimates and the current figures had been juggled around with, we had not really tinkered with our data base, if I can use that jargonistic word. And—and Danny Graham was asking us to do it, and we didn't like it. . . .

*General Graham:* Oh, for crying out loud. I never asked anybody (to) wipe out the computer—computer's memory. I don't know what he—I honestly haven't got any idea what he's talking about.

*Wallace:* We stress that Colonel Graham denies the allegation and insists that he never falsified nor suppressed any intelligence reports on the enemy. But Commander Meacham and Colonel Cooley insist that Graham did alter the record. And they suggest that because of this, we may never be able to go back and understand exactly what happened.[49]

The material aired leaves the clear impression that Meacham thought Graham was acting dishonestly by changing the computer database. It also implies that he charged Graham with altering the "record," a word Meacham specifically rejected as too strong. As a result, viewers were led to think that Meacham supported the documentary's minor premise that Graham intended to falsify the enemy order of battle. Yet Meacham repeatedly observed that even though he disagreed with Graham about whether there was justification for altering the database, Graham had access to more intelligence and might have been right.

Crile denies that he intentionally deceived viewers in his use of the Meacham material. He insists Meacham told him things off camera that justified the way in which the interview was edited. But Crile failed to reconcile the contradictions between what Meacham said off camera and on. Instead he chose to use selected on-camera material to support the program's premise. If Meacham contradicted himself, Crile could have dropped him from the show or perhaps tried to prove conclusively that he was lying. Instead, he used comments taken out of context in a biased fashion, and he elected not to use an evaluation by a source with solid credentials (Meacham) that cast grave doubt on the documentary's major premise.

We could provide numerous additional examples of such editing, and we could devote pages to describing biased visual techniques that were used to make Westmoreland look bad, such as excessive tight shots of him emphasizing his facial tics and his growing anger, discomfort, and impatience under Wallace's sustained grilling. These television techniques are often used to heighten drama, but when their intent is to slant the story being presented, they are a visual expression of bias.

An astonishing political conclusion is also almost inevitably inferred by the viewer. Without explicitly saying so, the show leaves the impression that Lyndon Johnson decided not to run for reelection because he was deceived about the enemy order of battle for the months leading up to Tet. (Evidence uncovered during the trial discovery process indicates that this was not the case.) Crile has disavowed that it was his intention to demonstrate that Westmoreland's alleged conspiracy was meant to "conceal this discovery [of an allegedly larger enemy force] from the American public, the Congress and perhaps even the President." But the program was orchestrated to make this conclusion almost unavoidable. Its climax went like this:

> *Wallace:* What had happened is that after Tet the CIA had regained the courage of its convictions, and among other things, they told the wise men [a small group selected by the President to advise him on the conduct of the war] of the CIA's belief that we were fighting a dramatically larger enemy. That was at least one of the reasons why Lyndon Johnson's advisors concluded that despite the military's insistence that we were winning, the enemy could not in fact be defeated at any acceptable cost. The wise men then stunned the President by urging him to begin pulling out of the war. Five days later, a sobered Lyndon Johnson addressed the nation.
>
> *President Johnson* (3/31/68): I shall not seek, and I will not accept, the nomination of my party for another term as your President.
>
> *Wallace:* Two months after the President's speech, General William Westmoreland was transferred back to Washington and promoted to become chief of the army. To this day, General Westmoreland insists that the enemy was virtually destroyed at Tet. Be that as it may, the fighting went on for seven more years after the Tet offensive. Twenty-seven thousand more American soldiers were killed; over a hundred thousand more were wounded. And on April 30, 1975, that same enemy entered Saigon once again, only this time it was called Ho Chi Minh City.[50]

What are we to infer from Wallace's reciting those two speeches and sandwiching between them the brief but emotional Johnson statement? There is certainly an implication that the alleged Westmoreland conspiracy to "cook the books" was the decisive triggering cause and Johnson's decision not to run was the effect. The documentary also hints that Westmoreland was responsible for seven more years of war, 27,000 additional American deaths, and 100,000 more U.S. wounded. Many viewers almost certainly rose from their chairs at the end of the show with this message embedded in their minds, although no such inference is ever explicitly drawn by CBS. These inferences may not be inevitable in that they do not flow logically from the evidence, but they are implicit in the selection and juxtaposition of the information, and in Wallace's portentous delivery.

It would be difficult, we think, to prove conclusively that Crile intentionally pilloried Westmoreland. We are not convinced of this intention after interviewing Crile and reading through thousands of pages of documents pertaining to his work. But we are confident that a charge of bias can be sustained. By stacking the interviews 9–2 against Westmoreland, which made the Adams thesis seem impregnable—even though there were plenty of knowledgeable participants prepared to support Westmoreland's viewpoint—Crile failed to present a substantial amount of available counterevidence. No prudent journalist, no matter what his or her personal views, would handle the evidence so unfairly. Crile displayed bias by deleting highly relevant material from the interviews that were conducted, by not asking a whole range of important questions, by failing to put the order-of-battle question in proper context, and by creating the impression that Johnson decided not to run again because he was misinformed about enemy troop levels as the result of a consipiracy led by Westmoreland.

Crile's first obligation was neither to history nor to CBS. His principal responsibility as a journalist was to accurately represent to the public a complex controversy. He should not have become an advocate for a cause, no matter how noble he believed it to be. If a cause is just, in the end it will be best served by reporters through unbiased presentation. By taking up Adams's cause—some would say his obsession—Crile lost too much of the fair-mindedness, truthfulness, and objectivity that is vital to maintaining journalistic integrity. He also publicly crucified a man who, based on the available evidence, almost certainly deserved a fairer hearing.

## Conclusion

The philosopher David Hume considered a "moderate" species of skepticism an antidote to bias. He maintained that we should check and recheck our basic observations, our data derived from the testimony of others, and our inferences from both observations and testimony. Skepticism on every level, where reason corrects our untrustworthy observations and inferences, is the only method, Hume argued, "by which we can ever hope to reach truth, and attain a proper stability and certainty in our determinations." He saw skepticism as "a necessary preparative to the study of philosophy, by preserving a proper *impartiality* in our judgments, and weaning our mind from *all those prejudices,* which we may have imbibed from education or rash opinion."[51] To Hume's recommendation we add only that skepticism is as suited to journalism as to epistemology.

Today there is an ongoing debate among journalists and the public about whether unbiased reporting is possible even by skeptical journalists. James J. Kilpatrick—as we have seen—does not believe unbiased reporting is possible, while *Washington Post* reporter Spencer Rich has argued that journalists not only should but can maintain sufficient distance from their subject matter to prevent personal bias.[52] We concur with Rich, but with the understanding that unbiased coverage can be achieved only if journalists maintain a skeptical awareness of their own personal biases and follow practices designed to prevent those biases from infecting their articles and broadcasts.

NOTES

1. Editorial, "CBS's Problems," *The Wall Street Journal,* March 28, 1985, p. 32; Walter Cronkite, "News and Views at CBS," *The Wall Street Journal,* April 5, 1985, p. 17 (with a supporting comment on the same page by Richard Salant); "News and Views at CBS," Letters to the Editor, *The Wall Street Journal,* April 18, 1985, p. 17.

2. Robert J. Samuelson, "On Journalists, the Reforming Instinct, and Saying Something Nice," *The Washington Post,* January 2, 1985, p. B8.

3. Jean McNair (Associated Press), "Christian Network Plans Nightly News Broadcast," *The Washington Post,* December 20, 1985 p. E1.

4. See Robert C. Stevenson and Mark T. Greene, "A Reconsideration of Bias in the News," *Journalism Quarterly,* Spring 1980, vol. 57: 116–17.

5. See Peggy Berkowitz, "Canada Sets Oil, Gas Exploration Plan to End Bias Against Foreign Companies," *The Wall Street Journal,* October 31, 1985, p. 6.

6. Anthony Spaeth, *The Wall Street Journal,* October 30, 1985, p. 32.

7. *Personal Investor,* September 1985, p. 9.

8. Compare Jane Wallace, "CBS Morning News," December 10, 1982 and John Kemeny, *Report of the President's Commission on the Accident at Three Mile Island* (Washington, D.C., 1979).

9. Bill Powell, Carolyn Friday, and Rich Thomas, "Is the Junk Party Over?" *Newsweek,* December 16, 1985, p. 52.

10. These bonds range widely in quality, although all are below what is often called investment grade. These categories spring from a conservative perspective on investing, which in effect denigrates any investment of funds in an instrument that is below "investment grade." However, many successful and often highly promising corporations are swept under this umbrella of junk. Only 675 U.S. companies are rated investment grade, although over 20,000 have assets above $25 million. Moreover, mutual funds that are dedicated to investing in these high-yielding bonds have shown excellent results, without undue risk from the perspective of even many cautious investors. Drexel Burnham has always insisted that they thoroughly investigate the actual quality of a bond before recommending it. See Frederick H. Joseph, "High-Yield Bonds Aren't 'Junk'," *The Wall Street Journal,* May 31, 1985, p. 22; and Anthony Bianco, "The Growing Respectability of the Junk Heap," *Business Week,* April 22, 1985, p. 66.

11. Gary Lee and Don Oberdorfer, "Shultz Expresses Pessimism After Talk with Gorbachev," *The Washington Post,* November 6, 1985, p. A1. Emphasis added.

12. Bernard Gwertzman, "Schultz Says No Significant Results Were Achieved in Moscow Talks," *The New York Times,* November 6, 1985, p. 1.

13. "Eye-Catching Numbers," *Money,* March 1985, p. 13.

14. Ibid.

15. Midge Decter, "More Bullying on Campus," *The New York Times*, December 10, 1985, p. A31.

16. R. G. Collingwood, *An Essay On Metaphysics* (Oxford: Oxford University Press, 1940), p. 304.

17. C. Richard Hofstetter, *Bias in the News* (Columbus: Ohio State University Press, 1976), p. 19.

18. James J. Kilpatrick, as voiced often on the weekly television program "Agronsky and Company"; see also his "The Post's Rain Clouds," *The Washington Post*, February 1, 1983, p. A17.

19. Stevenson and Greene, "A Reconsideration of Bias," p. 121. Emphasis added.

20. Ibid, pp. 118–29; and Albert R. Hunt, "Media Bias Is in Eye of the Beholder," *The Wall Street Journal*, July 23, 1985, p. 32.

21. William Schneider and I. A. Lewis, "Views on the News," *Public Opinion* (August/September 1985): 6–11, 58–59, esp. 6–7.

22. Sidney Hook, "All Is Not Fair in News Reporting," *The Wall Street Journal*, February 21, 1985, p. 33. Emphasis added.

23. Jonathan Friendly, "Chief U.S. Rights Official Says the Press Is Painting Distorted Picture," *The New York Times*, April 1, 1984, p. 18.

24. William Keyserling, "Longshot Democrats Never Had a Chance in the Media," *The Washington Post*, December 25, 1983, p. B1.

25. Hodding Carter III, "On TV One Picture Is Worth a Thousand Lies," *The Wall Street Journal*, May 10, 1984, p. 35.

26. David K. Shipler, "Gorbachev and Geneva: The Burden's Back Home," *The New York Times Magazine*, November 11, 1985, p. A8.

27. Blaine Harden, "Magic Rules Rural Life in Liberia," *The Washington Post*, December 7, 1985, p. A17; Randolph Nunnelee, "Magic—or Stereotype?" *The Washington Post*, December 14, 1985, p. A21.

28. Rachel Vincent, Letter, *The Washington Post*, December 14, 1985, p. A21.

29. See Nicholas D. Kristof, "Japan Trade Barriers Called Mainly Cultural," *The New York Times*, April 4, 1985, p. 1; Susan Chira, "Can U.S. Goods Succeed in Japan," *The New York Times*, April 7, 1985, sec. 3, p. 1.

30. Samuel Adams, "Vietnam Cover-Up: Playing War with Numbers," *Harper's*, May 1975, p. 41.

31. George Crile, Blue Sheet, November 24, 1980, p. 1.

32. According to the 1964 *New York Times* v. *Sullivan* case, to libel a public official a journalist would have to willfully lie or act in "reckless disregard of the truth." That standard was later extended to public figures.

33. CBS, "Lenell Geter's In Jail," "60 Minutes," December 4, 1983, produced by Suzanne St. Pierre.

34. George Crile, Letter to CBS President Van Gordon Sauter, July 7, 1982.

35. George Crile, White Paper, "Response to TV Guide," June 3, 1982, p. 1.

36. Ibid., pp. 10–11.

37. Don Kowet and Sally Bedell, "Anatomy of a Smear," *TV Guide*, May 29, 1982, pp. 3–15.

38. Burton Benjamin, *CBS Reports: "The Uncounted Enemy: A Vietnam Deception": An Examination*, July 8, 1982, pp. 52–53, (CBS internal report).

39. Ibid. p. 6.

40. Ibid.

41. Ibid., p. 57.

42. Transcript, Westmoreland interview with Mike Wallace, May 27, 1981, pp. 35–36.

43. Transcript, Hawkins interview with George Crile, March 12, 1981, p. 32; transcript, Meacham interview with George Crile, March 6, 1981, p. 21.

44. Transcript, McChristian interview with George Crile, March 24, 1981, pp. 4–6.

45. Aside from Adams, Hawkins, Meacham, and McChristian, there were Lieut. Col. Russell Cooley, a military intelligence officer, Joseph Hovey, a CIA analyst, George Allen, the CIA's number two man on Vietnam, Lieut. Richard McArthur, an order-of-battle analyst, and Col. George Hamscher, a military intelligence officer; Benjamin report, pp. 1, 57.

46. Photocopy of Department of Defense cable.

47 Benjamin report, p. 29.

48. Benjamin report, pp. 23–24.

49. CBS, Transcript, "The Uncounted Enemy: A Vietnam Deception," p. 24.

50. Ibid., p. 26.

51. David Hume, *An Enquiry Concerning the Human Understanding,* 3d ed., ed. by L. A. Selby-Bigge (Oxford: Oxford University Press, 1975), section XII, pp. 149–50. Emphasis added.

52. Spencer Rich, lectures and conversations with authors.

# Chapter 4

# Avoiding Harm

> Newspapers, magazines, and broadcasting companies are businesses conducted for profit and often make very large ones. Like other enterprises that inflict damage in the course of performing a service highly useful to the public, such as providers of food or shelter or manufacturers of drugs designed to ease or prolong life, they must pay the freight.
>
> Judge Henry Friendly[1]

*Primum non nocere*—first, do no harm. This principle, or something like it, has served as a guideline for medical practitioners at least since the time of Hippocrates. Avoiding harm entails not injuring or doing wrong or evil to others, an indisputably worthy objective. But how far does the principle reach? Suppose a reporter on consumer affairs savages a new toy, or a theater critic writes a devastating review of a play. The consumer reporter harms the manufacturer of the product, retail shops that have stocked it, and owners of shares in the company. The theater critic harms the author of the play, the actors, the director, producer, investors, and many others connected with the production. In each case the harm done is avoidable, yet we would not say that journalists should avoid or temper their criticisms merely because they are harmful.

In the routine of their jobs, journalists regularly harm corrupt officials, unsuccessful athletes and actors, businesspersons whose companies perform poorly, and many others. If the harm is done in the service of a greater good, such as exposing corruption or advising the public not to waste its money, then it is an acceptable side effect, just as in medicine an amputated leg is generally an acceptable side effect if the alternative is death. But there are flaws in this analogy. In clinical medicine both the risks and the benefits can be discussed with and refused by the patient. In journalism the risk of harm to a person or institution being reported on is rarely disclosed, not always evident, and virtually never refusable. Furthermore, the potential beneficiary is not the subject of the story who will suffer the harm; the beneficiary is usually the public.

The harmful effects of journalists' activities seldom lead to disciplinary action (except in libel suits), even if the public benefits of the journalists' work fails to justify the harm done. This situation is tolerated because of the axiom that the harmful effects of placing legal or other external restraints on journalistic freedom would outweigh the harmful effects of virtually any instance of journalistic malpractice. This danger justifies the zone of legal freedom defended in Chapter 1, but it does not dispose of the moral responsibility of journalists to avoid unjustifiable harms to subjects of their stories, sources, institutions, and the public.

On a superficial level the moral problems involved in causing and avoiding harm seem uncomplicated. Almost everyone would agree that damaging another person's interests if there is little compensating benefit and the damage could easily be avoided shows poor character. But journalists rarely confront such a clear, relatively uncomplicated scenario. There usually are benefits that offset the harm, which cannot always easily be avoided.

## Harm and the Harm Principle

*The Harm Principle.* John Stuart Mill's monograph, *On Liberty,* has long been regarded as a classic on the subjects of free speech and the rights of a free press. However, it has gone almost unnoticed in journalism that this work discusses harm as much as it does liberty. Mill argues that while it is difficult to determine a set of right and wrong exercises of liberty, some valid restrictions are necessary, and they all turn on protecting persons against the harmful actions of others. Mill devised the harm principle, as it is now called, to delineate the valid grounds for the limitation of individual liberties.

The harm principle says that *a person's liberty may justifiably be restricted to prevent harm that the person's actions would cause to others.* The principle says that liberty may be overriden if a harm is sufficient, but it does not say that any harm is sufficient to justify a restriction of liberty. It merely provides a principle to be balanced against principles protecting liberty. Whether a particular harm outweighs a particular liberty depends on considerations such as the gravity of the harm, the significance of the liberty, the efficiency with which a liberty-limiting intervention can occur, and the resources available for such an intervention.

We tend to think today almost exclusively in terms of legal coercion as the power that should be used to protect us against the harmful actions of others. But Mill thought the restriction of liberty could also legitimately be enforced by physical force or by force of public opinion. Indeed, Mill relied heavily on public opinion, custom, and private friendships and associations as powers to control harmful behavior. He believed that they were more pervasively influential social forces than legal coercion.[2] Mill thus viewed the category of social influence as so broad that manipulative and coercive structures of almost any kind could qualify as legitimate powers over individuals. We too give *power* and related terms such as *influence* a wide range in this chapter (and in Chapter 7).

Because of the advantages of maintaining a maximally free press, it almost always would be undesirable to rely on legal coercion of journalists, which suggests that Mill's idea of moral pressures and mechanisms may be the most plausible resource for the limitation of press liberties (see Chapter 8). For example, although the watchdog role played by the press is generally applauded, many believe that in its zeal to identify and condemn wrongdoers the press often oversteps the bounds of propriety and does more damage than good. To the extent this occurs, the harm principle provides grounds for some form of restriction on journalists' activities.

*The Nature of Harm.* It is difficult to apply the harm principle unless it is clear what counts as a harm. There are competing conceptions, some of which are highly explicit and broad enough to encompass invasion of liberty, damage to or theft of property, damage to reputation, and more. Other definitions do not make clear such things as whether to cause someone embarrassment is to harm them or whether one can harm by negligence, innuendo, and insinuation. Such uncertainties make use of the harm principle tenuous. Without a tighter understanding it could be argued, for example, that under the harm principle liberty may be restricted to prevent slander, defamation of character, and group libel (a practice better known in law and journalism as prior restraint). An even more problematic claim is that various invasions of privacy constitute harms. For example, does an embarrassing disclosure of the names of rape victims constitute a harmful invasion of privacy if those names are taken from the public record? Questions of that kind must be answered before we can use the concept of harm.

Our analysis will not dispose of all or even most conceptual and moral controversy about the nature of harm. But we will provide a general working definition. Our account relies heavily on Joel Feinberg's contention that a harm involves thwarting, defeating, or setting back an interest.

> [Interests] can be blocked or defeated by events in impersonal nature or by plain bad luck. But they can only be "invaded" by human beings, either by myself, acting negligently or perversely, or by others, singly, or in groups and organizations. It is only when an interest is thwarted through an invasion by self or others, that its possessor is harmed in the legal sense. . . . One person harms another in the present sense then by invading, and thereby thwarting or setting back, his interest. The test . . . of whether such an invasion has in fact set back an interest is whether that interest is in a worse condition than it would otherwise have been in had the invasion not occurred at all. . . .
>
> Not all invasions of interest are wrongs, since some actions invade another's interests excusably or justifiably, or invade interests that the other has no right to have respected.[3]

The specific kinds of interests Feinberg has in mind include property, privacy, confidentiality, friendship, reputation, health, and career. Indeed, a harm can be caused by any violation of rules essential to the stability or viability of society. A different and narrower range of definitions than Feinberg's might be limited to physical or mental impairment and might exclude interests like those in liberty, property, reputation, and the survival of society. One approach, for example, makes it essential that the setback to interests be an evil, or a morally indefensible action, or a violation of another's right. Harm then connotes moral wrong.

We will stick to Feinberg's broad analysis and will not try to untangle the philosophical knots of this controversy, because a broad definition based on nontrivial setbacks to interests is well suited to an analysis of the problems involving the harms that arise in journalism. Questions about the responsibility for the harm, or the justifiability of causing the harm, or the violation of another's right should, under this analysis, be kept entirely separate from the question of whether the harm occurred. Causing a setback to interests in health, financial goals, or recreational plans constitutes a harm, in our sense, even if no one has been wronged or violated. Thus, defamation counts as harm, but so does a newspaper article that discloses a fact about a person's life that causes serious embarrassment or financial loss.

Vagueness surrounding whether something qualifies as a harm often results from a lack of clarity about its cause or a failure to differentiate between causal and moral responsibility. Some years ago when Representative Wilbur Mills's automobile skidded into the tidal basin in the moonlight near the Jefferson Memorial and his relationship with a stripper named Fanne Foxe was discovered by an enterprising reporter, Mills suffered acute embarrassment and other setbacks to his interests (ultimately he had to retire). Had the story not been written, Mills would not have suffered the resultant harm, but we need to distinguish between the harm caused by the reporter's act and the harm that resulted from Mills's own action. Both caused harm, but assessing responsibility for the harm and deciding whether Mills was wronged by the reporter or unjustifiably harmed are quite different matters from assessing the cause of the harm.

Walter Shapiro, an editor of *The Washington Monthly*, has been quoted as saying that arguably "no role played by the press is more important than that of illuminating the character of public officials."[4] Shapiro suggested that such reporting was imperative irrespective of any harm to the official that might result. Shapiro went on to say:

> The canons of objective journalism insure that newspapers and television are full of stories which begin, "Wilbur Mills, the chairman of the powerful Ways and Means Committee, announced yesterday that . . ." For the intelligent reader to evaluate news like this he needs to have some sense of what kind of man Wilbur Mills is. . . . If the public has been led to believe that Mills is a dedicated man whose entire life shines with integrity, the average reader will probably conclude that whatever Mills does is motivated by his concern for the public interest. If, however, the reader has been given an impression that many of Mills' dealings are shady, he is likely to look at a Mills statement and wonder, "What's his angle?"[5]

Shapiro was writing even before Mills took his dive in the tidal basin, but he holds, as we do, that a journalist's proper concern is for the public interest even if serving that interest leads to harming a public official. We recognize, of course, the difference between a failure of character in an official's public and private life. Consider two stories from *The Wall Street Journal* that bring into focus this distinction and the distinctions between justifiably causing harm by reporting and unjustifiably causing the harm. The *Journal* regularly carries stories with a potential for causing financial harm, legal jeopardy, and loss of reputation. On February 25, 1985, a story appeared on page one about the private life of a public official, John Fedders, who was director of enforcement at the Securities and Exchange Commission, a job that involves supervision of 200 government lawyers. The *Journal* reported that Fedders had confessed in a public divorce trial to periodically beating his wife to the point of a broken eardrum, a neck injury, and numerous black eyes; that he had lived it up beyond his capacity to meet expenses on his government salary; and that he was haunted by an alleged cover-up of a corporate bribe scheme by a previous client. Fedders quit the next day, saying that the news reports of wife beating had been exaggerated and unfair and that the reports would, if continued, harm the SEC. This *Journal* article undoubtedly itself caused an increased harm beyond the considerable harm that had already been done to Fedders's reputation and standing, but it cannot be argued reasonably that the *Journal* was not justified in publishing information bearing on the character and therefore the fitness for service of a high-ranking public official, especially when a substantial basis for some of the harms was largely established before the paper reported the story.[6]

The story on Fedders contrasts with one carried ten days later in the *Journal*.[7] This story was about William L. Brown, chief executive officer of the Bank of Boston, the sixteenth largest bank in the United States and a bank with until then a stellar reputation. The bank had just pleaded guilty to a felony and paid a $500,000 fine for handling millions of dollars in cash for alleged leaders of organized crime, without notifying the government of the cash transactions involved, as required by law. These facts had been reported before the *Journal* story appeared, but in this particular article the *Journal* focused on *Brown's leadership,* not merely on illegal transactions at the bank.[8] The story presented an overwhelmingly negative view of Brown's character and mangerial skills. It recounted an unusually high bonus that Brown had paid himself in 1983, "sloppy controls" at the bank, a weak management style, local resentment at the bank's aloofness, illegal transactions unrelated to the organized crime link, a 1978 connection to a Miami-based legalized gambling concern that led Florida officials to question the bank's "moral character," a cavalier disregard of federal laws, and so on.

Brown and his bank's reputation were harmed by this story, and it is fair to say that because the story was enterprising and original, it caused the major part of the harm, at least to Brown. This contrasts with the story on Fedders, which only augmented an already present harm. What cannot be said in either case without more analysis is that these harms were unjustified. They may have been thoroughly justified and may have constituted a public service.

Questions about the justification of harmful publication and the right to print stories that will predictably be harmful lead naturally to questions about responsibility for the harm.

## Responsibility for Harm

In professional contexts it is often necessary to assess responsibility and liability for harm, usually because a client, patient, or customer seeks to punish the responsible party, be compensated, or both. We will not dwell on legal liability or compensation, but the legal model of responsibility for harm suggests a general framework that can be adapted to express the idea of moral responsibility in journalism.[9]

Taking due care is a central concept for assessing moral responsibility for harmful outcomes. Anyone who is not sufficiently careful automatically invites moral blame as well as legal penalty for omissions as well as for actions. To be morally blameworthy, however, a harm must be caused by carelessness resulting from failure to discharge a socially, legally, or morally imposed duty to take care or to behave reasonably toward others. Two important tests of reasonableness are that professionals should conform to the minimally acceptable standards practiced in the profession and that they should perform any actions that a reasonably prudent person would perform. Therefore, negligence or "careless" action can be analyzed in terms of the following essential elements:

1. an established duty to the affected party must exist;
2. someone must breach that duty;
3. the affected party must experience a harm; and
4. this harm must be caused by the breach of duty.

If these elements of negligence are to serve as a workable model for journalism, the established duty cannot be set at such a low level that virtually any conduct is acceptable, and, conversely, if the potential harm is so remote as to be unforeseeable, then causing the harm might not constitute negligence.

The duty breached by a negligent act or omission is based in law on a general standard of reasonable care in human interactions, which in turn is based on the same reasonable-person standard discussed in Chapter 2. Professional negligence, or malpractice, is an instance of negligence in which professional standards of care have been developed for persons possessing or claiming special knowledge, expertise, or skill. Such standards are relevant for journalists because journalists claim certain special skills and because they need some special knowledge and skills to deal competently with sources who have special knowledge and skills, such as high-level government officials, athletes, and scientists. Journalists also have colleagues who constitute a peer group and whose judgment and performance help set the standards applicable in their work. This account of journalistic negligence assumes, for example, that in almost all cases there is a professional duty of due care to make sure that sources know they are speaking to a reporter and that what they say might be published. Similarly, it assumes that journalists will present as factual only that information which is verifiable as factual.

This model is hardly a foolproof method of assessing responsibility for causing harm in journalism. For example, harm might be caused by a decision that many parties were involved in reaching, including editors, other reporters, perhaps even a publisher. Here a diffusion of responsibility occurs, and it is often difficult or even impossible to determine who, if anyone, made the decision or performed the action that caused the harm. Another limitation involves the fact that avoiding harm to others sometimes involves acts of exceptional courage of a kind that has not generally been required in the professions or elsewhere. Finally, there is some question about whether a customary standard of due care exists among journalists—and, if one does not, how much consensus would be required to establish such a standard.

One major area of uncertainty surrounding the question of due care involves responsibility for failure by a reporter to probe deeply enough. In other words, if persons are harmed by not having information that might have been uncovered had the journalist performed competently, does the journalist share the blame for the harm? Take as a comparison the reports of accountants who audit public corporations. Since a scandal at Mc-Kesson and Robbins in 1940, the Securities and Exchange Commission has held that an accountant doing an audit has a duty to uncover and disclose gross management misstatement. Although accountants have long resisted the idea that they are negligent if they fail to uncover management fraud (and as a result harm is caused to investors), some recent legal cases have indicated that the courts expect accountants to recognize and report fraud, no matter how subtle it is. Accordingly, auditors who fail to respond to red flags would be responsible for harms that result from their negligence.

This standard of duty and negligence would be far too high for journalists, who often have no privileged access to documents similar to the access provided to accountants. Nevertheless, there are reasonable expectations, if not professional standards, for investigations in journalism, and if these expectations are not met, journalists should share in the moral responsibility for any resultant harm. If, for example, a reporter suspects but does not investigate and report that a Defense Department official is showing favoritism by awarding helicopter spare-parts contracts to a company whose performance is poor, and a faulty part produced by that company causes a fatal crash, then the journalist shares responsibility for the harm.

Of course, a reasonable standard of due care should be applied to determine whether the journalist should have been able to uncover the relevant information that went unreported. Even when the utmost care is exercised in reporting and editing a story—when reporters and editors have good reason to believe that they have checked and rechecked every source and answered every relevant question—it is possible that some critical factor has been omitted or distorted. In a case like that, reporters and editors would have no moral responsibility for the harm, even if they share some causal responsibility, as long as due care has been exercised.

A more developed model of responsibility for harm would seek to resolve or eliminate all problems and qualifications such as those above. An analysis of that scope, however, is beyond the ambitions of this book. But our schematic model should take adequate account of the multiplicity of harms that regularly occur in journalism, some of which are avoidable, others of which are not. An example of a typical avoidable harm that a journalist might cause is the following. Suppose a reporter came across an electronics industry trade secret that appeared by mistake in an obscure court record. The highly technical information has little or no value to the public at large but would be of considerable value to the competitors of the firm whose secrets were inadvertently disclosed during a legal proceeding. Employees of the firm are under a strict obligation to keep the information confidential, a duty that remains in force even if the employee were to leave the firm. (A trade secret is, in effect, the intellectual property of the company.) If the secret is in the public record, there is no legal restraint on its publication. Yet publication may harm innocent parties, provide companies with information to which they are not entitled, and in no appreciable way serve the public. The reporter will benefit if an editor thinks the story has some value, and a few specialized readers will find the story interesting. In a situation of this kind, there is little doubt that the reporter and editor should be held responsible for harms resulting from the story.

There is no clear and present benefit for the public and no broadening or deepening of the pool of generally useful information that would justify the inevitable loss to the company that owned the secrets. The argument that newspapers are in the business of publishing news, not suppressing it, carries little, if any, weight, because this case is less a matter of publishing or suppressing news than of deciding whether something is news and whether the benefits to the public of its publication are worth the possible costs. Journalists are paid to make discretionary judgments of this kind, and when they do, various moral principles should and frequently do play a significant, if unacknowledged role.

The electronics industry example is based on a chance discovery of information in a public record. Many investigations, however—whether carried out by detectives, scientists, journalists, or anyone else—begin with a hypothesis and end with a harm, although often a justifiable one. The nature of the enterprise is to track down something the investigator strongly suspects is true and prove it. There is almost always some degree of psychological preference for confirmation rather than falsification of the hypothesis, which was developed out of the flash of insight, tip, or rumor that set off the investigation. While scientific inquiry demands that biases be set aside in the interest of discovering the truth, this is at least as psychologically difficult to achieve in journalism as in science.

Consider the case of Brian Taugher, an assistant attorney general of California. One day, without warning, he was arrested in his front yard and charged with child molesting. Seven months of emotional and legal torture followed before Taugher was finally acquitted. He was arrested, with no supporting evidence, on the word of a nine-year-old girl. The fact that an assistant attorney general was charged with child molesting was sufficient to evoke front-page coverage in *The Sacramento Bee*,[10] stories on the inside pages of papers elsewhere in the state, and numerous television reports, all strongly implying Taugher's guilt.

Jay Mathews of *The Washington Post* quoted Taugher as saying, "Once that publicity hit, there was no turning back for anybody." The district attorney who pursued the case denied that the decision to prosecute was influenced by media attention, which may or may not be true, but the notoriety resulting from the news coverage caused significant harm to Taugher's reputation. If the press coverage did influence the decision to prosecute—an uncertain matter—then it was also partly responsible for Taugher incurring $50,000 in legal costs. It is impossible to assess what portion of his mental anguish can fairly be blamed on the press, but some can. In the end, Taugher also worried about broader harms resulting from the reporting of his case. In an extraordinary statement for someone in his position, he told Mathews:

> There's no question that we ignored for far too long abuse within families. A dramatic, well-publicized acquittal like mine suggests that all of these things are ill-founded. And that's wrong. It's just simply wrong. The vast majority of people who get accused of this are guilty as hell.[11]

When reporting on a matter with the potential to do so much harm, a reasonable standard of due care would require considerably more evidence than the uncorroborated testimony of a child of nine before publishing or broadcasting the story. The Taugher case is atypical, because it involves an especially damaging harm; but lesser harms for which the press bears at least partial responsibility—many that are avoidable at no cost to the press or public—occur almost daily. For example, in early October 1985, *The Dallas Times Herald* carried a story that Dallas Cowboy football players Danny White, Tony Dorsett, Tony Hill, Butch Johnson, and Ron Springs might have shaved points in early 1980 games in exchange for supplies of cocaine. These allegations had surfaced through legal documents submitted in a trial in Pittsburgh in which a highly unreliable former FBI undercover agent, Anthony Mitrione, Jr., noted that some cocaine dealers had told him about the alleged deal. Although this former federal agent had pleaded guilty to charges of conspiracy, bribery, and possession of cocaine with intent to distribute, the *Times Herald* and numerous subsequent reports on radio and television throughout the country made it sound as if the charges were credible and under serious examination in the courts. The story embarrassed the football club and overshadowed Dorsett's attempt that same week to become only the sixth player in NFL history to rush for 10,000 yards. While these charges may have appeared credible to the *Times Herald*, there was no evidence to support them, and the paper should have questioned the credibility of the legal documents and their source.

Other fairly common harms in journalism for which the press is responsible include misquoting or quoting sources out of context; perpetuating embarrassing and possibly false rumors in gossip columns; misrepresenting a business's price structure; identifying sources, perhaps inadvertently, despite a promise not to disclose who they are; invading the privacy of a husband grieving for his murdered wife; or simplistically and misleadingly characterizing a transaction by a corporation as illegal.

## Calculating Harms and Benefits

In an ideal world we could supply a simple formula to journalists who must decide, on deadline, whether to include a paragraph in a story knowing both that it has some news value and that it might harm someone. There is no such formula, but we can indicate some ways to think about whether potential public benefits, or benefits to specific groups or individuals, deserve to outweigh potential harms, and how weighing harms and benefits can become part of the decision-making process.

The electronics industry case provides an example of how this process works. We concluded that the harms outweighed the benefits of publishing, because, although the calculable benefits were substantial, they would go to a small number of people who were not entitled to receive them— owners and managers in competing companies. The harms would also have been substantial, and those who suffered them would have done so undeservingly. There were no significant benefits for the public. If publishing the information would cause little or no harm, little or no moral justification would be needed, but that was not the case.

In this example, however, the calculation is too easy. In contrast, consider a circumstance in which a highly respected public official, who is also a husband and father and is known as a strong defender of traditional family values, is found to have a clandestine homosexual lover. Publication of that fact will destroy his career and do irreparable harm to his family, as a unit and as individuals. What public benefit, if any, would justify publishing information about a public official's private life that would do devastating harm to the official and the other individuals involved? The most obvious answer is that some information about the official's character would be relevant to the way he does his job. To make a judgment of that kind, journalists would need to know whether the official had ever been blackmailed or was vulnerable to blackmail because of the secrecy of the arrangement, and they would need to know something about the character of the lover—for example, whether the lover was a potentially bad influence on the official and whether he ever improperly influenced the official. The same standard would, of course, apply if the relationship were heterosexual.

It might not be possible to get the needed information, and the journalist would then still have to decide whether to publish the story. The fact that the person in question is a public official is a relevant consideration in the balancing that must be done at this point. By choosing public life he has given up some of his entitlement to privacy. If there is good reason to believe that some fact, situation, or circumstance in his private life has or is likely to have bearing on his public life, there is justification for weighing the public benefit of knowing about it against the potential harm to the official.

In short, if an official's actions are relevant to his position of public trust, then the duty of the press to provide the public with information it needs would outweigh the competing duty to avoid harm. As the details change, so will our judgment about what should be published, if anything. Suppose the person involved is a public figure such as a movie star—Rock Hudson, for example. Hudson's homosexuality was an open secret in Hollywood, but reporters did not write about it until he disclosed that he was dying of AIDS. Should they have kept his secret for all those years? Did his fans or the larger public have a right to know about his sexual practices? Or was he entitled to keep his private life private, even though as a movie star he was, among other things, in the business of seeking publicity?

The choice in this case would seem to be between giving movie fans titillating information about Hudson and an opportunity to boycott the actor's films because of his sexual preference, and doing some degree of harm to Hudson's career and perhaps causing him emotional pain. One pivotal difference between Hudson and the public official is that Hudson was not elected or appointed to carry out the public's business. The consequences for the public of not knowing about Hudson's homosexuality seem negligible. Furthermore, Hudson's homosexuality does not appear to be relevant to the way he performed his particular public service—entertainment—or to any public trust he might have had. We would argue, therefore, that the Hollywood press corps acted properly in not disclosing Hudson's homosexuality, while in a similar case the press could act properly in disclosing a congressman's homosexuality.

Because the basic responsibility of the press is to provide the public with information it needs, a central question in any process of decision making about whether to withhold publication will always be how much the public needs the information and how successfully that need competes with the principle that we should avoid the harm that would result from its publication. If the two seem roughly even, because journalism exists to benefit the public, preference ordinarily must be given by journalists to publishing in the public interest; but when the public benefit is marginal and the harm potentially great, the harm should usually be avoided, no matter how engaging or interesting a story might be to some readers or viewers.

We need to distinguish in these reflections between avoidable and unavoidable harms in stories that clearly are important and about which the public has an obvious need to know. The following case illustrates a series of harms that could have and should have been avoided, although the news was of considerable importance and the subject deserved extensive coverage.

## A Case Study: *The Washington Post*'s Cancer Series

In 1981 *The Washington Post* published a series of articles on an emotionally wrenching subject—the treatment of cancer with experimental drugs. The project was to have been the first of several investigative reports under the general heading of "The War on Cancer." The lead-off series of four articles appropriately, and ironically, ran under the subtitle, "First Do No Harm."[12]

Ted Gup and Jonathan Neumann, then members of the *Post*'s metropolitan staff, spent a full year reporting on one element of a single federal project—the Phase One trials of the experimental drug program of the National Cancer Institute. Their articles ran for four consecutive days, beginning on October 18, 1981. They started on page one each day and totaled 541 column inches. "First Do No Harm" was an investigative series. Its purpose was to root out and report abuses by physician–investigators. Based on preliminary reporting, Gup and Neumann hypothesized that there were significant, documentable problems with the experimental drug program. They set out to find the problems and determine whether they were bona fide. So far, we have potentially valuable investigative journalism, with admirable and appropriate goals.

In the face of the complexities of reporting on cancer research, it is unclear how extensive an obligation the *Post* had to carefully weigh the information gathered by Gup and Neumann, to try to assess the risks involved, and to publish a series that would be free of unjustified harm. On a subject so complex, a thoroughgoing exercise of oversight might have paralyzed the project or delayed it indefinitely. It does seem clear, however, that on a story that involved two person-years of reporting time, many hours and even days should have been spent in guaranteeing that the series was written, edited, and displayed so as to avoid much of the needless harm it ultimately caused. In appraising this series, we are not able to judge definitively the *Post*'s motives or those of Gup and Neumann as individuals, but we can evaluate their product.

The *Post* was investigating a subject that had traditionally intimidated journalists because of its scientific and social complexity, the many false reports of cures in the past, and its unremitting grimness. Violent wars provide their share of heroes and excitement; the war on cancer had provided few of the former and little of the latter. The project represented a leap of courage and imagination for the *Post,* as well as a major outlay of resources. But because the subject was so fraught with emotion and would touch the lives of so many persons—cancer patients, their families, physicians, nurses, researchers, and the whole community of people who fear cancer—it should have been obvious that there was a risk of causing harm to numerous persons.

After their extensive research Gup and Neumann reported that unwitting patients were being given experimental drugs with a primary purpose that was not therapeutic; rather, the purpose was predominantly *experimental,* trying to discover which levels of toxicity were reversible. Hundreds of patients had died as a result of the experimental drugs they had been given; others had suffered severe side effects. Such research, these reporters maintained, seemed to be in the interest of learning about drugs that could not help these specific patients and were virtually certain to hurt them. Furthermore, in some cases the patients were being fraudulently led to believe that these drugs were their last best hope for recovery.

Gup and Neumann recorded case after case in which they emphasized that experimental drugs were linked to the deaths of cancer patients. They placed less emphasis, however, on the fact that all of the patients they wrote about were classified as terminal, most with weeks or, at best, months to live. They chronicled these cases after talking to dying patients, their close relatives, their doctors, and their nurses. They also collected information on at least two success stories: the development of the drug cisplatin, which had been effective in curing testicular cancer, and the case of a a thirteen-year-old Maryland girl who was alive and leading a relatively active life, partly because of treatment with experimental drugs.

Gup and Neumann had a vast amount of material to organize and make readable. They used an anecdotal approach, which engaged readers directly in the drama and suffering of terminal cancer patients. The two reporters apparently had been profoundly affected by their many encounters with pain, dashed hopes, and people faced with deciding between certain death and a one-in-a-thousand chance of survival that carried with it the promise of weeks of significantly increased suffering. Understandably, they wanted to convey these findings in a way that would move readers as they had been moved.

They proceeded to organize their stories to reflect what they apparently believed to be a genuine scandal involving the abuse of dying and helpless people. The series took shape under the experienced editorial eye of Bob Woodward, the *Post* metropolitan editor who had won richly deserved renown as an investigative reporter for his work covering Watergate with Carl Bernstein. In final form the four main articles totaled about 450 column inches. There were also four short articles, totaling about 90 column inches. The long articles were tales of distress and suffering, strung together for column after column. The short articles consisted of the cisplatin story, the Maryland girl's story, the comments and criticisms of Dr. Vincent DeVita, head of the National Cancer Institute, and a brief excerpt from an interview with DeVita.

About a week before the series was scheduled for publication, Gup and Neumann conducted a second interview with DeVita, the man ultimately responsible for the experimental drug program. It lasted five hours. According to DeVita, it became clear during the interview that Gup and Neumann had written an anecdotal series of articles in which cancer researchers were portrayed as heartless scientists who had neither sympathy nor respect for the human subjects of their experiments. These scientists, the series would suggest, seemed concerned solely with the results of those experiments, results that had little to do with curing but involved only measuring toxicity and advancing science. DeVita maintained that he tried to correct what he believed were grievous misunderstandings on the part of the two reporters. He said that they acknowledged the merit of his statements but nevertheless told him they would not change the account they had written. The *Post* did agree, however, to print DeVita's comments and criticisms in a separate box next to the second day's article.

Despite this nod to fairness, the Gup–Neumann series is filled with examples of unfair, sloppy, and at times incompetent journalism. First, the articles are often vague, which, considering the time and resources devoted to the project, is difficult to justify. In a piece of crusading reporting that is essentially an indictment, vagueness may suggest that more precise evidence was lacking. For example, exact numbers of persons were rarely given; instead, groups were characterized as "some," "many," or "few." Yet it is as important in this kind of journalism as it is in social science to be precise.

Second, the articles used authoritative words such as "documented" and "verified," but it is often difficult to determine the process of confirmation or even to discover to what these words refer. What had been documented, what remained "undocumented," and who had verified what are left obscure. The precise meaning of and justification for words such as "implicated," as in "implicated in the deaths of cancer patients," is uncertain. DeVita told a joint hearing of two subcommittees of the House of Representatives that it is often difficult to distinguish the effects of the drug from the effects of the cancer itself. Does this complexity explain why Gup and Neumann say drugs are "implicated in" rather than "responsible for" the deaths of patients? If so, this important point should have been specified. If not, then whatever they did mean by "implicated in" should have been made explicit. Medical scientists generally use the phrase "implicated in" to designate a causal relationship, but those who live and work outside the culture of medicine are unlikely to grasp this usage.

Some genuine abuses discovered by these reporters may have been treated less seriously than they should have been because of shortcomings of the kind discussed thus far. Consider one allegation in particular. Gup and Neumann charged that the informed consent forms used at some hospitals were inadequate; as a result, patients had little idea of what they were authorizing when they "consented." There is merit in this observation: Patients often do not adequately understand the implications of the "Phase One" program in which they agree to participate and put more faith in the prospects for cure than previous experience with the drug being tested would warrant. Further, some experiments were conducted without clearance for human experimentation by either the NCI or the Food and Drug Administration, and the NCI may not have carefully monitored the management of experimental drug programs at some hospitals around the country.

Clearly there was something important to be gained by publicizing these problems in a way that might lead to their correction, but it is reasonable to believe that the abuses cited in the series would have been more seriously considered had the series been less susceptible to criticism. There is a need for serious, insightful reporting in this area, and the substantial failure of the series dried up at least one potentially fruitful source. There is no doubt that the two reporters brought considerable skill to some aspects of the project, and there is no reason to assume that they were malevolent or ill motivated. Yet they stacked the deck in their presentation so heavily, without proper qualification or exploration of counterevidence, that they failed in what should have been their primary task—providing an accurate, reasonably objective, substantially complete, and therefore fair account of the Phase One trials.

Despite the year they spent in preparing the series, they did not review their work with adequate perspective. Involved editors apparently failed to provide that perspective or to point to the serious omissions and overstatements in the work. For example, nowhere in the series is it said that the experimental drugs being tested for toxicity were able to kill cancer cells precisely *because* they were toxic and therefore potentially damaging to normal cells as well. Similarly, Gup and Neumann did not write that all drugs tested for toxicity in humans were drugs that the NCI believed held promise in the treatment of malignancy (as a result of tests with animals). Furthermore, nowhere in the series is it mentioned that cancer is not one disease, but tens, even hundreds—each resistant to conquest by medical research but some far more resistant than others. A drug that failed to cure one kind of cancer might succeed with another, and therefore it is not irrational to test it repeatedly, even in the face of a dismal record.

The articles also display apparent ignorance of many procedures of science and of the scientific data. Once an experiment is running, for example, the lack of positive results in intermediary stages does not necessarily indicate that the experiment should be aborted. Even more significantly, as DeVita pointed out in his published response to the series:

> Gup and Neumann totally missed the concept that anticancer drugs are meant to be used in combination with other forms of treatment, such as surgery and radiation, and that they are expected to be most effective in treating early cancers. For ethical reasons, all drugs are first tested against advanced cancers afflicting patients for whom no other hope exists. Even a few responses against advanced cancers can mean major effect against early cancers, particularly when the drugs are used in conjunction with surgery and radiation therapy.[13]

The series also said that only six experimental drugs had proved effective against cancer, but according to NCI, the correct number at the time was forty-nine. We do not know what "effective" means in this context and therefore what the correct number was, but at least NCI's figure should have been cited and examined. They also wrote that "the *official* rationale for this experimentation, despite the fatalities, is that these patients were already terminally ill and that scientific progress required the risks of subjecting functioning human beings to highly toxic drugs."[14] But there is at least as good a basis in fact to believe DeVita's statement, "Potential for beneficial effect exists and is an important part of the ethical base for conducting such studies."[15]

In their effort to indict the enterprise of drug research for the treatment of cancer, Gup and Neumann frequently dwelt on accurate but irrelevant facts that were in some way incongruous or bizarre. How else would one explain that the first article said three times that a drug was derived from a dye used in ballpoint-pen ink? One of the most widely known medications, penicillin, comes from bread mold. Should we indict the original research on penicillin for investigating that source? Gup and Neumann also digress at some length about a nurse's sloppy bookkeeping. In context, the desired inference seems to be that sloppy bookkeeping is characteristic of institutions engaged in cancer research.

There are also problems in the presentation of the series that are inextricably linked to the problems in the copy itself. As befits a project of such length, which involved so much time, effort, and money to produce, the cancer series was lavishly displayed, beginning in the Sunday paper, spreading across the entire page above the masthead. This is the paragon of news display for stories involving unusual enterprise by reporters. The series began on page one all four days. Stories ran at the top of the page for three days, dropping to the bottom only on the fourth—an unmistakable signal that *Post* editors had judged it a highly important series.

On projects of the magnitude of the cancer series, much of the editing at the *Post* is done by senior editors before the story gets to the copy desk, but desk editors write the headlines. The page-one headlines must be approved by the ranking editor in the newsroom. The headlines are meant to reflect the content of the stories, and the headlines in the cancer series did not fail to do that. The headline on the first article said: "Experimental Drugs: Death in the Search for Cures." The front-page headline the second day had to be compressed into one column. It read: "Risk, Rivalry and Research—And Error." The headline on the inside page where the story was continued said: "A Medical World of Risk, Rivalry, Research—and Serious Error." On the third day the page-one headline said bluntly: "The World of Shattered Hopes." And on the fourth and final day of the series, the wording was: "Spark of Hope vs. Ordeal of Pain: Dilemma of Drug Researchers." These headlines accurately signal the portrayal of a world of death, serious error, shattered hopes, and ordeals of pain—all balanced by a single, faint "spark of hope."

To get a feel for both the series and what the headline writers were asked to introduce, consider the opening paragraphs that ran over the masthead on page one on the first day:

On the fourth of July in Peoria, Ill., an 8-year-old cancer patient named Sheri Beck was rushed to Methodist Hospital. She died there the next day.

Cancer did not kill Sheri Beck. Her treatment for cancer did. She died of congestive heart failure brought on by Mitoxantrone, an experimental drug derived from a dye used in ballpoint pen ink. She was one of hundreds of cancer patients who have been given the experimental drug and one of a growing number who suffered heart failure as a result.

Those given Mitoxantrone are not alone. A one-year study by *The Washington Post* has *documented* 620 cases in which experimental drugs have been *implicated* in the deaths of cancer patients. Each of the drug-related deaths was *verified* by doctors and recorded in government accounts of the experiments. And they amounted to *merely a fraction* of the thousands of people who in recent years have died or suffered terribly from cancer experiments conducted in the nation's hospitals.

Over the last decade, more than 150 experimental drugs have been given to tens of thousands of cancer patients under the sponsorship of the federal government's National Cancer Institute. Many of these drugs have been derived from a list of *highly toxic industrial chemicals including pesticides, herbicides and dyes.* They have all been tested by the NCI and hospitals around the country in the hope that they would prove to be lifesavers against a disease that has ravaged America and frustrated its medical and scientific community.[16]

The headlines and the first four paragraphs of the lead article reflect the tone of the series as a whole. They also provide clues to its flaws. In the end, these substantive and technical defects constitute a presentation that is both harmful and unfair to cancer patients, doctors, families of patients, future cancer sufferers, and the public at large—all of whom, in varying degrees, had reason to put some faith, if not in the probable efficacy of these drugs, then in the future prospects for experimental drug research.

There is an additional harm: Negative reports on institutions almost inevitably taint the reputations of the professionals associated with the institution. Because of the powerfully emotional presentation in the *Post* articles, even patients with years of accumulated trust in a physician stood to have their established confidence eroded. Furthermore, the overall effect of segregating the critique by the head of the NCI and the two success stories from the much longer articles chronicling a succession of horror stories was to trivialize the former and intensify the indictment of the latter.

Like scholarship and research generally, almost any complex subject investigated by journalists is too rich in detail, and each situation too individual, to be captured by broad generalizations. Generalizations often are inadequately supported despite detailed investigative reporting, although they may become the most memorable elements of the story. How these generalizations are supported and how thoroughly they are qualified are frequently the keys to assessing the fairness of the story. Gup and Neumann were not setting out to learn enough to give a course in pharmacology or medicine; neither were they randomly vacuuming up information. They were investigative reporters looking for a story. Presumably they were looking for impact—human drama, scandal if any appeared, a major therapeutic development on the horizon—but not for the portrait that ultimately emerged.

In a symposium held by the *The New Republic* after the series was published, Woodward said the following in response to criticism of its content, mainly by physicians whose own work was not reported on by Gup and Neumann:

> And you look at this as some sort of semi-academic—either look at or attack on the system. It is not that. What we did—if we found out that the head of the cancer treatment center in Miami was stealing $500,000 out of NCI funds, we probably would have put that in the article. We were there to report what was going on. It was a slice, the best slice we could make at it.[17]

But if the object, as Woodward reports, was to offer the public "a slice, the best slice," the slice should be characteristic of the salami. If you are trying to give people who have never eaten salami an idea of what the meat tastes like, and you happen to have a salami that is mostly good but is rotten at one end, would you give them only a taste of the rotten end? Or would you give them a taste of the good part and warn them that sometimes it can be rotten? The press does have an obligation to report on rot and corruption, but there is in this case a competing obligation to avoid harming the subjects, sources, and readers who are innocently involved, as well as to present as objective a report as possible.

It seems odd that the result of a year-long investigation of the Phase One trials of the experimental drug program of the NCI should be almost exclusively a report on what has gone wrong. Failures in the program can only be presented fairly in a broader context that includes at least an accurate indication of what has gone right. In a series of this kind, to report only the abuses—even were the report entirely accurate—is to suggest that abuses are the whole story. It will not do to argue that the paper carried then, and still carries, some reports of positive developments in the war on cancer. Such stories are reported over many years, some have not been reported on at all, and no general reader can be expected to recall all or even most of them and relate them to current articles. Because the *Post* did not provide the proper context—a correct characterization of the goals of the program and the prospects for success measured by those goals—the press's much criticized "bad news bias" surfaced again.

Editors should be especially wary of a major series of articles on a

complex subject that indicates few positive aspects in an essentially negative picture. Dr. Philip Cohen raised a question reflecting this viewpoint at
the *New Republic* seminar. He asked:

> Is it fair or proper to list and stress only the side effects of the treatment
> without giving a fair picture of the denominator or percentage of patients
> when treated who did not have the side effects? If we physicians are ex-
> pected to discuss treatment options with our patients, giving a balanced
> view of risks and benefits, then is it not reasonable to ask the press to do
> the same? Is there any way we can resolve the disparity between the need
> for more impact and the need for balance in this type of reporting?
>
> And . . . what is the responsibility of the media to the public in ex-
> ploring these sensitive issues regarding cancer, for example, and in the
> manner and style it relates these facts to the public? It would be unwise
> for me to speak to a person with advanced cancer and give him unrea-
> sonably false hopes about the effectiveness of a particular experimental
> treatment. But on the other hand, if all I were to focus on were the dire
> consequences of the disease itself, or terrifying side effects of treatment, I
> suspect I'd be considered insensitive and unkind.[18]

Objectively reporting on risks so that patients will be forewarned of
the hazards involved in taking an experimental drug is a commendable
service, but it is another matter to create the impression that almost all
chemotherapy results in suffering from side effects or a painful death and
at the same time offers virtually no chance of a cure.[19] Dennis O'Leary of
George Washington University said at the same symposium that he had
been told by colleagues that several of their patients had been frightened
away from not only experimental drugs but also conventional chemotherapy because the articles blurred the difference between them. This occurred during a period when significant advances were being made in the
field of chemotherapy, developments reported in various other news
sources.[20]

In sum, the preponderance of available evidence in this case indicates
that the *Post* presented an unfair and harmful portrayal of an anticancer
program whose relatively meager results had been produced by slow and
painful methods. Gup and Neumann elected to weight their coverage too
heavily toward the mistakes and failures of the Phase One trials; they
misreported both the purpose and the nature of clinical trials of this kind;
they failed to communicate to readers that cancer is many diseases and
that a drug that fails to cure one kind might cure another; they sensation-
alized irrelevant but bizarre-sounding data; they did not incorporate in the
body of their series accurate information presented by the head of the
NCI; they did not make clear the difference between experimental and
conventional regimes of chemotherapy; and they stated as fact disputed
judgments such as the number of effective drugs in use at the time they

wrote their series. For all these reasons, they caused psychological pain and possibly physical harm to the community of cancer sufferers, and they damaged reputations in the cancer-care community.

In a journalistic effort of the magnitude of this *Post* series, can one justify the damage done and the losses suffered? We think not, and certainly not by an appeal to the positive effects of the series. Whatever good the series did could have been accomplished without the distortions, harms, and losses involved.

## Harms from Falsity and Duplicity

The cancer series and other examples discussed above present only a sample of the kinds of harms that can result from journalistic investigations. Another class of harms is caused by false or duplicitous statements, statements made by journalists to sources, to subjects of stories, or to the public. Consider, for example, the case that came to be known as "Tailgate," an account detailed by the "CBS Evening News" of alleged homosexuality and drug abuse by members of Congress. Dan Rather revealed portentously on the night of June 30, 1982, saying: "CBS News has learned that federal law enforcement officials have a wide-ranging investigation underway into allegations of illicit sex and drug use on Capitol Hill. The allegations include congressmen engaging in sex with underage employees, often members of the same sex."[21]

The CBS report was carefully hedged. Rather did not say that anyone had done anything illegal or even wrong; he said that an investigation was underway into allegations of wrongdoing. But he also failed to say that the "federal investigation" CBS used as the news peg for its report might have itself been prompted by CBS's own journalistic investigation. That charge was later explicitly made in a report to the House Ethics Committee by Joseph Califano, who was appointed special counsel to look into the allegations, only some of which were aired by CBS.[22]

John Ferrugia of CBS News, who reported the story, said that CBS had been satisfied before broadcasting his report that the network was not "chasing its own tail," which meant that it had not created the federal investigation by its reporting. Ferrugia said that CBS made "literally dozens of calls to federal agencies, law enforcement agencies, and congressional aides"; he said it was not "until we were totally satisfied" that the federal investigation was not spawned by CBS reporting that a decision had been reached to run the story. Ferrugia allows, however, that what Rather referred to on the air as a "wide-ranging investigation" might have been something less than a "formal investigation" at the time he questioned two teenage pages, both of whom appeared on the June 30 broadcast with their identities carefully masked.[23]

The following account, which is based largely on the Califano report, describes how duplicity with sources and the broadcasting of false allegations by unreliable sources played a part in harming in various degrees innocent members of Congress, the institution of Congress, congressional pages, and American taxpayers. On June 9, 1982, a sixteen-year-old page in the House of Representatives received a phone call from someone who asked for his address so that he could send him an invitation. The page, Jeffrey Opp, provided the address, and within five minutes he received not an invitation but a visitor. The caller, Opp testified under oath, was Ferrugia, who told Opp that he was investigating a ring of twenty-five to fifty gay congressmen who may have been involved in sexual perversion and child molestation. Opp later said, while still under oath, that Ferrugia told him that one congressman liked eight-year-olds and another cruised Washington's tacky 14th Street corridor for gay prostitutes. Opp said in his testimony before the House Ethics Committee that the reporter flattered him by saying he had heard he knew plenty and was "no air head." Ferrugia said in a telephone interview that he did not call Opp on the telephone before showing up at his door. However, he would not discuss precisely what he said to Opp when he interviewed the sixteen-year-old page in his Capitol Hill apartment.

The day after Opp was visited by Ferrugia, the young page went to two aides of his congressional sponsor, Rep. Patricia Schroeder (D–Colo.). He told them that he knew of a homosexual ring involving pages and members of Congress, that he was working under cover for CBS, that his room was bugged, and that his roommate was a spy for the House doorkeeper. The aides were angry that CBS would use a sixteen-year-old as their undercover operative. They called to complain, but Ferrugia would not discuss the matter over the phone. They agreed to meet him in front of the East Wing of the National Gallery, just a few blocks from the Capitol. At that meeting, Ferrugia elaborated on the alleged scandal.

The next day the aides talked to Opp again. This time he admitted to them that he had lied the day before when he told them his room was bugged, and he said he had no evidence that his roommate was spying on him, as he had previously charged. But he stuck to his story about the homosexual ring. In the days to come, the aides, although skeptical of Opp's story, arranged for him to be interviewed by the Justice Department. CBS did an on-camera interview with him in which his identity was masked. Meanwhile, according to his testimony, one of the Schroeder aides told Ferrugia: "If you are basing your story on Opp's word, you are skating on thin ice. He may know something but he is not reliable, and a good deal of what he told us about this, . . . turned out not to be true."[24]

But Ferrugia told the aides he had other sources, too, and kept pursuing his story. He tracked down a former page, Leroy Williams, and then turned up unannounced at Williams's home in Little Rock, Arkansas. According to Williams's testimony, Ferrugia told him that Opp was accusing him of being involved in homosexual activity and drug dealing and that the House doorkeeper, who is in charge of pages, was telling reporters that Williams had been fired because he was "a bad apple."[25] Ferrugia would not discuss with us what he said to Williams, but Williams consented to appear on-camera, in the shadows so that he could not be identified. He said he had engaged in homosexual relations with three members of Congress and one staff employee. Later he said he had procured a gay prostitute for a senator.

The two interviews with Opp and Williams formed the backbone of Ferrugia's June 30 broadcast. But, as it turned out, Williams was lying and Opp exaggerating in such a way that it was tantamount to lying. The Ethics Committee report, prepared by Califano, said that Opp "twisted minor, at best ambiguous conversations with three Congressmen and one lobbyist and characterized them as 'homosexual advances.' "[26] Califano's report implies that Ferrugia was guilty of duplicity in his approaches to both pages. It suggests that by flattering Opp and leading him to believe that there was a major scandal he might have drawn the highly impressionable teenager into a fantasy world of spies, electronic bugs, and investigative journalism. Ferrugia also primed Williams at his home in Little Rock by telling him he was there to give him a chance to be cleared of accusations Opp had made about Williams's sexual involvement with male congressmen and allegations the House doorkeeper had made.

From Williams's or Opp's perspectives it hardly matters whether Ferrugia was acting out of malice—we have no reason to believe that he was—or whether he was negligent or possibly incompetent in carrying out his assignment. Both teenagers, although hardly innocents, were harmed. While they contributed substantially to harming themselves, if Ferrugia had not pushed them much of the harm done would have been avoided, as would whatever harm was done to Ferrugia's reputation as a result of broadcasting a story based on unfounded rumors.

The Congress and the public's perception of its members is also a part of the larger picture of the harm that resulted from this story. The implication of the CBS story was that the Congress of the United States was a den of iniquity, many of whose members engaged regularly in illicit sexual activity. Although Califano's investigation found that there had been no wrongdoing, and although no members were mentioned by name, Ferrugia and CBS editors were derelict in not taking sufficient account of the damage that might be done to the institution and its members as a result of an inflammatory report based on the allegations of highly questionable sources. Some specific individuals in Congress—such as Robert Bauman (R–Md.) or Fred Richmond (D–N.Y.)—were especially vulnerable to innuendos because of previous disclosures about their sexual preferences. One can reasonably argue that their particular vulnerability was their own fault and that politics is a rough business, but that argument is better advanced in defense of an accurate story based on solid information provided by reliable sources.

More than the public's perception of Congress is involved in this list of harms. The Ethics Committee investigation, which was prompted by the CBS report, cost taxpayers almost half a million dollars. A legal liability to pay the costs may be too high a burden to place on a news organization in a case of this kind, but a moral responsibility is inescapable. Ferrugia reported both too much and too little, and he bears responsibility for the harms caused by both. Had Ferrugia and CBS exercised better judgment and due care about the use of information provided by suspect sources, many of the resultant harms need not have occurred.

## Harms by Insinuation and Innuendo

Another common problem in journalism is causing harm by either innuendo or insinuation. We do not mean to imply that the press always causes such harm intentionally. The primary problem seems to be a failure to scrutinize what has been written for hidden or subtle meanings and consequences. But the press does sometimes use insinuation and innuendo intentionally, and there are many cases of unascertainable motives and mixed intent.

Consider, for example, the press accounts during the 1984 presidential campaign of alleged Mafia connections in the family of Democratic vice-presidential candidate Geraldine Ferraro's husband, John Zaccaro. An article that appeared on the editorial page of *The Wall Street Journal,* under the headline "Rep. Ferraro and a Painful Legacy," seemed to hold that Ferraro, who was then running for vice-president, might be the heir to, or at least be deeply influenced by, the actions of her deceased father-in-law, Philip Zaccaro.[27] These actions had taken place at least thirteen years earlier.

There is little doubt that some readers were interested in knowing details about the family background of a wealthy New York real estate developer whose wife happened to be the first woman majority-party candidate for vice-president. If the presumption is in favor of the publication of relevant data about public figures, as we have argued above, then the burden is on those who think an article ought not be published to persuade the others that they are right. Such a balancing and persuading process seems to have been attempted at the *Journal.* The article was originally reported for the news pages, was subjected to analysis by editors, and finally ran on the editorial page. Some uncertainty remains about whether it was turned down by the news department or whether the authors offered it to the editorial page at their own initiative, but it is certain that several reporters and editors in the news department were opposed to the *Journal*'s running the article anywhere.

Jonathan Neumann, coauthor of the *Post* cancer series, offered a highly positive, retrospective evaluation of the *Journal*'s behavior: "I thought the piece was extremely responsible, exceedingly careful and open-minded," he said. "Normally an article like that would be out of place—one that raises questions and does not answer them. To pull it off is really hard, and I think *The Wall Street Journal* did pull it off.[28] We believe, however, that Neumann's assessment suggests an inability to distinguish relevant information and analysis from unfair commentary and innuendo. By publishing the article, the *Journal* seemed to suggest that those events, none of which was illegal, were relevant to the 1984 campaign and somehow tainted Ferraro's qualifications for office. Although the *Journal* noted that "the known facts are all capable of sympathetic explanation, as well as of sinister explanation," the paper pursued "unanswered questions" about Philip Zaccaro's real estate dealings and his character reference for a Mafia figure. Reporters Jonathan Kwitny and Anthony M. De Stefano of the *Journal*'s New York bureau wrote as follows:

> The connections involve only legitimate business transactions that don't appear *in themselves* to have been illegal, although a *subsequent* sale of one of the Mafia-connected properties is currently being investigated by a federal grand jury in Manhattan. There isn't any evidence that the connections have ever affected Rep. Ferraro's behavior in public life or that she even met people like Mr. Profaci [allegedly a Mafia don].
>
> Nor is there any evidence that the Zaccaro family has developed new links to Mafia characters since John Zaccaro took over the business in 1971 at age 38. In fact, there is evidence that he may have gone out of his way to sever *some* connections he inherited.[29]

Assuming the above is true, why devote a lengthy article on the *Journal*'s editorial page to a dead man's marginal links with members of the Mafia? The history of the relationship had not been exhaustively uncovered, and the reports contained more hints than relevant facts. The article justified the inquiry as follows:

A Zaccaro-Ferraro defense might . . . point out that some of President Reagan's backers and appointees, including his close friend and campaign manager, Sen. Paul Laxalt, have befriended people with reputations right on a par with those of people the Zaccaro family has helped. But questions of the president's sensitivities on such matters have been dealt with in detail in this newspaper. The Zaccaro family's associations with the New York underworld deserves no less. The perniciousness of organized crime is a public issue. It is entirely believable that the underworld connections died with Philip Zaccaro, but voters are entitled to enough facts to decide for themselves if that is the case.[30]

In suggesting that Ferraro and her husband need to mount a "defense," the *Journal* is subtly suggesting that they are on trial, as indeed they were. Trial by press, in this instance, involved no charge of criminal wrongdoing, only allegations of guilt by association, and even the association was inherited by the candidate's husband from his father. Even the charge is presented in loaded language. Phrases like "transactions that don't appear *in themselves* to have been illegal" imply that together with still undisclosed information some illegal action occurred. And by saying that John Zaccaro "may have gone out of his way to sever *some* connections he inherited," the implication remains that he still has some Mafia ties. It is also unclear what "facts" are provided in the *Journal* article to help voters "decide for themselves" if the Zaccaro family's "underworld connections" died with Philip Zaccaro.

Newspapers have a right, even a duty, to raise questions they cannot answer in the hope that the questions will enhance the public's awareness of important issues, and that airing the questions might produce answers. But in the Ferraro case there is good reason to believe that simply raising the questions might significantly harm the interests of the article's subject or subjects, with no clear compensating benefit for the public. There is a substantial possibility that the malfeasance, immorality, and illegality implied by the questions posed was nonexistent; but even if there had been wrongdoing of some sort, it was irrelevant to the public's legitimate interest in the primary subject of the story. In this case, the real target was Ferraro. Had she not been running for vice-president, there would have been no story and no objective.

Kwitny and De Stefano did consider some of the concerns we have raised but reached the conclusion that the public was entitled to decide for itself whether the Zaccaro–Ferraro family was still connected to the Mafia. We do not concur with this balancing of potential harms and benefits, for two reasons. First, the paper's analogy to reporting on allegations involving Paul Laxalt fails to take account of two relevant facts: Laxalt, unlike Philip Zaccaro, was a U.S. senator, and, unlike Zaccaro, Laxalt was very much alive. Second, and far more importantly, the *Journal* did not provide any evidence to show that Ferraro or her husband were linked to the Mafia. It is not enough to lard the article with disclaimers to the effect that "we are just raising questions, not making accusations." The fact that Zaccaro and Ferraro refused to answer many of the *Journal*'s questions does not make it legitimate to raise them in public unless there is some reason to believe that the damning implications are reasonably likely to be true, that they are relevant to the campaign, or that the public has some other legitimate interest in the information. None of these justifications seems to apply to the *Journal*'s publication.

The *Journal* quickly ran into a cascade of mounting criticism,[31] not only for this story but for two other, near simultaneous negative stories on Ferraro: one on her financial affairs and one on her husband's real estate transactions. After two weeks of criticism had passed, the *Journal* succumbed to temptation and responded in an editorial of unusual vigor and length.[32] The *Journal* seemed to suggest that somehow two wrongs make a right. It argued that media publications like *The New York Times, The Washington Post,* and *Newsweek* use a double standard by hounding conservatives and leaving liberals in benign neglect. The *Journal* editors compared the treatment that had been given in "liberal" publications to conservative Edwin Meese with its treatment of Ferraro. But again, there is an important difference that bears directly on the distinction between legitimate criticism and innuendo: The criticisms of Meese were of Meese, whereas those of Ferraro were of a distant and dead relative by marriage.

Even if the double-standard accusation were correct, it would not justify the *Journal*'s behavior, and the problem is compounded by an apparent inconsistency at the *Journal*. The editors and columnists of this newspaper have repeatedly argued on the editorial and op-ed pages that journalists and members of Congress have attempted unjustifiably to hound public officials out of office or prevent them from obtaining office, using insufficient evidence as a basis for their stories or hearings.[33] Because their treatment of Ferraro seems to be paradigmatic of their own objections, they fell prey to their own line of argument.

In a separate incident with an ironic twist, the *Journal* noted in a front-page article on Australian press lord Rupert Murdoch, that Murdoch's "930,000-circulation *New York Post* featured negative front-page headlines about Ms. Ferraro in 10 issues, most of them insinuating that the vice-presidential candidate was linked to organized crime."[34] The article observed that "On Oct. 18, one story in the tabloid detailed how her father was in fact indicted just before his death some 40 years ago. This was news not just to *Post* readers, but also to Ms. Ferraro, who was eight years old at the time. Ms. Ferraro called Oct. 18 'the worst day of my political life.' And in private, the iron lady broke down and cried."[35]

*Journal* reporter Jane Mayer noted that "such partisan journalism [as *The New York Post*'s] is still commonplace in Europe, but not in this country." Her concern for Ferraro is touching, but, for whatever purpose, she and the *Journal* wound up reprinting the *Post*'s allegation about Ferraro's father on the front page of the million-plus-circulation *Journal.* Mayer went on to discuss Murdoch's approach to newspapering, which exhibits a concern about harm by insinuation and innuendo similar to concerns about the morality of killing exhibited by a coyote in pursuit of a rabbit. Mayer quoted Jack Newfield of the Murdoch-owned *Village Voice,* who said *The New York Post* "doesn't just endorse you, it campaigns for you. And if they're against you, they just kill you, like they're doing to Ferraro now."[36] Toward the end of her article, Mayer quoted a series of *Post* headlines, almost all of which linked Ferraro or Zaccaro to organized crime. Then Mayer wrote: "Even those who criticize *The New York Post* concede that some of the stories are legitimate. But they question the paper's front-page pre-election play of some stories that even Mr. [Roger] Wood [executive editor of the *Post*] admits 'don't prove anything but simply raise a lot of questions.' "[37]

Why did *The Wall Street Journal* decide to run its story on Murdoch, with its repetitions of *Post* slurs, innuendo, and insinuation about Ferraro, just four days before the election? One reason is that the story would have been stale after the election, with more of the flavor of history than news. But surely a newspaper as resourceful and ordinarily as responsible as the *Journal* could find another peg besides the Ferraro story on which to hang a story about a hardy perennial like Murdoch. The *Journal* remained unrepentant. In an editorial exclusively on the subject of its treatment of Ferraro that was published over a year later, the *Journal* could offer only the following as a justification of the article by Kwitny and De Stefano.

> In terms of journalism, . . . Mr. Zaccaro has pleaded guilty to a fraud, a circumstance to which the moral standards of P. Zaccaro & Co. are clearly relevant. . . . Back when this mattered, voters could learn about it only in a few places. For being one of them, we offer no apologies. Indeed, we stand ready to accept them.[38]

We think, of course, that an apology by this newspaper rather than to it is in order, which takes us to the subject of appropriate apologies and retractions.

## Inevitable Harm and the Retraction of Mistakes

Some harm-causing mistakes are inevitable. Reporting and editing are often done under extreme time pressure, with inadequate resources. Even with-

out these constraints, human error is sometimes unavoidable. Once it occurs the harm probably cannot be completely corrected or compensated
for, because not everyone who has read or viewed the original report will
see a later correction. However, the issuing of corrections—as some newspapers now do on a regular institutionalized basis—is essential.

A case in which a perceived error was corrected properly, and as effectively as possible within reasonable parameters, involved television station
WDVM in Washington, D.C., which is owned by the Evening News Association of Detroit. WDVM broadcast a four-part series beginning November 7, 1983, charging that the Vietnam Veterans Memorial Fund misappropriated money intended for construction of the monument. The series
prompted a General Accounting Office audit, which found no evidence of
any wrongdoing. One year to the day after the appearance of the first story
in the series (by investigative reporter Carlton Sherwood), WDVM news
director Dave Pearce made a statement at the close of the 6:00 P.M. and
11:00 P.M. news programs that said:

> We aired the series because we believed it accurately represented the facts
> as we knew them at the time. While we continue to believe that we have
> acted responsibly throughout this controversy, it is obvious that the Me-
> morial Fund may have been harmed by our reports and that at least some
> of its officers may have suffered personally as a result. The bottom line is
> that the suspicions aroused in our reports about the fund were un-
> founded.
>
> To officially set the record straight, we would like to correct any
> impression left from our broadcasts last November that the Memorial
> Fund or its officers have done anything improper. We regret any harm
> that may have been caused to the Memorial Fund and its officers. The
> evidence indicates they performed a great public service.
>
> The GAO investigation turned up no evidence which supported the
> statement made in our series. In addition, our own internal investigation
> into the story has turned up no evidence to support the charges made
> during last year's reports.
>
> Once again, we sincerely regret and apologize for any harm these re-
> ports may have caused to the Memorial Fund, John Wheeler, Jan Scruggs
> or any other officers or directors of the Memorial Fund.[39]

This statement, in its explicit and forthright recognition of the errors
made and the injustice and possible harm done, is a model apology. There
is no reason to doubt Pearce's assertion that WDVM aired the series because they believed it to be accurate at the time. We did not investigate
whether Sherwood's research and reporting were sufficient or whether the
reporting was of sufficient quality to justify the station's confidence. Our
concern is not with evaluating Sherwood's journalism but with finding effective ways to correct mistakes and mitigate harm. Furthermore, we do
not know WDVM's motive in issuing its correction-cum-apology. The last

sentence in *The Washington Post*'s article on the subject said however: "Pearce declined to elaborate on his remarks following the 6 p.m. broadcast but did confirm that the Fund had threatened to sue before the settlement."[40]

## Conclusion

We have tried in this chapter not to impose an alien model of responsibility on journalism, but we have argued that journalists, like other relevantly similar occupational groups, must live up to basic standards of due care and due diligence. In the following chapter we make the leap from the duty to avoid harm to a consideration of whether the general-interest media has a specific duty to benefit the public, one that transcends the option to provide merely that information which the media sees fit to provide.

NOTES

1. Judge Henry Friendly, *Buckley* v. *New York Post*, 373 F.2d 175 (1967), p. 182.

2. See C. L. Ten, *Mill on Liberty* (Oxford: Clarendon Press, 1980), p. 2, for interpretation of relevant passages in Mill.

3. Joel Feinberg, *Harm to Others* (New York: Oxford University Press, 1984), pp. 34–35. Compare R. M. Hare, "Wrongness and Harm," in his *Essays on the Moral Concepts* (Berkeley: University of California Press, 1972).

4. Morton Mintz and Jerry S. Cohen, *Power, Inc.* (New York: Bantam, 1977), p. 446.

5. Walter Shapiro, "Wilbur Mills: The Ways and Means of Conning the Press," *Washington Monthly*, December 1974.

6. Brooks Jackson, "Storm Center: John Fedders of SEC is Pummelled by Legal and Personal Problems," *The Wall Street Journal*, February 25, 1985, p. 1. See also Brooks Jackson, "SEC Enforcement Chief Fedders Quits, Says Reports on Marital Violence Unfair," *The Wall Street Journal*, February 27, 1985, p. 3.

7. David Wessel and Bob Davis, "Under a Cloud: Bank of Boston Faces Image Problem Likely to Linger for Years," *The Wall Street Journal*, March 7, 1985, p. 1.

8. See the *Journal*'s own previous reports of the story: Bob Davis, "U.S. Bank of Boston Unit Was Told It Broke Law 2 Years Before Compliance," *The Wall Street Journal*, February 28, 1985, p. 16; and Bob Davis, "Bank of Boston Says It Knew of Change in Cash-Reporting but Didn't Obey," *The Wall Street Journal*, March 5, 1985, p. 5.

9. This strategy is used in Martin Curd and Larry May, *Professional Responsibility for Harmful Actions* (Dubuque: Kendall/Hunt, 1984), from which our analysis has benefited.

10. Mary Crystal Cage, "Key Van de Kamp Aide Arrested on Molestation Charge," *The Sacramento Bee*, July 25, 1984, p. Al.

11. Jay Mathews, "Child's Charges Brand Innocent Man," *The Washington Post*, March 19, 1985, p. Al.

12. Ted Gup and Jonathan Neumann, *The Washington Post*, October 18–21, 1981, p. Al each day.

13. Vincent DeVita, "DeVita Responds to Post Article," *The Washington Post*, October 19, 1981, p. A27.

14. Gup and Neuman, October 18, 1981, p. Al. Emphasis added.

15. DeVita, "DeVita Responds to Post Article," p. A27.

16. Gup and Neuman, October 18, 1981, p. Al. Emphasis added.

17. Bob Woodward, answering questions at *New Republic* seminar, November 12, 1981, p. 52 of transcript.

18. Philip Cohen, remarks at *New Republic* seminar, November 12, 1981, pp. 5–6.

19. Marcia Angell, remarks at *New Republic* seminar, November 12, 1981, p. 22.

20. See, e.g., Jane Brody, "Chemotherapy Moves to Fore as Cure for Cancer," *The New York Times*, May 15, 1984, p. Cl. Brody listed drawbacks along with the advances made in chemotherapy in recent years, but the first three paragraphs set the tone for two carefully written articles:

> Chemotherapy, once the black sheep of cancer treatments, has become the leading weapon for increasing the number of patients who can be cured of cancer.
>
> At the same time, researchers are reducing the debilitating side effects that chemotherapy patients have typically had to endure.
>
> Furthermore, new drugs, and new methods of using old ones, hold out the promise that there will soon be significant improvements in fighting some of the most common cancer killers.

21. Dan Rather, "CBS Evening News," June 30, 1982.

22. Report of the Committee on Standards of Official Conduct, House of Representatives, "Investigation Pursuant to House Resolution 12 Concerning Alleged Illicit Use or Distributions of Drugs by Members, Officers, or Employees of the House" (Washington: U.S. Government Printing Office, November 17, 1983) and *Report by Committee on Standards of Official Conduct, House of Representatives*, Pursuant to House Resolution 518, "Report on Investigation" (Washington: U.S. Government Printing Office, December 14, 1982).

23. John Ferrugia, telephone interview, 1985.

24. Report of the Committee on Standards of Official Conduct, p. 282.

25. Ibid., pp. 286–87.

26. "Report on Investigation," p. 11.

27. Jonathan Kwitny and Anthony M. De Stefano, "Rep. Ferraro and a Painful Legacy," *The Wall Street Journal*, September 13, 1984, editorial page.

28. As quoted by Eleanor Randolph, "Journal Article on Ferraro Family Background Stirs Up a Furor," *The Washington Post*, September 22, 1984, p. A3.

29. Kwitney and De Stefano, "Rep. Ferraro and a Painful Legacy." Emphasis added.

30. Ibid.

31. Ibid. For an outspoken criticism, see Jonathan Alter, *Newsweek*, September 24, 1984, p. 55.

32. Editorial, "About Press Vendettas" *The Wall Street Journal*, October 1, 1984, p. 28. See also an insightful letter to the editor by Michael E. McGurkin, "Press Standards," *The Wall Street Journal*, October 12, 1984, op-ed page.

33. An example of this well-known stance at the *Journal* is the editorial "Scandal Time Again," *The Wall Street Journal*, December 5, 1985. A typical summary comment appeared in Suzanne Garment's "Capital Chronicle" column: "For the past 10 years some politicians and journalists have used the issue of ethics as a big political club. . . . More commonly, . . . the defendant really isn't guilty of anything very exciting." "Watergate-style Sleuthing Gets a Bit Harder," *The Wall Street Journal*, November 8, 1985, p. 32. See also the editorials "Cowboys and Indiana" (June 30, 1986) and "Judicial Restraint" (July 11, 1986).

34. Jane Mayer, "Australia's Murdoch Is Getting His Kicks in U.S. Political Races," *The Wall Street Journal*, November 2, 1984, pp. 1, 18.

35. Ibid.

36. Ibid.

37. Ibid.

38. Editorial, "Pardon Gerry Ferraro," *The Wall Street Journal*, December 13, 1985, p. 30.

39. WDVM (Washington, D.C.), "Eyewitness News," November 7, 1984.

40. John Carmody, "Channel 9 Apologizes to Fund," *The Washington Post*, November 8, 1984, p. D15.

# Chapter 5

# Serving the Public

In 1823, when journalism in the United States was still in its formative stages, Thomas Jefferson wrote, "The press is the best instrument for enlightening the mind of man, and improving him as a rational, moral, and social being."[1] Jefferson's sentiment is mildly hyperbolic, but the press, more than any other institution, is able to add to the knowledge and understanding of vast numbers of individuals. It is a short step from this fact to the conclusion that it is part of the media's mandate in democracies to provide a public benefit by circulating useful information and promoting the public's understanding.

We will not provide a detailed definition of public benefit, nor will we provide a list of criteria for the kinds of benefits that journalism might offer. Rather, we will try to capture the conception of public benefit that from the Founding Fathers onward has been invoked to justify special privileges and protections for the press. Jefferson, Madison, Adams, and the other framers of the Constitution conceived the press's obligations in terms of an implied contract with the public; journalists were given the role of supplying the information people need to be good citizens. In working terms, this can be translated to mean that an editor who is deciding what to publish on deadline should ask this question: "Do people *need* to know this?" If the answer is yes, there is a strong presumption in favor of publishing. If two items about which the public has a need to know must compete for the space, the question becomes, "Which do they need to know more?" or, "Which do they need to know first?"

To attempt to give exact criteria for the information the public needs absent the specific context and to try to express the idea of public benefit in capsule form would be to invite ridicule. Moreover, it would involve potentially tedious inquiry into the distinction between what the public wants to know (e.g., Washington and Hollywood gossip) and what it needs to know. Instead, we will do what we have done elsewhere in this book—sketch the historical background and then offer a few examples and arguments to try to show why certain kinds of stories do or do not provide appropriate benefits and whether a good argument can be made on moral grounds for an obligation to publish them.

## Historical Considerations

In the eighteenth century, when the United States was emerging as a nation, the debate on the role of the press was focused on various questions of freedom and rights. The emerging justification for freedom of the press, as distinct from freedom of speech and its attendant rights, was implicitly grounded in a duty to provide public benefits. For example, in making its case for independence, the Continental Congress touched on the rationale for an independent press:

> The importance of this [press freedom] consists, besides the advancement of truth, science, morality and arts in general, in its diffusion of liberal sentiments on the administration of government, its ready communication of thoughts between subjects, and its consequential promotion of union among them, whereby oppressive officials are shamed or intimidated into more honorable and just modes of conducting affairs.[2]

The Continental Congress thus offered a catalogue of benefits the press can be expected to provide the public as a justification of the press's special freedoms.

Another example is contained in correspondence between William Cushing, an influential member of the convention that framed the Massachusetts Constitution, and John Adams. The details of the correspondence relevant to our inquiry are embedded in a discussion on libeling public officials, but a central conclusion is that the policy of allowing a free press can be justified by its consequences for the public good. Cushing wrote in 1789:

> What is that liberty of the press, which is essential to the security of freedom? The propagating [of] literature and knowledge by printing or otherwise tends to illuminate men's minds and to establish them in principles in freedom. But it cannot be denied also, that a free scanning of the conduct of administration and shewing the tendency of it, and where truth will warrant making it manifest that it is subversive of all law, liberty, and the Constitution; it can't be denied. I think that the liberty tends to the *security of freedom in a State;* even more directly and essentially than the liberty of printing upon literary and speculative subjects in general.[3]

Cushing's justification of a free press rests on the premise that the press provides direct benefits in its role as a monitor of the public's business and as an educator. His is not a conception based on the right to speak freely but rather on the benefits that flow from a particular genus of speech—news reporting on the activities of public officials.

Adams, while responding to Cushing's points about whether truth should be a defense in a libel suit brought against a public official, wrote the following:

> Our chief magistrates and Senators &c are annually eligible by the people. How are their characters and conduct to be known to their constituents but by the press? If the press is stopped and the people kept in Ignorance we had much better have the first magistrates and Senators hereditary. I therefore, am very clear that under the Articles of our Constitution which you have quoted, it would be safest to admit evidence to the jury of the Truth of accusations, and if the jury found them true *and that they were published for the Public good,* they would readily acquit.[4]

"Published for the Public good." With that phrase Adams captured the rationale for a free press that was quietly emerging during this period: Freedom entails a responsibility to report or comment on the activities of public officials, and journalists should do so with a concern for benefiting the public. Adams was also concerned that the reputations of public officials be protected from libel, but his primary interest was to ensure that the public would benefit from legal protections bestowed upon the press.

Adams, Cushing, and the members of the Continental Congress all concentrated on the importance to the public of the watchdog aspects of providing public benefits. However, Adams's use of the broad phrase "public good," Cushing's reference to "the propagating of literature and knowledge by printing," and the Continental Congress's reference to "the advancement of truth, science, morality and arts in general" strongly suggest that these early and prominent figures in American history envisioned a much more expansive role for the press as a provider of public benefits and that the press clause of the First Amendment was born in a climate in which such freedoms were bestowed to ensure that those benefits would continue to flow to the public.

Although the language is slightly updated, those who write thought-fully on this issue continue to present arguments similar to those of the Founding Fathers. Consider Alan Barth, for example:

> A free press—that is, a press free from government regulation or con-trol—serves as a censor of the government in two ways. First, it is *supposed* to give the people of a democratic society the information about the world they live in and about what their government is doing without which they cannot possibly, in any real sense, be self-governing. This is, of course, the business of the news pages.
>
> Second, a free press is *supposed* to speak out in defense of the rights and liberties of the people whenever these are threatened—even in the name of national security—and to give warning of any extension of gov-ernmental power beyond the perimeters fixed for it by the Constitution. It is *supposed*, in short, to speak for the people and against the govern-ment. This is, of course, the business of the editorial pages.[5]

The point is that the press is "supposed"—that is, has a role responsibil-ity—to benefit the public.

## The Duty to Benefit

The special liberties granted the press are based on the expectation that it will provide public benefits. All that is necessary to illuminate the point is a moment's reflection on Samuel Johnson's epigram, "A newswriter is a man without virtue, who writes lies at home for his own profit."[6] If we accepted Johnson's view we would waste little time in revoking the press's rights and privileges. To justify those special privileges and protections, journalists must meet this obligation to benefit the public.

The use of words like *obligation, duty,* and *requirement* sends most journalists running for cover under the First Amendment. The operative assumption seems to be that if obligations are accepted, regulations will follow. Yet in journalism—unlike some vocations—the objective of pro-viding public benefits through the provision of timely, relevant, and ade-quate information is built into the very rationale for the institution, con-ceptually no less than historically. The implicit contract between press and society, on which the privileges of the press are based, is that the press is to provide adequate information for readers or viewers, not only about political affairs but in other spheres as well. The measure of the adequacy of the information published and broadcast by the media is the benefit it provides toward the understanding that is essential to autonomous delib-eration and choice. To the extent that it fails to provide this benefit, free-dom of choice in politics and all other areas becomes a sham, and the justification for any special treatment of the press is substantially undermined.

Even though many journalists are uncomfortable with the language of obligation, the American Society of Newspaper Editors says in its statement of principles, "The primary purpose of gathering and distributing news and opinion is to *serve the general welfare* by informing the people and enabling them to make judgments on the issues of the time."[7] It is notable that this statement specifies "the general welfare" and does not specify "the *political* issues of the time." Traditionally the value of the press as a means to free and informed political choice has been used as the justification for press freedom, but deliberation and choice in economic and social spheres are no less fundamental. There is no good reason in the rationale of a free press to hold that the press has less of a duty to provide information in these areas. Among the subjects we would include within the scope of this broad duty are matters that bear on health, from hurricane warnings to new developments in cancer research to environmental hazards to consumer and occupational safety; general economic news about employment and unemployment, interest rates, and taxes; news about education ranging from developments in local schools to national educational policy and trends in education; and important social trends such as crime patterns, drug abuse, birth rates, changing racial attitudes, and demographic movements.

This list is far from complete, and it includes nothing that the general media do not already cover, although not always adequately. We intend to be neither comprehensive nor critical but only to emphasize that the general media have an obligation to report this kind of news just as they have an obligation to report political news. We realize, of course, that some media outlets serve special constituencies, some of whose interests may conflict with the prevailing conception of the public interest. As a result, we do not suggest that, on balance, everyone's interests must be served by any one journalist's efforts, or even by the efforts of any one journalistic institution. There are different roles and commitments in journalism, and benefits can legitimately be construed as applying to discrete groups or special interests. What we do advocate is that providing information that benefits the public is a fundamental obligation of journalism, not a matter confined to editorial discretion.

A distinction relevant to this discussion is sometimes drawn in moral philosophy between perfect duties and imperfect duties. A perfect duty is strictly defined in regard to a specific person or group—for example, reporters have specific duties to identifiable editors that must be discharged in specific ways. Imperfect duties, by contrast, are more open-ended, less strictly defined with respect to the persons or groups owed the duty, and sometimes indeterminate regarding how the duty must be discharged. We will argue that journalists often have only imperfect obligations to serve the public and therefore are not always bound to provide benefits in specific ways to specific populations. Journalists who accept the protection of the First Amendment are morally bound to produce public benefits, but they must be given discretion in deciding how to serve the public.

Many journalists recognize a duty of providing public benefits analogous to the duty of public health officials to care for the public's health. In a 1949 speech titled "Wake Up Angry," James Polk, the managing editor of *The Louisville Courier-Journal,* said, "The good editor . . . has to wake up angry every morning. He does not wait for the moment to crusade on a spectacular scale. He does not await an epidemic. He spots and cauterizes civic germs, regardless of the enemies gained, before an infection takes root."[8] Polk uses a health-care analogy to characterize one kind of benefit journalists can provide. By saying that journalists should do so "regardless of the enemies" they acquire, he makes the point that it is a basic duty to provide the benefit.

In a talk to a group of Newspaper Guild members, former *Washington Post* reporter Murrey Marder quoted Polk's speech and used the quotation to introduce an example from his own experience of reporting during the period in which Senator Joseph McCarthy was wreaking havoc by labeling innocent public servants Communists. Because of their appropriateness to the discussion of providing public benefits, we quote Marder's remarks at considerable length:

> In the McCarthy era . . . the practice of journalism . . . was to report what people said; it did not essentially go beyond, behind, around what people said, especially if they were members of Congress. You reported what a senator said, what a representative said on a day-to-day basis. You didn't . . . question it, you didn't challenge it. . . .
>
> Joe McCarthy . . . exploited to an extraordinary degree the built-in limitations of the American press, which were, as I said, essentially in the case of public figures to report what they said, not to go beyond. He learned . . . that if he made charges late in the day he could hit late editions and people would not have time to question and challenge what he said. . . . And he learned that he could exploit the competitiveness between the Associated Press, United Press, and what was then International News Service. He could play one against the other. And the press did not seem to know what to do about this. . . . Al Friendly [then assistant managing editor of *The Washington Post*] . . . tried . . . to take a couple of cases and pursue them and talk to the people and find out the essence of the charges. But meanwhile, McCarthy was rolling along on a day-to-day basis with new charges against new people and you could never catch up with that. . . .
>
> I found that the only way to deal with this was on a constant running

basis. A McCarthy charge would come up a couple of hours before the deadline, we would report whatever we could in the paper of that day, of that edition rather, and the normal practice would have been then to go home. Instead we would keep at the thing. We'd try to call sources to find out the seriousness or shallowness of the charge, to find out what evidence there was behind it. We'd make some corrections, changes in the story in the next edition, and then in the next edition, and in the next edition, and this would go on all through the evening. The result was it completely changed the pattern of coverage. Of course it also meant working until midnight every day and fighting, fighting literally, for understandable reasons, with the news desk, with the makeup editors, with everyone, because this is a very costly venture. At the time the *Post* was really in a very strained financial condition. And it meant each night going back into the paper to change something with a great struggle over how much it cost to remake a page, and the time cost in slowing deliveries of newspapers, and it was a terribly frenetic process.

And during that process, which literally went on for four years, I can remember one of my very respected colleagues, Ferdy Kuhn, Ferdinand Kuhn . . . came back to me one night about 11 o'clock when I was sitting at the desk trying to call people to check on some of the charges saying, "Murrey, what are you doing? This is a hopeless cause. How can you possibly win? You're beating your brains out. You can't possibly keep up with the charges. The paper can't keep up with the charges. Where do you think you will come out on it?" And, I said, "Frankly, I don't know, Ferdy, I really don't know. The only principle I can operate on as a newspaperman is, if I keep throwing enough facts out there hopefully eventually it will have some effect on the situation." And he said, "I don't think it will." And I said, "Well, if it doesn't, if I thought that, then what's the point of the whole business?" So of course actually it did have some impact and some of the articles contributed to bringing on the Army-McCarthy hearings and eventually the downfall of McCarthy.[9]

Marder was concerned with having "some effect on the situation" and ultimately with "the point of the whole business." He saw his role as journalist as that of providing benefits far beyond the basic provision of information. The information he was making available—the facts he kept throwing out—were intended to produce a beneficial effect, or else it would miss "the point of the whole business." Marder and his colleagues, with the support of the *Post*'s management, pursued McCarthy for four difficult, costly years, and in the end their efforts paid dividends, for them and for the public. Marder does not use the language of duty or obligation. Nevertheless, he is implicitly expressing what he considers to be his duty as a journalist to provide a public benefit once he has accepted an assignment like the one to report on McCarthy's activities. This is a duty not merely to provide information and to tell the truth, but to benefit the public by providing information and telling the truth in a certain way for a public purpose, even if a price must be paid by him and his paper. Marder did not view his sacrifice as beyond duty when he worked until midnight week after week, month after month. He viewed the sacrifice as resting on a duty flowing from his acceptance of the assignment, and the *Post* viewed support as part of its duty as a newspaper.[10]

References to the general idea that the press has obligations are often treated by journalists as attacks on their freedom on the ground that obligations express what you must do rather than what you are free to do. On reflection and in practice, however, these same journalists frequently reach a different conclusion. For example, discussions among reporters and among editorial writers often center on benefits that should be provided and harms that should be avoided. An instance is found in the debate over whether television news programs should broadcast the results of election-day exit polls when it is still early enough for the findings to influence election results in other parts of the country. The public debate on this issue has focused on whether the public would benefit more from having the survey results as soon as they were available or from having them withheld until they could no longer influence state or local elections. Some television executives may have argued internally that the broadcasting of exit-poll results improves the ratings of their news programs, but the public debate was conducted on the moral high ground of what most benefits the public.

When considering issues such as health hazards, journalists are often willing to concede that the criterion of what counts as news should be expanded to include information of direct personal benefit to readers or viewers. Networks, stations, and papers may even voluntarily share information that, in other circumstances, would be viewed as competitive. In discussing how journalists were covering AIDS, Joseph Lovett, an ABC-TV producer, said, "Reporters help each other. There's a war going on" against a vicious disease.[11] Some journalists even see stories that provide direct benefits to the public as often transcending in importance the political news that provides most of the grist for most newspapers. They argue, correctly in our view, that much so-called political news is gossip, that political stories are often highly repetitive, and that this kind of political entertainment crowds out stories that are essential to personal understanding of and decision making about urgent matters such as health and finances.

One nationally prominent reporter agreed to let us quote from memos on this subject that he wrote to his editors over the years, on the condition that neither the individuals nor the publication were identified. We agreed because, with or without names, these memos illustrate that good journalists are concerned with providing public benefits. In this memo only the names and one sentence are deleted:

In the Winter 1967/1968 issue of *Columbia Journalism Review,* in connection with the coverage by us and the noncoverage by others of the
antibiotics antitrust trial, this editorial statement was made: . . . "Newspapers still underestimate stories that cut close to readers' essential concerns of life and health. . . ."

I was reminded of this today when I picked up the paper and found
that a story given exclusively to me and . . . on an Agriculture Department survey of filthy meat plants had been cut into an item [a story only
a few paragraphs long carried in a roundup column of relatively minor
national news], with evisceration of the names of the cities in which plants
were closed and in which corrections were ordered, and with deletion also
of the brief summaries of the reasons for these actions.

I suppose you will be able to justify this on the ground of more pressing news? I say that we are among those newspapers that "still underestimate stories that cut close to readers' essential concerns of life and health.
. . ." If you want more evidence, look at the pile of good drug stories
that have been lying around for weeks. . . . Christ Almighty."

This reporter makes the point emphatically that information alerting
the public in an accurate and substantially complete way about health threats
such as filthy meat plants should not be crowded out of the paper, because
the benefit is too important. The reporter goes on to express the press's
duties to provide benefits in another memo. Here is an edited but essentially undistorted text:

The morning [paper] devotes:
* 89 column inches, many of them on page one, to the indictment of Rep.
[Charles] Diggs [D–Mich.] for the illegal diversion of $101,000 in federal
payroll monies.
* 1 3/16 inches . . . inside, . . . to the indictment of Olin Corp. and
three former officials, for concealing the dumping of 38 tons of mercury
into the Niagara River over a period of seven years.

*The [New York] Times* account said: "State environmental officials
said the dumped mercury, which can cause nervous disorders and harm
the human reproductive system of anyone eating fish from the waters,
represented a serious and continuing hazard to people in Niagara Falls
and scores of communities along the Niagara River and the southern shore
of Lake Ontario into which it empties."

Disregarding prominence, headlines and photos, the systematic thefts
of the Hon. Diggs got 75 times as much attention as the "serious and
continuing hazard" to a very large number of human beings created by
systematic poisoning of the Niagara by Olin.

My submission is that the disproportion in attention given the two
events reflects, in fairly extreme form, a problem with chronically distorted news values.

To be sure, I believe that if a member of the staff had gotten an exclusive story conveying the substance of the Olin indictment, we would
have given it a big ride. I do not believe this fact (which I believe it to be)
redeems a performance such as today's, in terms of our *obligation to our
readers* [emphasis added].

Here the reporter explicitly reflects on journalists' obligations to readers to report fully on events that have a direct bearing on their well-being. He thinks people need to know about corruption in government as well, but he does not think that 89 column inches on Diggs's corruption should overshadow the activities of the Olin Corporation. We agree.

Although journalists are often defensive when outsiders tell them they are responsible for providing specific benefits to the public, they tend internally to justify their professional behavior in terms of just such benefits provided or harms avoided. Consider the following excerpt from a column by Lou Cannon, White House correspondent of *The Washington Post,* which focused on coverage of the hijacking of TWA Flight 847:

> Several freed hostages thanked reporters for keeping the public focus on their plight. And it is also worth noting that the media refrained from publishing or airing information that could have been damaging to the hostages.
>
> For starters, the press suppressed the fact that one hostage was a member of the National Security Agency. Everyone involved in the coverage recognized that revealing this information would have endangered his life.
>
> Another potentially important confidence was also withheld. On the day the Secretary of State George P. Shultz raised the ante and tried to obtain release of the seven Americans held hostage before the TWA hijacking, some of us were told that the U.S. government did not expect this maneuver to succeed. We suppressed this assessment at administration request since publishing it could have ruined whatever slim chances existed for the release of the missing seven.
>
> At *The Washington Post,* as the crisis deepened, editors decided on their own to forgo stories about military options and possible targets for reprisal. Such stories were simply considered too risky.[12]

Cannon describes a situation in which journalists acted on principles of avoiding harm and of providing benefit to a specific individual or specific individuals, at the cost of depriving the general public of information that, by almost any standard, would be considered newsworthy. Such cost–benefit judgments are essential to responsible journalism, as we explore below.

## Avoiding Harms and Providing Benefits

Philosophers have often argued that the obligation to avoid harm is more stringent than the obligation to provide benefits, but this claim, and the distinction on which it rests, are of dubious merit. To be sure, the claim that avoiding harm is a more stringent duty has a strong intuitive appeal.

For example, a physician's duty not to injure a patient by abandonment intuitively seems stronger than the duty to prevent injury to a patient who has been abandoned by another physician. Similarly, the duty not to drown someone seems stronger than the duty to save someone from drowning. But these examples only show that in some cases the duty to avoid harm overrides the duty to provide benefits. It is implausible to claim that avoiding harm is always a more stringent duty than providing benefits, or even that the two activities are always distinct. As noted in Chapter 4, there are many occasions when providing a benefit easily outweighs avoiding a harm, such as when a person's reputation is unavoidably harmed by a thoroughly justified news story.

There is also an important conceptual problem in analyzing the distinction between avoiding harm and providing benefits that is illustrated by the following examples. If a journalist writes a story about someone's desperate need for money or free medical care because of an exotic disease, and the money or care is provided by donors as a result of the story, has the journalist provided a benefit, contributed to avoiding a harm, contributed to removing a harm, or all of the above? Similarly, if a journalist refrains from writing a story that is likely to ruin a career, even though it is based on compelling (but exclusively circumstantial) evidence, has the journalist simply prevented a harm, or has he or she also provided a benefit to the party who would have been injured? These examples indicate that the distinction between providing benefits and avoiding harms does not have sharp conceptual boundaries. We therefore ought to view the obligation to provide benefits more as continuous with the obligation to avoid harm than as different from it.

The obligation to avoid harms and the obligation to provide benefits may conflict. Similarly, two obligations to avoid harm may conflict and two obligations to provide benefits may conflict, resulting in dilemmas over which harms to avoid and which benefits to provide. Practitioners of any profession will face similar choices. Physicians, for example, who pledge to do no harm are not pledging never to cause harm but rather to strive for a balance of benefits over harms. The Nuremberg Code developed at the trials of Nazi physicians advanced the principle that even in human experimentation "the degree of risk to be taken should never exceed that determined by the humanitarian importance of the problem to be solved by the experiment."[13] The relevant analogy for journalists is that the weight of the harm and the degree of risk should be balanced directly against the public benefit of the reporting. The obligation is to weigh benefits against harms, benefits against alternative benefits, and harms against alternative harms.

A typical and also commendable example of a newspaper's handling of this problem is found in a front-page 1977 story in *The Boston Globe*. The *Globe* reported that a South African affiliate of the Polaroid Corporation has been clandestinely selling Polaroid products to the South African government in direct violation of a 1971 agreement with Polaroid that such sales were forbidden. The story emerged through the whistle-blowing efforts of a former employee in the shipping department of the affiliate company (Frank & Hirsch). The employee had made photostatic copies of invoices documenting the delivery of Polaroid products to the Bantu Reference Bureau, the agency that issues passbooks for nonwhites in South Africa. An American source then gave the documentation to the *Globe*. The *Globe* was aware that publishing the story entailed risks that numerous South African employees would lose their jobs, the Polaroid's business relationship with the affiliate would be severed, that distress and embarrassment would be caused to Polaroid (a company with a history of opposition to apartheid), that the affiliate would be driven out of business, and that the whistle-blower would be punished. Yet the editors also recognized that publication of the story would be a major public benefit. The *Globe* handled the situation by informing Polaroid executives about the story five days before the planned date of publication. Polaroid then sent its export sales manager to South Africa to investigate, and he was able to document the charges. Polaroid and the *Globe* were able to secure the safety of the whistle-blower, and Polaroid was also able to announce that it was terminating its distributorship and all involvement in South Africa on the same day as the *Globe* published the story. This we suggest, is a model balancing of risks and benefits.[14]

It is tempting to say that the general maxim that should be followed in such balancing is that causing or not preventing a harm is justified only if there is a compensating benefit of greater weight; or, to substitute a similar maxim drawn from risk–benefit analysis, a journalist can legitimately place persons at risk only if the risk is offset by a benefit that is at least commensurate. But what is to count as a compensating benefit or as a commensurate benefit? Is either a reasonable criterion? These goals are worthy, but we are inclined to think that there will be cases where there is sufficient justification to publish or broadcast a story that is likely to produce a significant benefit, even if there is no reasonable way of calculating that the story will actually outweigh related risks to which various parties are vulnerable.

Calculation of benefits is inherently unpredictable and therefore unreliable in many instances. The French newspaper *Le Monde* once published an account of how senior government officials knew about and may have authorized an effort to sabotage a campaign to halt French nuclear testing in the Pacific Ocean. Although *Le Monde* was cautious in making its accusations, the intent was to identify those involved in a major cover-up of clandestine activities. Both the defense minister and the head of the French secret services were ultimately driven from office, and even President François Mitterand was imperiled. Apparent harms were everywhere, and the U.S. media quickly took note of them: *Newsweek* focused on how the story had been "damaging in political terms," and *The Washington Post*'s Michael Dobbs wrote that the so-called Greenpeace affair had "damaged French prestige around the world and shaken the country's Socialist government."[15]

These assessments are generally accurate, but should *Le Monde* have weighed the potential harms to government officials and the French state against the public benefits of publishing its reports? Would it be wrong to publish the story even if the harms seemed to outweigh the benefits—or even if there was no clear compensating benefit? After all, the officials had created the situation and had hidden it from the French public. Besides, journalists rarely can assess with any precision the likely consequences of their stories. In this case, for example, Olivier Todd, former editor of *L'Express* magazine, said "that the press brought down Charles Hernu,"[16] but it is possible that the political fortunes of the dismissed defense minister, were actually advanced by his subsequent dismissal from the Mitterand government, because his popularity and reputation flourished almost immediately thereafter. In circumstances of this kind, the press is valued principally because of the free flow of information it facilitates and not because of any specific, predictable public good that might flow from it.

To attempt to carefully balance benefits against harms in every story would place an impossible burden on reporters and editors. Even experts often disagree over the nature of the risks involved and over how to weigh the various factors. A journalist might have to make a decision where there is no objective evidence that dictates one course of action rather than another, and intangible benefits to one group might have to be traded off against tangible benefits to a different group. If the press is to remain free from being manipulated or coerced, the burden of proof in cases of this kind must rest on those who would suppress a story rather than on those who would publish it.

## The Scope of the Obligation to Provide a Benefit

The principle that journalists are obligated to provide benefits raises questions about the extent to which reporters or editors are required to take personal risks or to suffer harm themselves to provide the benefit. This subject is illustrated by an article headlined "Newspapering and Courage," in which Gerald Shaw reported that "in South Africa, the truth can put you in prison":

> As editor of the *Cape Times*, . . . Anthony Heard, 48, finds himself having to reconcile a host of conflicting demands, the most pressing of which is to ensure the paper's survival in the teeth of an economic recession, a mine-field of restrictive legal measures and a political onslaught of great ferocity. . . .
>
> He is currently facing the threat of prosecution and imprisonment because of his decision to publish a full-page interview with Oliver Tambo, president of the African National Congress. . . . It is an offense in South Africa to publish the words of Tambo or anyone else who is a banned person in terms of South African security laws.
>
> In Heard's view, his primary responsibility is to ensure the survival of the *Cape Times*—but survival, not as a conformist journal acquiescing in a conspiracy to suppress the news, but as [a] trusted newspaper . . . telling its readers what they have a right to know. . . .
>
> Heard is at the same time desperately anxious about the safety of his reporters and photographers, who are in danger of harassment and arrest or, in situations of mob violence, injury or worse at the hands of the police and stone-throwing rioters alike. . . .
>
> Infringement of the Police Act means risking a 10-year prison sentence. . . .
>
> There are death threats to staff members and their families and the risk cannot be wholly discounted that the odd lunatic might seek to give effect to such threats.[17]

These conditions are extreme, but they are not unusual conditions for reporters to labor under in many parts of the world. Earlier we discussed the difficulties Murrey Marder and the *Post* encountered in reporting on Joseph McCarthy, and we noted that Marder did not regard his sacrifice as "beyond duty" once he had accepted the assignment. The plight of Anthony Heard and his staff prompts a return to this topic and to reflection on the extent to which journalists are obligated to sacrifice, including whether they have a duty to place themselves at significant personal risk or inconvenience to provide a public benefit.

Morality suggests that there are circumstances in which certain parties in certain roles are obligated to make a sacrifice. For example, there are conditions under which a parent might properly be accused of cowardice or neglect by failing to sacrifice in the interests of a child; and a policeman who failed to protect a colleague under a direct threat of death might properly be accused of cowardice. But do these parallels have any meaningful application to journalists? Did Marder, for example, have to accept his assignment and the extraordinary effort it demanded? Even if one accepts the proposition that journalists are morally required to provide benefits and not merely to avoid harms, can this principle be extended to require acts of heroism, extreme sacrifice, and the acceptance of more than minor risk?

The only fair answer to this question is a conventional one given in moral theory: Such acts are supererogatory (beyond duty) and thus are matters of an individual's personal ideals rather than a requirement of morality. They are more akin to acts of charity and acts of conscience that are discretionary decisions, rather than decisions governed by duty. When *The Wall Street Journal* carried out an investigation of "how [the] mafia controls air-cargo businesses at Kennedy Airport," the reporting required courage that transcends the paper's obligation to provide a public bene-fit.[18] Such acts of courage—which include various examples of war corre-spondence, coverage of civil disturbances, or on-scene reporting of epidem-ics—are laudable, but reporters and editors have no duty to take the risks involved. Just as no one is required to perform all possible acts of charity, journalists are not required to provide all possible benefits, and benefits obtained by running extreme risks are the most dispensable.

At about the time Heard was being threatened by the South African government, that same government put into effect regulations barring tele-vision cameras from scenes of racial violence. U.S. television networks, which had been covering South African street demonstrations intensively, suddenly found themselves in a bind. They were sometimes able to learn what happened by reporting at the scene or interviewing eyewitnesses, but they could not tape the action. With no pictures to show, what had been a major running story virtually disappeared from the air. "Nobody wants to be in the position of saying that what the South Africans did has worked," said Peter Jennings, anchorman of ABC's "World News Tonight," "but it has worked."[19] *The New York Times* added, "A comparison of television coverage during August and November [of 1985], the two most violent months of the year in South Africa, illustrates the point. In August, the three American networks broadcast 61 stories from South Africa on their evening newscasts. In November, the first month of the press restrictions, the total dropped to 20."[20]

What should the networks have done? It would have been both im-practical and morally indecent to expose their correspondents to the risk of arrest or worse at the hands of the South African police. But coverage of the story could have continued as intensively as before, without running any risk, by using more inventiveness and resourcefulness to piece together a compelling two minutes from interviews, file tape, and graphics, in lieu of action shots. Instead of focusing on the public benefit of their reporting, as opposed to its potential for producing high ratings and audience share, the networks allowed themselves to be coerced by the South African gov-

ernment into significantly reducing their coverage. In the spring and summer of 1986, however, the U.S. media, both print and electronic, responded much more vigorously and creatively when South Africa imposed
an even tougher ban on coverage.

## Blamable Failures to Provide Benefits

It is obvious that the press should be the source of important news, but
controversy sets in when it is asserted that the press is subject to blame if
it fails to provide benefits that it could provide. Consider this example. An
Alabama House member named Kenneth A. Roberts held a series of hearings from 1956 to 1963 on automobile safety. At the time the hearings
opened more than a million people had died on U.S. roads, and millions
of others had been injured. As the hearings progressed they moved into
the virgin territory of automobile design and its consequences for safety.
Physicians, engineers, and other specialists in crash-injury research said at
the hearings that the industry was capable of designing cars that could
significantly reduce the number of deaths and injuries in auto accidents
and reduce the severity of injuries suffered. For example, it was said to be
a simple matter to eliminate protruding dashboards knobs that sometimes
penetrated the skulls of infants or the kneecaps of adults.

The general news media paid little attention to these hearings. *Washington Post* reporter Morton Mintz argued in a speech that the failure to
report on them could have been responsible for the deaths of "tens of
thousands of people." Mintz contended that the significance of just one
safety device, the energy-absorbing steering assembly, provides evidence of
the literal truth of this projection:

> They were first patented in the 1920s. Yet they were not offered until the
> 1960s—initially on certain 1967 models, and then of all new cars manu-
> factured after December 31, 1967. Suppose that, at that point in time,
> all, rather than a negligible proportion, of motor vehicles had been equipped
> with the assemblies. The result, National Highway Traffic and Safety Ad-
> ministration has said, would have been that "instead of 53,000 annual
> traffic deaths, there could be 40,000, a saving of 13,000 lives a year."[21]

In the crush of other news, Representative Roberts's auto-safety hearings
did not attract much notice. If editors had considered the potential benefits
that could result from covering those hearings, however, they might have
received more attention, a possibility that suggests a revision of the criteria
most editors use for determining what constitutes news.

In cases involving national security, journalists often directly confront

a conflict between their apparent duty to provide a public benefit by withholding information and the traditional and fundamental journalistic duty
to benefit the public by providing information. A difficult judgment may
be required to determine whether withholding the information would constitute a public benefit and, if so, whether the benefit produced in that way
would outweigh any public need for or right to the information. National
security reporters often operate in such difficult circumstances. They either
are given or ferret out information that is hard to verify and where the full
context is either unknown or inadequately known. If information is vol-
unteered, they do not always know the motive for the leak, which may be
to manipulate journalists for the source's purposes irrespective of the implications for national security. It may also be impossible to tell if the
information endangers intelligence agents who may be either Americans or
foreign nationals and whether it compromises effective means of gathering
important intelligence electronically.

We recognize the constraints under which journalists operate in these
situations. Nevertheless, before publishing or broadcasting they must (and
often do) ask whether the public would benefit more from having the information released or withheld. Columnist Jack Anderson made such a
judgment when he decided to write about an electronic intelligence-gathering
operation code-named Gamma Guppy that allowed the National Security
Agency to eavesdrop on telephone conversations between Soviet leaders
and pass on the information to the CIA. To demonstrate that he had some
concern for not compromising national security, Anderson wrote: "For
obvious security reasons, we can't give a clue as to how it's done." He
then went on to say: "But we can state categorically that, for years, the
CIA has been able to listen to the kingpins of the Kremlin banter, bicker
and backbite among themselves."[22]

Anderson's report almost certainly compromised the agency's ability to
receive and evaluate these private, high-level conversations, in which one
of the parties was speaking from his official car. Anderson's column itself
arguably provides evidence that important information was gleaned from
these conversations. For example, information on the health and drinking
habits of Leonid Brezhnev, the party chief, and Premier Aleksei Kosygin
was disclosed.[23] Anderson said that he decided to publish the story—without reference to the limousines—because his source, whom he said he had
developed himself and whom he said he trusted, told him the Russians
already knew about it. He said he thought he had checked with a second
source, but that he no longer remembered who that second source was.[24]

According to Laurence Stern, writing more than two years later, "A
former intelligence official who monitored the Gamma Guppy interception
traffic said that the conversations revealed few major strategic secrets but
'gave us extremely valuable information on the personalities and health of

top Soviet leaders.' "[25] Stern also noted that "a former intelligence official who had access to the Gamma Guppy traffic characterized the original 1971 leak [to Anderson] as 'completely gratuitous—it served no purpose and blew our best intelligence source in the Soviet Union.' "[26]

We do not know whether this official's characterization was entirely accurate. But we are convinced that both the publication and the leak were gratuitous and that they contributed to blowing, if not the best, then at least a good source of intelligence. Even if the Soviet officials knew their calls were being monitored, there was, for example, the possibility that the U.S. government knew they knew, that the Soviet officials were using the calls to pass disinformation, and that the U.S. government wanted the Soviet officials to think the disinformation was being factored into U.S. policy decisions. The only benefit to the public in publishing the information was exposure to a bit of intrigue of the kind that is as easily found in spy fiction. This is a case in which the benefit of not publishing very likely outweighed the benefit of publishing (and that judgment could have been made before publication).

A similar case, which might have been partly responsible for the deaths of American servicemen, was recounted by Katharine Graham, chairman of the board of the Washington Post Company, in a lecture delivered in London in December 1985 and later published in the *Post:*

> In April 1983, some 60 people were killed in a bomb attack on the U.S. embassy in Beirut. At the time, there was coded radio traffic between Syria, where the operation was being run, and Iran, which was supporting it. . . . One television network and a newspaper columnist reported that the U.S. government had intercepted the traffic. Shortly thereafter the traffic ceased. This undermined efforts to capture the terrorist leaders and eliminated a source of information about future attacks. Five months later, apparently the same terrorists struck again at the Marine barracks in Beirut; 241 servicemen were killed.[27]

Although it is not possible to ascertain whether broadcasting and publishing the fact that the United States was intercepting messages between two terrorism centers was responsible for the deaths of the marines, there is good evidence that a source of intelligence that had the potential for frustrating terrorist activities was eliminated. Here the benefit of not publishing outweighed the benefit of publishing.[28]

## Withholding the Full Benefit

Sometimes the press covers an event or issue but fails to provide the full benefit that ought to have been provided, as coverage of the dangers of smoking can again illustrate. *The New Republic* once commissioned David

Owen to write an article on cancer and the cigarette lobby. He wrote a blunt piece that *The New Republic*'s editors killed. According to *USA Today*, "In the candid (and no doubt regretted) words of Leon Wieseltier, the editor who assigned it, the threat of 'massive losses of advertising revenue' did it in."[29]

Apparently the editors of *The New Republic* had been willing to report on the dangers of smoking and on the pressures brought by lobbyists but were not willing to support the forcefulness with which Owen stated his case. Owen later published his piece in *The Washington Monthly*, where he wrote, "The transcendent achievement of the cigarette lobby had been to establish the cancer issue as a 'controversy' or a 'debate' rather than as the clear-cut scientific case that it is."[30] He went on to portray an industry that, among other things, tries to enhance its appeal by portraying the young smoker as healthy and sexy. According to extensive research conducted by Kenneth E. Warner, this example of the death of Owen's article is but one of many documentable failures by the American press to cover the story of the dangers of smoking for fear of loss of advertising revenue.[31]

Predictably, the American Newspaper Publishers Association and the Magazine Publishers Association ducked under the cover of First Amendment protections of the right to advertise and to present the facts as newspapers see fit. This response prompted *Washington Post* ombudsman Sam Zagoria to chide newspapers for failure to see the issues as moral rather than legal:

> In this era of voluntarism, when the business community is constantly urging Congress and regulatory agencies to stand aside and "let us take care of this problem ourselves," couldn't the newspapers of the country agree—voluntarily and collectively—to refuse cigarette advertising? Couldn't they do what is right rather than only what is not prohibited by law?
>
> Most papers take great pride in the service they render to their communities, not only in providing information but also in philanthropic activities that provide scholarships and underwrite athletic tournaments. Is not helping some youngster avert the tortures of life-shortening lung cancer even a greater gift? A greater service? . . . Is there any media group for social responsibility?[32]

The question stands whether the issue is the negative one of not publishing advertising or the positive one of the obligation to report on the specific health dangers of smoking. On either count, very few papers (6 out of 1,700 daily American newspapers, using Zagoria's statistics for advertising, which were taken from the *New York State Journal of Medicine*) seem at present to be attempting wholeheartedly to provide the range of benefits that they might.

Consumer needs as well as health-care needs deserve attention from the press. Here the particular benefit may be in the form of advice about how to avoid a harm. During National Consumer Week in 1985, Zagoria wrote a column in which he took the position that the press has a watch-dog role to play not only in government but in consumer safety as well.[33] Few journalists would disagree with Zagoria's judgment that this role is a legitimate one for the media. But is it as we have proposed in this chapter, a morally obligatory role?

In discussing specific risks related to the use of certain consumer goods, Zagoria argued that the media often rely on unreliable sources and noted: "Some hazards are so hidden that even the companies that make the prod-ucts are unaware of the dangers. A rubber pacifier on a store shelf seems harmless, but while an infant is sucking on it, cancer-causing nitrosamines could enter the tiny body." On the face of it, merely listing or mentioning a cancer-causing agent in baby pacifiers, as Zagoria did, would appear to be a beneficial if possibly insufficient warning for parents of infants.

A few months later, however, one of Zagoria's colleagues, Robert J. Samuelson, who writes a weekly column for the *Post*'s financial section, took a starkly different view of reporting on a cancer-causing agent in pacifiers:

> Just about the best thing that ever happened to me is nine months old and 18 pounds. Her name is Ruth. Like any parent, I worry about my child. I don't need careless government agencies, incompetent reporters and insensitive scientists manufacturing artificial anxieties to go with my real or imagined ones. But that's what happened last week.
>
> The Consumer Product Safety Commission released a study by a panel of scientists concluding that a chemical used in some children's prod-ucts—including pacifiers—is potentially cancerous. The media reports of this study, mostly on television, raised the specter of parents (including me) and baby-product companies exposing children to a huge cancer risk. Being a reporter is a license to poke around. So I did. My conclusion is that the cancer risk is negligible at worst, and may not exist at all.
>
> What happened was a great media hype, but one that needlessly alarmed many parents. This was journalism by innuendo: Although the facts were correct, their presentation conveyed a picture that's untrue. But it wasn't only sloppy reporters who were at fault. The scientists who wrote the report did not explain their conclusions in understandable English, and the CPSC didn't clarify their scientific mumbo-jumbo.
>
> The issue here is broader than children's pacifiers. How do we inform ourselves about dangerous products or substances? As the cliche goes, there is no easy answer. Especially when cancer is involved, many mys-teries remain. But there are better and worse ways of coping with these uncertainties. And the great pacifier scare is an almost-textbook case of what not to do.[34]

Samuelson goes on, in admirable detail, to document what parents were not told in various press reports on the subject: that the maximum danger of cancer by the consensus estimate was .003 percent (around 50 extra liver cancers per 3.6 million births), that most manufacturers have already stopped using the hazardous chemicals cited, and that only rats have been tested so that any inference to humans is highly conjectural.

As Samuelson points out, the underlying journalistic problems are those not merely of innuendo but of fundamental competence, comprehensiveness, and accuracy. Although coverage of this kind is often complicated by its very nature and by the technical jargon used in many scientific journals, and even in press releases and interviews, journalists are both professionally and morally obliged to ask questions until they understand the material adequately. Samuelson's question, "How do we inform ourselves about dangerous products or substances?" is profoundly important. The easy answer is that the press informs us. But the easy answer, as is often the case, is superficial and only partly true. The press gives us some information about some dangerous products and substances. It is obvious that the press cannot give everyone all the information all the time that is necessary to make informed decisions on every health and safety issue of personal concern. But by now it should be equally obvious that benefiting the public by providing a substantial amount of information that helps people decide whether to buy a particular pacifier, to take calcium pills, or to eat fish from the Kanawha River is part of the press's fundamental responsibility.

Sound health-risk reporting and consumer reporting often require a commitment to understanding the methods of science, a willingness to master scientific and technical information and jargon, and an understanding of risk analysis. In a demonstration of this level of commitment, *The New York Times, The Washington Post,* and ABC News have found physicians—Lawrence Altman, Susan Okie, and Timothy Johnson—who are competent reporters and writers. Health-risk reporting has also been done especially well by reporters such as Jane Brody, Stuart Diamond, Erik Eckholm, and Philip Boffey of *The New York Times;* Cristine Russell and Victor Cohn of *The Washington Post;* Ruth SoRelle of *The Houston Chronicle;* George Strait of ABC News; Robert Bazell of NBC News; Susan Spencer of CBS News, and others.

What sets these reporters apart from many colleagues, aside from their general reporting and writing ability, is that they have taken the trouble to learn how science works and to acquire the requisite special knowledge. But even substantial commitment, knowledge, and writing skill are often not enough to satisfy readers and viewers who want a reasoned evaluation of whether a product is safe, a substance in the water is dangerous to humans, or they are at risk for a particular disease. Generally speaking, health-risk reporting cannot provide definitive evaluations because science has not provided them. The media can most effectively benefit the public by helping people understand the limits of risk analysis, by using precise language, by avoiding sensationalism (e.g., by not giving undue prominence to very low-probability events, or using worst cases in leads), by using clear analogies to more familiar situations, by avoiding studies that have not gone through peer review, and by seeking the relevant scientific consensus.

## The Cost of Providing Benefits: A Case Study in AIDS Reporting

With the criteria outlined above in mind, over the next few pages we will examine AIDS coverage by the national media. In the early reporting on AIDS, the disease was widely treated as an affliction of homosexuals. Soon afterward it was linked to intravenous drug abusers. However, not until it was recognized that AIDS represented a greater than negligible threat to the general public—the non-drug-abusing heterosexual community—did media coverage increase significantly. And it was not until the so-called Rock effect—a sharp increase in coverage set off by actor Rock Hudson's announcement that he had AIDS—that most of the media began making prominent in its coverage the kind of sexually explicit information that might help those both at high and at low risk to avoid contracting the disease.

When AIDS was perceived as an epidemic almost exclusively affecting homosexuals, it was not given coverage comparable to that received by other recent epidemic-like health scares perceived as affecting the heterosexual population, such as Legionnaire's disease and toxic shock syndrome, although by mid-1982 AIDS had already caused the deaths of more persons than those two diseases combined.[35] In a symposium on press coverage of health risks at the Columbia School of Journalism (April 22, 1986) both Strait and Bazell, science correspondents for ABC News and NBC News respectively, said that in the early days of the AIDS epidemic they had a hard time convincing anyone at their networks that AIDS was an extremely important public health story. Bazell, who has a degree in immunology, said he was told: "Look, it ain't us. We don't want to hear stories about drug addicts. We don't want to hear stories about homosexuals, and that's the way it is." It may be that this reporting reflected a bias in the press based on sexual preferences, or it may be that the number of persons ultimately believed to be at risk was treated as the dominant factor in determining the importance of the story. If the latter were the case, it helps explain why coverage exploded onto the front pages and into prominence in the network news when journalists concluded that, to some un-known degree, the entire population—gay and straight alike—was at risk of contracting AIDS.

Newspaper space and radio and television time must be allocated like any other scarce commodity, according to some set of standards intended to efficiently foster the goal of the enterprise. But what is the goal of the enterprise of journalism when reporting on a disease like AIDS? Is it to tell the general reader or viewer what has traditionally been considered most newsworthy—such things as how many new cases were reported in the previous week and that 73 percent of them were homosexual men? Or is it to help members of high-risk groups avoid harm by telling them how they might avoid contracting the disease? Obviously these choices are not the only ones available, nor are they mutually exclusive, but they do rep-resent the polar options. One approach is that there is no duty to provide a benefit to, for example, gay readers and viewers by helping them stay healthy, while another, less common approach has recognized the exis-tence of a duty to benefit the most directly threatened communities.

In 1981 and 1982, shortly after the disease was identified in the United States, most of the newspaper coverage of AIDS tracked by the public affairs office of the Department of Health and Human Services was pitched at the general reader. Its objective was not to provide information that would be helpful to those believed to be at risk of contracting the disease. As it became clear that AIDS was always fatal, that the number of cases was doubling annually, and that more than a quarter of its victims might not be homosexuals, the emphasis of the coverage began to shift. More and more stories described how AIDS spread and emphasized that it al-most certainly was not spread by "casual contact," which was referred to in various ways such as "hugging," "kissing," and "drinking from the same glass" (or it was left to the reader's imagination).[36]

From our review of AIDS stories in about a dozen newspapers across the country, it appears that the attitudes of editors about what constituted news about AIDS was constantly changing. Blood transfusions quickly be-came part of the story because AIDS was transmitted through the blood-stream. But AIDS was also transmitted through semen, which posed a problem for editors of general-circulation publications on grounds of taste. Editors ask themselves questions like, "Would our subscribers like to read that at the breakfast table?" If the answer is no, they look for ways to make the story more palatable. Many editors apparently concluded that stories would not be tasteful if they involved mention of semen and, more pointedly, homosexual anal intercourse. As a result, editors, who usually dislike euphemisms, began to use ambiguous phrases like "the exchange of bodily fluids" to describe how AIDS was transmitted. To avoid saying explicitly that the disease was easily transmitted through anal intercourse, they often used another technique editors generally avoided—a negative construction—and said that it was not transmitted by casual contact.[37]

When conflict occurred between providing a potentially life-saving benefit to the less well-informed members of a limited and to some extent an outcast community, and offending the taste of the larger community, many editors came down, at least initially, in favor of taste. But by the middle of 1983 headlines such as the following were beginning to appear in a wide range of publications: "The AIDS Hysteria," "AIDS Panic: Who's to Blame?" "AIDS Possibly Can Spread by Family Contact," "Mysterious, Lethal Disease Spreads in U.S.," "Study: AIDS Also Threatens Heterosexuals," "Mysterious Fever Now an Epidemic," and "A Mystery in the Blood."[38] In these stories AIDS was presented as a threat to non-drug-abusing heterosexuals who were neither Haitians nor hemophiliacs. But there were still almost no direct references to anal intercourse, although this sexual practice was by then recognized as perhaps the most likely way in which the disease was being passed from person to person in the gay community. Stories also rarely provided addresses and phone numbers of organizations where additional information about AIDS was available.

However, as it became increasingly evident that AIDS would spread into the general population if people were not made aware of the kinds of precautions that would prevent it, the media, both print and electronic, began devoting more space in stories about AIDS to ways to provide protection against it. By late 1985 (especially after Hudson announced that he had AIDS), more and more editors decided that taste should give way to explicit, potentially life-saving information involving blunt language. Even Ann Landers referred directly to "the receiving partner in anal sex" in her syndicated column, which is undoubtedly common fare at breakfast tables around the country. Her sister, Abigail Van Buren, was even more explicit. She wrote: "How is AIDS transmitted? The most significant route is by anal sex, oral sex and 'old fashioned' sexual intercourse with a person who has been infected by the AIDS virus."[39]

*The New York Times* provided an easy-to-understand question-and-answer explanation of how AIDS may and may not be contracted, a lengthy article on the ways in which women are at risk, and an article on an AIDS support organization.[40] Roughly from the time of the Hudson announcement onward, the overall trend was toward including in all lengthy news stories a capsule account of the ways in which the disease is most easily contracted.

The AIDS coverage we have traced provides some modest evidence that there comes a time when editors recognize that providing a direct benefit to the public is in effect part of the story. This benefit may be late in coming, but if the public wants and needs the information, editors tend to respond. Back in 1982 and 1983, however, several million gay Americans were eager if not desperate to have that same information, when much of it was available from physicians and researchers but rarely included in stories because it was not perceived to be part of the story. (One notable exception was the coverage by Randy Shilts, a reporter for *The San Francisco Chronicle*, who is gay himself and who works for the paper that probably has a higher proportion of gay readers than any other general-circulation daily in the country.)

We have, of course, argued that the institution of journalism in the American tradition has always been and remains based on a goal of providing public benefits that transcends quirky or frivolous notions about what constitutes news. If so, then once the benefit or writing about how AIDS is contracted was evident to editors—which it should have been as soon as it was known that the disease was lethal and spreading rapidly—they had an obligation to inform their readers about how it spreads. The potential cost of devoting substantial space to AIDS coverage when it was perceived by many readers as a disease of homosexuals and drug addicts was that such coverage would not appeal to large numbers of readers. Moreover, if the sexual dimensions of the disease were treated explicitly, many readers might be offended. In this case, however, the duty to provide a public benefit to those at risk clearly outweighed the cost of doing so.


## Conclusion

In this chapter we have argued that the duty to provide public benefits is foundational in the traditions of American journalism and political life but is rarely explicitly acknowledged by the media, which tend to be preoccupied with their rights more than with their responsibilities. Unless the media provide accurate, objective, and substantially complete reports on matters such as personal health, environmental hazards, demographic trends, taxes, interest rates, and political developments, autonomous choice for many people becomes unlikely, because choice in the absence of adequate understanding is not autonomous. Of the many values we discuss in this volume, none is more important than this public-service responsibility.

This value is, of course, not absolute or overriding on all occasions. It must compete with other values such as the allocation of a news organization's resources and the obligation to avoid placing reporters at undue risk. Nevertheless, in pondering this value, journalists might consider the following advice from one of their own:

[The media] need to develop new attitudes and innovative techniques to serve the special informational demands of a violently unstable world. The profession's smug defense of its present reactive, adversarial, and action-oriented system should not blind journalists to its grave deficiencies.

Among other things, I would specifically recommend a new kind of journalism—"preventive journalism" as opposed to the popular investigative journalism—that would approach the world in a very different way from what the press does now. Instead of only describing the ruins that follow disaster, preventive journalism would search in advance for the hidden forces of change; it would try to identify the underlying causes of crises before, rather than after, they explode so that an altered society might have time to protect itself from the ambushes of history. It is not enough for the media to provide videotapes of war; they should also patrol ahead to uncover the hissing fuses.

This would require a different mindset and new techniques. It would mean looking deeply into social trends, on a sustained, long-term basis, so that the public can see and hear the grinding gears that precede the crises which the media eventually cover so fully. To their credit, *The New York Times* and *The Los Angeles Times* are doing some of this kind of reporting. But television and most newspapers are still dominated by an action-reaction mentality. And that is a worry.[41]

## NOTES

1. Thomas Jefferson, Letter to M. Coray (1823), in *The Papers of Thomas Jefferson* (Princeton: Princeton University Press), ed. Charles T. Cullen, forthcoming.

2. "To the Inhabitants of the Providence of Quebec," October 24, 1774, in Worthington Chavney Ford et al., eds., *Journals of the Continental Congress, 1774–1789* (Washington, 1904–37), 1:108, as quoted in Leonard W. Levy, *Emergence of a Free Press* (New York: Oxford University Press, 1985), p. 174.

3. Ibid., p. 199.

4. Ibid., p. 200.

5. Alan Barth, *The Rights of Free Men* (New York: Knopf, 1984), p. 293. Emphasis added.

6. Samuel Johnson, *The Idler*, November 11, 1758.

7. "ASNE Statement of Principles," as reprinted in John L. Hulteng, *Playing It Straight* (Chester, Conn.: American Society of Newspaper Editors), p. 85.

8. James Polk, "Wake Up Angry," *Nieman Reports* (January 1950): 7–8.

9. Murrey Marder, Speech to Newspaper Guild, December 16, 1985.

10. Ibid.

11. Joseph Lovett, telephone interview, November 25, 1985.

12. Lou Cannon, "A Convenient Double Standard," *The Washington Post*, July 8, 1985, p. A2.

13. *United States v. Karl Brandt*, in *Trials of War Criminals Before the Nuremberg Military Tribunals Under Control Council Law No. 10*, "The Medical Case" (Washington, Government Printing Office, 1948–49).

14. A comprehensive account of the events is found in George M. Houser, "Polaroid's Dramatic Withdrawal from South Africa," *The Christian Century*, April 12, 1978, pp. 392–93. See also David Vogel, *Lobbying the Corporation: Citizen Challenges to Business Authority* (New York: Basic Books, 1978), p. 173.

15. Spencer Reiss et al., "A 'French Watergate,' " *Newsweek*, September 30, 1985, pp. 36–37; Michael Dobbs, "Paris Stands Pat on Greenpeace," *The Washington Post*, September 29, 1985, p. A21; and Michael Dobbs, "French Minister Resigns in Greenpeace Scandal," *The Washington Post*, September 21, 1985, p. A1.

16. Frank Prial, "Greenpeace and the Paris Press: A Trickle of Words Turns into a Torrent," *The New York Times*, September 26, 1985, p. A12.

17. Gerald Shaw, "Newspapering and Courage," *The Washington Post*, November 10, 1985, p. D5.

18. Stanley Penn, "Mob Rule: How Mafia Controls Air-Cargo Business at Kennedy Airport," *The Wall Street Journal*, May 22, 1985, pp. 1, 23.

19. Peter J. Boyer, "South Africa and TV: The Coverage Changes," *The New York Times*, December 29, 1985, pp. 1, 14.

20. Ibid.

21. Morton Mintz, "Professionalism in the Newsroom" Second Annual Consumers Union Lecture, delivered at the Graduate School of Journalism, Columbia University, May 18, 1972, p. 8.

22. Jack Anderson, "CIA Eavesdrops on Kremlin Chiefs," *The Washington Post*, September 14, 1971, p. F7.

23. Ibid.

24. Jack Anderson, telephone interview, November 25, 1985.

25. Laurence Stern, "U.S. Tapped Top Russians' Car Phones," *The Washington Post*, December 5, 1973, p. A1.

26. Ibid., p. A16.

27. Katharine Graham "Safeguarding Our Freedoms as We Cover Terrorist Acts," *The Washington Post*, April 20, 1986, p. C2.

28. The network referred to by Graham appears to have been CBS, which on May 16, 1983, broadcast on "The Evening News with Dan Rather" a report by its Pentagon correspondent, David Martin, that U.S. intelligence had intercepted "a series of cables . . . from the Iranian Foreign Ministry in Tehran to the Iranian embassy in Damascus." The column apparently was by Jack Anderson. It appeared in *The Washington Post* on May 10, 1983, under the headline: "U.S. Was Warned of Bombing of Beirut Embassy." The key sentence in the column was: "The National Security Agency's code breakers had intercepted some alarming communications in the Middle East."

29. Charles Trueheart, "The Tobacco Industry's Advertising Smoke Screen," *USA Today*, March 15, 1985, p. 3D.

30. Ibid.

31. Kenneth E. Warner, "Cigarette Advertising and Media Coverage of Smoking and Health," *New England Journal of Medicine* 312 (February 7, 1985): pp. 384–88. Warner does not cite the particular case of Owen's article. Rather, Warner focuses on national weeklies such as *Time* and *Newsweek*.

32. Sam Zagoria, "Smoking and the Media's Responsibility," *The Washington Post*, December 18, 1985, p. A26. For a measured and balanced approach to the problem, see Elizabeth Whelan, "Second Thoughts on a Cigarette-Ad Ban," *The Wall Street Journal*, December 18, 1985, p. 28.

33. Sam Zagoria, "Consumer Watchdogs," *The Washington Post,* April 24, 1985, p. A24.

34. Robert J. Samuelson, "Pacifying Media Hype," *The Washington Post,* October 9, 1985, pp. F1, F12.

35. "Gay Disease Outbreak Gets Meager Attention, Critics Say," *Medical World News,* May 10, 1982, pp. 13–15.

36. The progress can be tracked in stories such as "AIDS: Prisons 'Deadly Plague'?" *USA Today,* June 6, 1983, p. 3A, in which the reporter, Richard Benedetto, used the following quotation in the fourth paragraph of his story to describe what was known about transmission of AIDS: "Our officers are frightened to death that they are going to catch this disease because there's no medical consensus on how it's transmitted." On June 1, 1983, *USA Today* carried a box headlined "Disease with no Cure," which carried these lines: "Common forms of transmission: Sexual contact; contaminated hypodermic needles." By mid-1985, however, many newspapers were carrying much more detailed accounts of how the disease is and is not transmitted. See, for example, Carl Rowan, "What scientists know and don't know how AIDS," *The Atlanta Constitution,* August 26, 1985, p. 11-A.

37. In telephone interviews on January 2, 1986, editors such as Richard Smyser of *The Oak Ridger* in Oak Ridge, Tennessee, and Harry M. Rosenfeld of *The Albany Times* and *The Knickerbocker News* in Albany, New York, concurred that considerations of "taste" at first kept their papers from providing explicit information about how AIDS was most likely to be transmitted, but that as the potential impact of the disease became clearer they responded to the need for more thorough and detailed accounts.

38. The headlines appeared in the following publications on the following dates (respectively): *Newsweek,* May 30, 1983: *Medical World News,* August 8, 1983; *The Atlanta Constitution,* May 6, 1983; *The Washington Post,* February 7, 1983; *The Atlanta Journal,* May 19, 1983; *The Los Angeles Times,* May 31, 1982; and *The Philadelphia Inquirer,* Reprint of AIDS Series, 1983.

39. Ann Landers, "Methods of Protection Against AIDS," *The Oakland Tribune,* October 29, 1985, p. C6; Abigail Van Buren, "Getting the Facts Straight on AIDS," *The Chicago Tribune,* August 12, 1985, sect. 5, p. 3.

40. Erik Eckholm, "Fear of AIDS Termed Largely Without Cause," *The New York Times,* September 13, 1985, p. B3; Erik Eckholm, "Women and AIDS: Assessing the Risks," *The New York Times,* October 28, 1985, p. A16; Glenn Collins, "AIDS Hotline Is Busy in City," *The New York Times,* October 7, 1985, p. B12.

41. Michael J. O'Neill, "Media Power and the Dangers of Mass Information," *Nieman Reports* (Summer 1985): 35.

# Chapter 6

# Maintaining Trust

The media need not ever be loved or even fully understood to
carry out their function in society. But they must be trusted if
they are to be credible in their watchdog role over the government, which has the power—with public backing—to restrict press
freedom.

Advisory Committee
on Public Opinion of the Society
of Professional Journalists[1]

Norman Pearlstine, managing editor of *The Wall Street Journal*, told his
colleagues at an annual meeting of the American Society of Newspaper
Editors (ASNE) that when he discovered that one of his reporters had
given outsiders prepublication access to sensitive investment information,
it was "every editor's nightmare come true." Pearlstine explained that the
resultant SEC investigation and prison sentence for the reporter, R. Foster
Winans, had occurred because "one reporter betrayed our trust." Bill Green,
the *Washington Post* ombudsman who investigated the fraud in which a
*Post* reporter invented an eight-year-old heroin addict, told the same group
of editors that both cases demonstrated how a news organization's need
to trust reporters made it vulnerable. Pearlstine, who was criticized by
some editors for the way in which the *Journal* investigated and reported
on the Winans case, added that the final judge of the *Journal*'s trustworthiness would be the paper's readers.[2]

Both of these cases are discussed later in this chapter, in the twin contexts of trust between reporters and their news organizations and trust
between news organizations and the public. They illustrate one of the most
pervasive and pressing moral concerns in journalism. Without the public's
trust, the press's social function of providing useful information cannot be

fulfilled. And without trust within the profession—between editors and reporters and between reporters and sources—that function is also endangered.

The foundation for trust in journalism is truthfulness, but trustworthiness does not rest solely on truthfulness. There is, for example, substantial public concern about "reporters' lack of concern whether their stories hurt people."[3] Skepticism of this kind erodes trust, too. Even a reporter or editor who is scrupulously truthful and concerned abut causing harm may be careless, have poor judgment, or be unable to keep confidences. These character flaws all discourage trust.

## Trust and Trustworthiness as Concepts and Values

Given the importance of trust for social cooperation generally, literature on its nature is surprisingly thin.[4] We use the term here to refer to an attitude of confidence, reliance, and approval placed in persons, institutions, statements, or even objects such as computers or automobiles. Usually trust is based on the expectation that persons, institutions, and so on will act as anticipated.

Because trust is an attitude, it can exist with little actual evidence of real trustworthiness to support it. Trustworthiness, however, is a virtue, and persons can be trustworthy even if no one places trust in them. Trustworthiness is the quality or character trait of reliability. A trustworthy person or institution must deserve the confidence that underlies trust, not merely have another's trust. Trustworthiness is also closely associated with fidelity and loyalty. A trustworthy person may be given a responsibility without having to investigate his or her credentials and without undue concern about the consequences (beyond inherent risks).

Certain forms of skepticism about how persons and institutions will act are logically incompatible with trust, but it is not illogical to trust persons in some respects while remaining skeptical about them in others. Competent journalism calls for a judicious blend of skepticism and trust. Sophisticated consumers of news also understand that, because of the constraints of journalism, uncritical trust in news reports is unjustified.

Frank Sutherland, managing editor of *The Hattiesburg* (Mississippi) *American* recounted a case that helps to make concrete the value placed on trust in journalism while at the same time illustrating some difficulties in handling the related dilemmas.[5] Sutherland's particular problem turned on whether a newspaper and television station in Hattiesburg should cooperate with a police operation. The police maintained that press cooper-

ation was essential to protect an innocent life. But the requested cooperation entailed lying in print and on the air, a fundamental breach of trust
between the press and the public.

The sequence of events was the following. A reporter for *The Hattiesburg American* received a telephone call from a man who identified himself
as a private investigator named Pete. He told the reporter that "there's
going to be a hit [killing] in Hattiesburg." Sutherland contacted the police,
who asked that the reporter maintain contact with Pete, which she did.
Pete then asked the reporter if she could get the police to supply someone
to pose as a hit man. The police agreed. They supplied a bogus hit man
who contracted to kill the target in Hattiesburg. A meeting was then called,
which was attended by the U.S. attorney, the district attorney, Sutherland,
his reporter, and the station manager of the local television station, WDAM-
TV. The U.S. attorney explained that the man who was behind the planned
killing was prepared to pay $35,000 for the hit "24 hours after he read it
in the news."

The U.S. attorney then asked Sutherland and the WDAM station manager to "help us out if you can." He said, "I know what we are asking is
tough, but we need your help." The U.S. attorney proposed that the killing
be staged and that the newspaper and television station give it full coverage as if it had happened so that the man behind the killing could be
tricked into making the payment and thereby be caught. The U.S. attorney
also said the bogus hit man had been told that if the killing had not taken
place by the weekend, another hit man would be hired to do the job. In
other words, unless the hoax worked a man might be murdered.

Sutherland asked if the attorney realized that he was "asking us to
knowingly present a falsehood. You are, in effect, asking us to tell a lie."
The U.S. attorney said he understood: "In law enforcement we call it deception. We have to use it all the time. It's part of our work, the way we
work. We wouldn't ask you to do it except that there are lives at stake."
Cliff Brown, the WDAM station manager, knew that Sutherland was president of the Society of Professional Journalists. Brown asked Sutherland
what kind of policy the organization had to cover cases of this kind. Sutherland told Brown that the SPJ code of ethics "says we should tell the
truth."

Sutherland then went outside with his reporter, Janet Braswell, and
they had the following conversation, as recorded by Sutherland:

> *Sutherland:* "What do you think we should do?"
> *Braswell:* "I think we should cooperate and do what the police want."
> *Sutherland:* "But what about lying to our readers? I have an awfully
> hard time telling a lie, even if we do come back later and say it was for a
> good cause."

> *Braswell:* "I think the majority of the people in [the] Hattiesburg area would understand and approve of us cooperating with the police." (A subsequent poll indicated that Braswell was right.)
>
> *Sutherland:* "That may be true for the short term, but that still leaves us with a credibility problem. Once you tell a lie, no matter for how good a reason, your readers will always remember it. They will never know for sure about us again, whether we will ever tell a lie again under another circumstance. We will have lost our effectiveness with the readers."
>
> *Braswell:* "I understand what you mean. It's a bad choice, because lives are at stake."
>
> *Sutherland:* "There are no good choices in this one. It's cold. Let's go back inside."

Sutherland discussed the matter further with the law-enforcement officers and then with his publisher. He was leaning against cooperation. His implicit evaluation was that the certain loss of a substantial measure of public trust if his newspaper lied outweighed the possibility that someone might get killed as a result of his not taking part in the deception. In the end, Sutherland's publisher compromised minimally—in a way that did not satisfy the law-enforcement officers, but also in a way that did not involve a blatant lie. The Hattiesburg paper published this sentence: "Police are seeking information concerning suspected foul play directed toward Oscar Black III" (the intended victim of the murder plot). The television station, by contrast, cooperated fully. Nevertheless, the man who had tried to finance the killing said he did not believe it had taken place and therefore did not make the payment. Several months later he tried to hire another hit man and was caught by the police without involving the media.

The outcome of this case tells us nothing about who was right—Sutherland or the television station manager. It could have gone the other way, ending in the death of an innocent man. But these events indicate that keeping the public's trust is such an important consideration in journalism that responsible editors can validly put trust in the balance with a possible risk to human life and come out on the side of doing what is required in order to retain the public's trust.

"Tailgate"—a story recounted in Chapter 4 (pp. 114-17)—illustrates other aspects of trustworthiness. In this television news investigation a reporter apparently trusted sources whose judgment and reliability were tainted by their youth, inexperience, and possible motives of revenge. Yet the story was aired as authoritative. Because of the way in which the story was presented and the way in which television audiences apprehend such information, many viewers concluded that the sources, two sixteen-year-old congressional pages, had been certified by CBS as trustworthy and therefore that the charges against unnamed members of Congress were based on reliable evidence that could be trusted. As it turned out, the pages were thoroughly untrustworthy, and the reporter had thoroughly inadequate grounds for the trust he apparently placed in them. When a story of this kind turns out to be untrue, as "Tailgate" did, it contributes to a slow but continuing erosion of public trust in the media generally.

As background to an analysis of the value of trust in journalism, we will examine briefly the nature and scope of the public's distrust of journalists.

## Distrust and Skepticism

Many Americans view the press with ambivalence. Their attitudes express a mixture of trust and distrust, as well as respect and disrespect. Different people cite different reasons for their distrust. Some think that journalists are too frequently biased, inaccurate, sensationalistic, negligent, callous, careerist, arrogant, incompetent, or contemptuous of the public. Others believe that the press frequently abuses its privileges and that other rights and values such as national security, reputation, privacy, and fair trial suffer disproportionately as a result.

There is undoubtedly skepticism and even cynicism about many aspects of news reporting, but neither we nor the polls find it symptomatic of a broad, corrosive distrust. The problem, rather, is that a steady erosion of public trust in journalism could result from a widening public perception that the media are untrustworthy. This outcome would have two negative consequences: The public would pay less attention to the press and would therefore be less well informed, and press freedoms would come under heavier attack. Although these problems are serious, public distrust of the press should be kept in perspective. Several recent polls indicate that the public is distrustful of the press's performance or attitude for all of the reasons mentioned above. But because there appears to be an underlying general trust in the media to present the news in a reasonably fair and unbiased fashion, there seems to be little threat of an overall breakdown of public trust. The polls we cite below show that by comparison to many national institutions and traditionally respected professions, the press is regarded as relatively trustworthy.

Several surveys and related reports on press credibility have been commissioned by journalism institutions. A study commissioned by ASNE concluded that "Three-fourths of all adults have some problem with the credibility of the media . . . [and] one-fifth of all adults deeply distrust their news media."[6] The study indicates that "Many people feels that the press . . . is a . . . self-serving, powerful and frightening institution."[7] The survey also concluded that significant percentages of Americans believe the press regularly invades the privacy of subjects, shows disrespect for standard news sources, is insensitive to harms caused by reporting, overdramatizes the news, tends to cover what supports the reporter's point of view, is not careful to separate fact from opinion, and often provides conflicting reports of the same story. In addition, this survey suggests that how consumers of journalism rate the credibility of both television and print journalism depends to some degree on their socioeconomic status. For example, "The credibility of television shows some tendency to decline as [the] education [of viewers] increases." [8]

An earlier study (1984) commissioned by ASNE showed that 57 percent of newspaper readers "do not believe that newspapers in general are usually fair." [9] The same study also said, "If there is any gap between editors and readers, it is based on questions about the fairness and accuracy of newspapers and on the feeling among 42 percent of readers that even their own newspaper attempts to manipulate them." An extensive poll by the Gallup Organization (commissioned by the Times Mirror Co.) that was released in early 1986 partially corroborated these findings. This poll gave the press high marks for "believability" (about 90 percent of those polled), fairly low marks for resistance to manipulation (53 percent said the press is too easily manipulated), and mixed signals about bias (45 percent said the press was biased in reporting, but those polled were split on the nature of the bias). [10] Although these polls indicate that substantial numbers of Americans distrust the media, it is difficult to assess how deeply the feelings run or how reliable the polls are.

Seymour Martin Lipset points out that distrust found in polls and elsewhere is not a new crisis. [11] In the 1960s and early 1970s the press was ranked ninth in public confidence among ten institutions surveyed. The press has long labored under a watchful and skeptical public eye, and yet it also maintains a wide, faithful, and often trusting audience. Although it would be wrong to conclude that trust in the press is about to collapse under the weight of recent criticism, many editors and publishers have become increasingly sensitive to the need to strengthen public trust in the media. For example, the Gannett Center for Media Studies at Columbia University has held a workshop on trust and the media, and Richard Clurman, former chief of correspondents at *Time,* is preparing a book on the subject. Publishers and institutions such as the Associated Press are financially supporting credibility studies, and the issue of trust has been high on the agenda of recent national meetings of editors, publishers, and reporters, including ASNE, the Associated Press Managing Editors Association (APME), and Sigma Delta Chi, the Society of Professional Journalists.

This sample is too thin to permit a judgment about how publications and broadcasting outlets will be affected by this newfound concern. But one thing is clear: There is no consensus in the journalism community about the scope of the trust problem and some question about whether there is a problem at all. Howard Simons, curator of the Nieman Foundation at Harvard and former managing editor of *The Washington Post*, says he goes into a "defensive crouch" every time the issue is raised, because he thinks the problem is both exaggerated and inevitable. Others disagree. Editors such as David Lawrence of *The Detroit Free Press* and John Seigenthaler of *USA Today* place lack of fairness and bias as among the most serious problems causing distrust of the press. Few of these journalists disagree about what constitutes untrustworthy journalism, but there is a deep concern among some in the profession that acknowledging even minimal irresponsibility or untrustworthiness will stimulate demands for repression and censorship.[12]

The media are also divided against themselves. Print journalists often blame television news for the increasing gap in credibility or public trust. Creed Black, a former president of ASNE, elaborated on why television news practices are responsible for eroding public trust in journalism generally:

> What the networks call news is in fact a mixture of news, analysis, opinion and speculation. The public lumps the printed press and television together in something called "the media" and makes little if any distinction between the two. The result is that we are blamed for the sins and shortcomings of what television, which remains basically an entertainment medium, calls news.[13]

However, Jody Powell—President Jimmy Carter's press secretary and later a syndicated columnist—was quoted at the same time as saying that the print media are as guilty as television of sensationalizing the news for commercial gain and should be held no less responsible for the press's loss of credibility.[14]

It seems to us wasted effort to pawn off problems of trust on one segment of the media or another. The biggest single problem is found everywhere. It is the truthfulness issue we have focused on from the outset. Public trust cannot flourish unless accuracy, comprehensiveness, and objectivity flourish in journalism.

## The Public Trust

Thomas Jefferson once observed, "When a man assumes a public trust, he should consider himself as public property."[15] The American press has implicitly assumed a public trust and can therefore legitimately be considered public property in the following respect: It is obligated to serve the public and is accountable to the public. This obligation and the nature of press accountability are the subjects of Chapters 5 and 8. But we can explore here what this Jeffersonian conception entails for public trust.

The right to seek information on behalf of the public has been entrusted to the press, and the press in turn is expected to present the information to the public fairly, truthfully, and competently. Robert Maynard, editor of *The Oakland Tribune,* has described what a legitimate public expectation of trustworthiness might entail: "When newspapers are perceived by the public to have an agenda different from the public's agenda, then they lose credibility and relevance in the public's eye. . . . Our motto at the *Tribune* is: We respect all and neglect none. We try to live that."[16] Maynard points out correctly that when the public comes to believe that a newspaper has an agenda that fails to respect the legitimate interests of, say, business or labor, or neglects some political figures to the advantage of others, the public, little by little, sector by sector, will lose faith in the paper, as it has every right to do. In Jefferson's terms, the paper will come to be perceived more as private property than public property. While newspapers are private property, there is a crucial difference between their serving the private interests of the owners (a private agenda) and serving the public interest (the public's agenda for a newspaper).

The press can betray the public's trust in many ways. Consider the case of R. Foster Winans of *The Wall Street Journal,* who was convicted of securities fraud for exploiting his position of public trust as a reporter for personal financial gain (not very effectively) and to help his friends and associates gain financially (very effectively). Winans was one of the reporters who wrote the column "Heard on the Street," which frequently influenced stock prices. A Winans-recommended stock jumped, on average, 6.5 percent on the day it was touted in his column.[17] But Winans was not content with his journalistic success, and he shared unpublished information collected for the column with three friends who used it for investment purposes. Winans and his friends enjoyed a trading advantage over members of the general public, who did not have access to the same information until a day or more later.

The management of the *Journal* judged Winans's advantages to be morally unacceptable. Stewart Pinkerton, an assistant managing editor of the newspaper, testified that he warned Winans when he was hired in 1982—and repeatedly thereafter—not to trade in stocks about which he wrote and not to discuss what he planned to write with anyone. Because Winans had betrayed this trust, he was fired and later sentenced to eighteen months in prison, although his lawyer—and a dissenting judge, on appeal—maintained that the prosecution sought to make a crime out of an offense against the paper's ethical standards.[18] (Winans said he knew of the *Journal*'s "practice," but denied that the *Journal*'s policy had been explained to him by Pinkerton or anyone else.[19])

Clearly there is a valid distinction between the legal issues and the moral issues in this case. The legal issue is whether Winans engaged in unlawful insider trading, an unsettled area of law. The moral question—at least the one ripe for our discussion here—is whether there is anything wrong with a journalist covering the value of stocks taking advantage of inside information to profit by trading securities before the general public obtains the information. Winans said he did not think his trading would "hurt the *Journal* in any way."[20] But the *Journal* has a policy precluding such conduct in order to avoid conflict of interest—particularly in the tempting case of the "Heard on the Street" column—because of the opportunity to precipitate sharp movements in the price of a stock.

There is ample moral ambiguity surrounding insider trading in general, as *Business Week* pointed out in a cover story:

> Executives do it. Bankers do it. Accountants, secretaries, and messengers do it. And so do printers, cabdrivers, waiters, housewives, hairdressers—and mistresses. Some do it on their own. Others work in rings with connections as far away as Switzerland and Hong Kong. But they all work the shadowy side of Wall Street by trading on inside information to make money in the stock market. Insider trading is running rampant, despite a major law enforcement crackdown and toughened penalties.[21]

*Business Week* maintained in an editorial in the same issue that "Insider trading violates a felt ethical sense," but was unable to offer convincing reasons for its conclusion that it is ethically improper.

Most persons in a position to engage in insider trading are not, in the same respect as journalists, in a position of public trust. But how does the simple fact that inside information has been passed to a journalist, with the understanding that it might be published, change the circumstance to one of public trust? Winans gathered the information as a surrogate for the public and was presumed to hold it in trust for the public until it was published. The central and perhaps sole matter of moral significance is that Winans compromised his trust with the *Journal* and with the public by taking unfair advantage of his position as a journalist. Over the long term, such conduct would, if recurrent and known, seriously impair the public's confidence in the fairness of journalists and in their papers, magazines, or networks.

Winans also broke trust with the sources who gave him the information to publish and who had trusted him not to trade on or share the information for investment purposes. One of his sources for prior stories testified during the trial that he would never have talked with Winans had he known the reporter might use the information for personal reasons—a position that doubtlessly would be widely shared by potential sources.[22]

## The Relationship of Reciprocity Between Journalists and Sources

Of all the relationships in journalism there is perhaps none in which trust plays a more central role than the reporter–source relationship. If reporters cannot trust sources to be candid—not only to tell the truth, albeit from the source's perspective, and not to deceive them (except on rare occasions)—the sources are virtually unusable. Similarly, if sources cannot trust reporters to accurately convey their information to the public and to keep confidences, the sources will cease to be sources.

Confidentiality is at the heart of trust in regular reporter–source relationships. But relationships of confidentiality between reporters and sources are different from those found in other professional settings such as between lawyers and clients, physicians and patients, and clergy and parishioners. In these relationships, the right of confidentiality exists to protect privacy and to encourage the openness that is required to guarantee the client, patient, or parishioner the full benefit of the professional's services. In the case of reporters and sources, by contrast, there are nonfiduciary and even adversarial elements in the relationship, with the reporter angling to learn more than the source wants to tell and the source trying to promote a particular view; and, of course, from the standpoint of the journalist, the public's interests, not the source's, should be paramount.

David Shaw, the thoughtful media reporter and critic for *The Los Angeles Times,* has pointed out that the failure to name sources is one way the press has run afoul of the public's trust: "Reporters who write stories based on statements they do not identify for their readers are, in effect, asking their readers to trust them, to assume that the reporters (and their editors) have evaluated the source's credentials and credibility. Good reporters from good newspapers figure they have earned that trust."[23] Shaw has also called attention to the sometimes mindless abuse of the privileges of confidentiality and anonymity, saying that journalists should recognize that the names of sources are often an important part of the story and essential to maintaining broad public trust. Editors such as A. M. Rosenthal of *The New York Times* and Benjamin C. Bradlee of *The Washington Post* have consistently, and properly, pressed their reporters to find ways to persuade their sources to speak "on the record" as often as possible, and *USA Today* has argued in a lead editorial that the public trust depends, in important respects, on the naming of sources.[24]

Many other editors have criticized journalists for substantially the same flaw. Gene Foreman, managing editor of *The Philadelphia Inquirer*, notes: "By the very act of taking someone else into our confidence, we strain the confidence our readers have in us. . . . A few readers may readily grant us [trust], most, I fear, resent being asked. Just as our profession has matured and become more sophisticated in the last generation, so, too, has our readership. There is skepticism, even cynicism, among our readers. We invite their wrath when we keep secrets from them, when we tell them: 'Trust us.' "[25] Eugene Patterson, president and editor of *The St. Petersburg Times*, adds that many editors think a reduction in the use of unnamed sources might help "rebuild that valued trust."[26]

Despite these criticisms, we are persuaded that if reporters could not provide a limited guarantee of confidentiality, much important news would never be reported. Reporters who break the trust put in them by sources are rare, even though a clash of values may sometimes justify doing so. We will discuss such a case later, but first consider two cases involving problems of confidentiality and trustworthiness.

*Protecting Confidentiality.* The case of *New York Times* reporter Myron Farber and Dr. Mario Jascalevich is now something of a classic in the literature of free press versus fair trial, but the case is also instructive about trustworthiness and confidentiality. Farber and the *Times* led authorities to reopen a legal case against Jascalevich, who was eventually accused of having murdered five patients in 1965 and 1966 by injecting them with the powerful muscle relaxant curare. The lawyer for the defense requested that the judge order Farber to turn over his files and notes, to ensure that Jascalevich received a fair trial. Farber refused, on grounds that his confidential sources would be compromised.

Farber and the *Times* argued that their duty to protect their sources and thereby the principle of confidentiality outweighed any duty they might have had to Jascalevich, to the criminal justice system, or to any specific law, and that it was their right—guaranteed by the First Amendment—to make that determination. The defense countered that not to turn the files over would deny a citizen his right to a fair trial, as guaranteed by the Sixth Amendment.[27] The underlying argument by Farber and the *Times* was that a breach of confidence in this case would undermine all reporter–source confidential relationships, which are based on trust, and thereby undermine an institution without which a free press cannot survive.

Jascalevich's indictment resulted from a series of articles written by Farber ten years after the purported murders. During the trial Judge W. J.

Arnold ordered Farber's notes to be submitted for the judge's private inspection. Farber refused; he was cited for contempt and fined $2,000. Eventually Farber went to jail and the *Times* paid substantial fines. Jascalevich was acquitted, while Farber and the *Times*—both of whom had been found guilty of criminal contempt—were subsequently pardoned by Governor Brendan Byrne of New Jersey.

Is the *Times*'s and Farber's claim that sources will dry up if judges are allowed to review confidential information valid? To some degree, almost certainly. But trust entails an element of risk of disclosure; if there were no risk there would be no need for trust. And there are times when a competing value overrides an obligation such as confidentiality that is based on trust. The inability to promise absolute confidentiality should not undermine trust. Rather, it should alert sources to the rules of the game. There can be no pledge of confidentiality that carries an unconditional guarantee. All a reporter can guarantee is that a promise of confidentiality will be broken only for morally overriding reasons that are extraordinarily compelling. There will be cases, especially those involving potential prosecution, in which certain sources will refuse to talk to certain reporters for fear that they will be identified. But good reporters will generally be able to offer important sources adequate protection from the risk of identification so that a high level of trust will be maintained. Even if a few sources evaporate, journalism as we know it will survive.

Consider this case, as recounted by James D. Squires, editor of *The Chicago Tribune:*

> It all started when a friendly but not too well-intentioned political operative dropped into the eager hands of an unsuspecting *Tribune* columnist a tape recording of a meeting between Mayor Harold Washington and two minor political figures. The mayor, the source whispered, had made some unflattering and potentially explosive comments about one of his political allies, a controversial alderwoman. . . .
>
> Instinctively, as too many reporters are apt to do, the columnist promised confidentiality to the source. And that was the second mistake. The first was accepting the tape without knowing the circumstances under which it was obtained. Unlike most states, Illinois makes the taping of anyone without their knowledge a crime.[28]

Squires said that he had no difficulty in deciding how to handle the story. He called Washington to find out if he knew he was being taped; when the mayor said he did not, the editor had his lead. He included in the story the unflattering remarks about the alderwoman and also a promise by the mayor of a city job to an opponent if he dropped out of the race. But, Squires said:

> [The story] also acknowledged high and unequivocally that the tape had been deliberately leaked to the *Tribune* by the opposing political camp in

hopes of embarrassing the mayor on the eve of a special aldermanic election. Failure to include the motivation of the leaker would have misled the reader, left the story in an incomplete if not erroneous perspective desired by the leaker and further abused the system of protecting anonymous sources.

Squires said that the principle of confidentiality of sources "remains critical to the conduct of complete and responsible reporting," and that the *Tribune*, "even in this case," did what it could to honor the reporter's commitment. But, Squires continued:

> [The] time has long since passed when the pledge of an individual reporter can bind and incapacitate a news organization to [a] point where it supersedes all other ethical considerations. Readers deserve honesty as much as sources deserve loyalty. And there is no greater editor's responsibility than the life and credibility of the newspaper.

Squires correctly sees that the competing values are loyalty to a source and the public's need for information about the source. In this case, the source provided the information for partisan purposes, not to benefit the public, so the argument for protecting that source is less compelling than for protecting, for example, a whistle-blower who acts at risk to himself or herself and in the public interest. As Squires noted, the only way the *Tribune* could fulfill its public trust was to report on the motivation of the source, an obligation that seems weightier than any obligation to protect the source's interests by obscuring or suppressing his motives. There is also little risk that a decision like the one Squires made will undermine the principle of trust between sources and reporters, but even if it should, it is a risk worth taking.

We affirm, of course, that trust is essential for the reporter–source relationship to flourish and that every such arrangement of trust involves an implicit contract whose terms express an arrangement of cooperation and confidence. However, if the terms are violated by either party, the other party's obligations are nullified. The source may legitimately have motives beyond the provision of information to the public, but the implied contract between the reporter and the source is that the source will not grossly deceive or mislead the reporter to further political, bureaucratic, career, ideological, or other goals at the reporter's expense. Similarly, the reporter is obliged to keep confidentiality and promises, as well as to exercise sufficient care to ensure that the source's information is not misrepresented in print or on the air.

As most reporters, sources, and editors agree, if the press is to provide the public with vital information that it needs and to which it is entitled, there is no practical alternative to the existing system, which sometimes entails not identifying sources to the public. The point is not to dispense with these "contracts" and protections, but to present them to sources and to the public for what they are, which takes us to a perplexing case where a problem of this kind turned out to be more difficult to resolve than those discussed thus far.

*Jesse Jackson on "Hymietown."* This case involved a journalist's decision that the public's right to a particular piece of information took precedence over an understanding of confidentiality with his source. Milton Coleman, a national reporter covering politics for *The Washington Post,* had a conversation with Jesse Jackson during the 1984 presidential campaign when Jackson was seeking the Democratic nomination. During this private conversation, Jackson referred to Jews as "Hymies" and to New York as "Hymietown." Coleman later wrote that Jackson said, " 'Let's talk black talk,' " which Coleman understood to mean talk "on background," or not for direct attribution. Coleman signaled Jackson to proceed. According to Coleman:

> Jackson then talked about the preoccupation of some [Jews] with Israel. He said something to the effect of the following: "That's all Hymie wants to talk about is Israel; every time you go to Hymietown, that's all they want to talk about." The conversation was not tape recorded and I did not take notes. But I am certain of the thrust of his remarks and the use of the words "Hymie" and "Hymietown."' I had not heard him use them before. I made a mental note of the conversation.[29]

Coleman did not use the material in one of his stories. Instead, he turned it over to another *Post* reporter, Rick Atkinson, who was assigned to do a story about, in Coleman's words, "Jesse and the Jews."[30] This story appeared on page one of the *Post* on February 13, 1984. It was fifty-two paragraphs long, and in paragraph 37 it said that Jackson referred to Jews as "Hymies" and to New York as "Hymietown" in "private conversations with reporters." The thirty-eighth paragraph contained a denial by Jackson, but Jackson subsequently acknowledged making the remarks.

The issue of immediate interest is whether Coleman was justified in breaking an implicit but nonetheless acknowledged agreement of confidentiality with Jackson, thereby potentially shattering a relationship based on trust that was of value to the *Post* and its readers. We will not concern ourselves here with the deplorable subsequent treatment of Coleman by Jackson and Louis Farrakhan—the latter of whom allegedly threatened the reporter's life[31]—or with the fact that many blacks perceived Coleman's reporting of Jackson's remarks as breaking trust with a black brother. We are concerned, rather, with a perspective on public trust advanced on the

*Post* op-ed page by Meg Greenfield, which said in effect that the real record is usually "off the record," while the so-called record the media publish and broadcast is often little more than a manipulation of the public:

> What we call the record often tends to be the precise opposite of a record. It is, rather, the artifice, the cooked-up part, the image that the politician, with our connivance, hopes to convey and generally does. The off-the-record part is where the reality and authenticity are to be found and where they are generally supposed to remain forever obscure. . . .
>
> I don't think we contribute nearly enough to making the real record available, the one people need to see if they are to make a genuine choice. Forgive me if I can't get sufficiently exercised about the ground rules under which Jesse Jackson uttered his remarks. Those remarks were *part of the actual record.* I think they also *belonged on the one we put out for public consumption.*[32]

Greenfield's proposal is similar to Squires's assertion that violating accepted guidelines regarding confidentiality "is precisely what newspaper editors and reporters should have been doing for a long time—refusing to be duped and manipulated into the kind of irresponsible journalism that has caused a lot of our credibility problems."[33]

Greenfield's argument raises profoundly important questions. What is it, after all, that the public has a need and a right to know? Should a reporter enter into blanket contracts of confidentiality with presidential candidates, public officials, and public figures that allow them to manage what filters through to the public in an attempt to manipulate the public's perception? Should the trust of a source be violated if it is essential for the "actual record" to be published or broadcast? If a politician is manipulating a reporter by selectively releasing information, does the reporter have any obligation of trust? How should journalists resolve conflicts between a source's rights and the public interest?

Much more is morally at stake in these questions than trust between reporters and their sources. Coleman's dilemma concerns the public's entitlement to relevant information as much as the bounds of confidentiality and the conditions of its possibility. Greenfield says she cannot get too exercised over violating the ground rules in such cases, but she does not elaborate beyond the quotation above. One possible argument is that what Jackson said was nasty enough to justify voiding the normal duty to fulfill a commitment of confidentiality. Another is that the casual way in which these commitments are entered into represents a poor service to the public, and therefore they need not always be honored. In some circumstances we would accept both rationales. But cases of this kind are comparatively rare, and they often involve exceptions to the moral principles that sustain relationships of confidentiality and trust.

To find an acceptable balance of the values in conflict in this thorny case is unusually difficult. Jackson's anti-Semitic remarks provide a clear-cut example of the kind of information a journalist is obligated to report to the public. Nevertheless, Coleman did promise confidentiality, and it is rarely acceptable to achieve a desirable goal by the morally perilous means of breaking a promise. Coleman's justification was that Jackson was intentionally concealing revealing and relevant information and thereby manipulating the public. The question, then, is whether it is justifiable to break a promise because a political candidate has made racist remarks in your presence (in circumstances, we note, where the candidate clearly has no chance to win). Is it not the reporter's moral obligation to keep promises to honor attribution agreements with politicians, no matter what the politicians say?

Syndicated columnist Carl Rowan wrote a column that only deepened the dilemma presented to Coleman when he questioned whether any moral rule applies to this case:

> I have had senators, Supreme Court justices, top White House officials say things at my luncheon or diner tables that, if written, would have embarrassed them terribly. The Rev. Jackson has said things to me in telephone calls that I knew were private and "off the record." But when a reporter covers a candidate for the presidency, *there is no clear rule* that says "this is reportable" or "this I shall swallow and forget."[34]

Rowan is saying, in effect, that the rules for covering a presidential campaign are different from the rules normally understood to be in effect between reporters and sources. However, in twenty-four years in daily journalism, one author of this book never heard anyone voice such a view, in private or in public, nor do reporters conventionally act on such a premise. In most circumstances, other journalists challenge a reporter's right to break promises that stand to endanger the prospects for trust in the future. Some would also question Greenfield's argument that Jackson's remarks were "part of the actual record" and therefore provide a sufficient reason for breaking promises and damaging relationships of trust. Greenfield herself points out that much of the "actual record" is regularly concealed from the public. Even if one takes the view that reporters should exercise more discretion in granting confidentiality, that viewpoint does not justify a leap to the proposition that promises of this kind, once made, may be broken because the source has provided juicier information than expected.

There are also practical drawbacks to breaking a promise, some with moral implications. Identifying a confidential source could shut down that particular fount of information, thereby depriving the public of other important news. It might also taint the reporter in the community of sources, resulting in a reputation for the reporter and even his or her publishing or broadcasting outlet as untrustworthy. The taint could spread beyond the paper or network, turning off sources for other reporters. These are serious concerns, and they strongly support the view that a source should not be compromised by breaching confidentiality except with powerful justification. Coleman's commitment to Jackson, therefore, should have been judiciously balanced against the importance of the information and the strength of the public's need for that information.

The case *for* Coleman's action is as follows. Jackson's comment was outside the realm of morally acceptable political discourse, and it showed an unbecoming side of his character that it was important for readers to know. It also had an indirect bearing on his views in an important policy area. Its coarseness and general relevance tend to undermine any moral claim on its concealment that Jackson might make. Coleman knew that Jackson wanted to talk on background because it would be politically damaging if he were publicly identified with anti-Semitic language and views. The public's need to know and the nature of the information therefore provided a clear and in some respects very compelling reason for Coleman's decision to allow the information to be used.

Nonetheless, we do not find Coleman's case totally compelling. We acknowledge the force and truth of Greenfield's and Squires's observations that the press too often aids and abets public officials in their manipulation of the public (see Chapter 7), but we cannot agree with Rowan that the rules are loose and different in a presidential campaign. True, the stakes are often higher in presidential politics by comparison to other contexts, and citizens need to know more than in most situations. But, granting that premise, trust between journalists and sources remains an exceptionally important value. Should it have been treated with more respect by Coleman than it was? We admire his courage and his legal right to choose the course of disclosure, and we acknowledge the immorality of Jackson's comment, but Coleman's decision still casts some doubt on his trustworthiness in reporter–source relationships, and it is difficult to estimate the consequences of the skepticism that naturally arises as a result. In the short term, the public utility was undoubtedly served by Coleman's disclosure. But public service is not always an overriding moral value, and the long-term judgment is more difficult to make.

We could persevere in this vein, but the fact is that in this particular case, we—the two authors of this book—agree on the principles but disagree on the decision. Disagreement in cases even when there is agreement on principles will occur occasionally, because the moral machinery for balancing conflicting reasons operates with less than precision. Even careful moral reflection will not always yield an outcome free of hesitancy or uncertainty.

*A Comparison to "Billygate."*  A case about trustworthiness that turns on deception rather than on breaking promises emerged in 1980 in the context of a phenomenon known as Billygate. It was alleged that President Carter's brother, Billy, received money in 1979 from Libya in connection with an oil transaction and also as part of a Libyan effort to influence U.S. policy in the Middle East. In an attempt to confirm elements of reports to that effect, American journalist Michael Ledeen was given access by a source he trusted to an intelligence file that referred to meetings between the president's brother, Yasser Arafat, head of the Palestinian Liberation Organization, and George Habash, leader of the Popular Front for the Liberation of Palestine. These meetings, had they taken place, would have been in conflict with U.S. policy and would have constituted a broken promise to Israel.

Ledeen trusted his source and believed the files to be authentic. However, he and his coauthor, Arnaud de Borchgrave, a former *Newsweek* foreign correspondent and later editor of *The Washington Times,* needed confirmation before writing the story, which was published by *The New Republic* on November 1, 1980.[35] A man who could provide the confirmation was Michele Papa, the head of an organization called the Sicilian-Arab Association, and the go-between for Billy Carter and the Libyans. Ledeen knew that Papa would not tell him or de Borchgrave what they needed to know, but an acquaintance of Ledeen's named Francesco Pazienza offered a possible solution. Pazienza was an Italian intelligence agent (although Ledeen said he did not know it at the time) and knew a Sicilian journalist who came from the same town as Papa and, as it turned out, was willing to interview Papa to obtain information for Ledeen and de Borchgrave. (Pazienza subsequently accused Ledeen of pursuing the story not as a journalist but on behalf of the Republican Party to help Ronald Reagan defeat Jimmy Carter in the 1980 election. Ledeen denied the charge and sued Pazienza for libel in an Italian court. As this book goes to print the case has not been decided.)

Although Ledeen agreed to this arrangement, he wanted a tape recording of the interview because he did not know the Sicilian journalist and he wanted to be certain that he was getting precisely the confirmation he needed. It was decided that the Sicilian journalist would have to use a hidden microrecorder to tape his interview with Papa, which he did. Papa confirmed during the conversation that Billy Carter had met with Arafat and Habash. The tape was given to Ledeen and de Borchgrave, who then wrote their article for *The New Republic.*

When asked whether he thought it was proper to deceive Papa by using a hidden tape recorder, Ledeen said there was no other way to get the confirmation and furthermore that in Italy the use of hidden tape recorders was so common that any sophisticated person would be aware of the possibility that a journalist might be clandestinely taping their conversation. Although we have been unable to confirm the premise that any sophisticated person would expect to be taped, we are convinced by our sources that secret taping is common enough in Italy to lend substance to Ledeen's claim that any sophisticated person would have been put on guard by an inquiring journalist.

But was the deception justified? And what were the trade-offs? Press advocates such as journalist Robert Sherrill would wonder what we are agonizing about. In cases of this kind, Sherrill wrote:

> I am inclined to pass over the ethical question entirely. If it works, I am generally for it. "Every government is run by liars and nothing they say should be believed," said I. F. Stone. That's right, and Stone could have said the same thing about every corporation. So long as reporters, vastly outnumbered and outgunned, are expected to penetrate these hostile areas to obtain useful information, they can, I think, be forgiven for using almost any device or tactic so long as it enables them to bring back the bacon.[36]

Sherrill's argument suggests that journalists can break moral rules because they are more virtuous than others. Clearly that premise is questionable. In any event, if journalists were to arrogate to themselves the right to use deception or "almost any device or tactic" to pursue what they think is important, however they want and whenever they want, the public's trust in the press would go into a tailspin.

We do not contend, however, that deception is never justified. There is only a presumption against it, just as there is a presumption against breaking promises. Sometimes enough is at stake that a deception is warranted. We think Billygate may have been such a case, because the American public had a clear need to know if the Carter administration—or even the president's brother on his own—was violating a national policy and breaking a promise to an important ally. Furthermore, given the climate for such activities in Italy, the deception itself could be classified as a more or less routine practice. (This observation is not meant as an attempt to justify the practice in all cases.) Journalists sometimes inflate the value of their stories and use the inflated part as justification for deception or promise-breaking, but we are not convinced that Ledeen and de Borchgrave were guilty of doing so.

Some pertinent facts are unknown in this case, of course, and it is also worth remembering that moral philosophy can only point to values in conflict and help us assess the weight of the arguments on each side. It cannot provide principles so rigid that they rule out all promise-keeping or deception. The award-winning, justly celebrated documentary film *Shoah* was possible only because of the deceptive use of hidden TV cameras and false promises told to former Nazi SS officers. But Claude Lanzmann's journalism was on such an enormously important set of themes (the attitudes and objectives underlying Nazi atrocities and the sympathetic attitudes of Polish citizens), and so revealing, that we find it impossible to deny the legitimacy of his deception and breaking of promises, especially since there was no other way to report the story.

The account in the next section—although used principally to illustrate the importance of trust in the working relationship between editors and reporters—is a prime example of an unjustified deception of editors, sources, and the public.

## Trust in the Editor–Reporter Relationship

Editors and reporters working in a cooperative venture aimed at informing the public must trust each other as much as they must trust sources, and probably more. When they trust each other and are working well together, each will enhance both the product and the other's professional standing. But trust suffers if reporters and editors suspect each other's motives or regularly disagree about the worth of stories and how they should be written. It may also suffer if an editor's authority to reward or punish reporters is exercised unfairly. Trust may break down completely if a reporter fails to live up to the expectations of an editor by inaccurate or incomplete reporting, a consistent lack of judgment, a failure to generate story ideas, regularly missing stories, or a failure of character such as laziness. The practical implication of such a complete failure of trust in a reporter by an editor is, of course, that the reporter must be either transferred or fired.

In the next few pages we discuss the Janet Cooke case, which illustrates some of these generalizations about trust in the reporter–editor relationship. This case has been mentioned earlier, (see pp. 52–53), but new issues are presented by placing it in the context of trust. Perhaps it is unfair to *The Washington Post* to recount again Cooke's fictitious reports on a mythical child heroin addict. Certainly the story can be generalized beyond the *Post*'s editors and presents a familiar problem that is not peculiar to the *Post*. For example, the day we completed the final draft of this chapter, the Associated Press reported that *The San Antonio Light* had declined to accept a newspaper column writing award conferred by the Headliners Club for an article by its reporter Betty Godfrey on a meeting between a bag lady and a businessman. The *Light*, it seems, discovered almost a year later that its reporter had published a fabricated story about a meeting in

San Antonio that had never occurred in that city (although some distantly related event had occurred in Germany). The *Light* profusely apologized for its reporter's "serious breach of ethics."[37]

Cooke was a twenty-six-year-old reporter who won a Pulitzer Prize for her gripping 1980 story about an eight-year-old addict. The prize was withdrawn when the *Post* discovered and immediately made public the fact that the subject of her story was not an individual child but rather a composite she had invented. We will set aside what a fraud of those dimensions does to public trust in the press to consider the relationship of trust between Cooke and her editors and the way in which she played on the theme of trust between a reporter and her sources to deceive them. Cooke, who had been at the *Post* for about two years as a reporter on the District Weekly (a zoned Metropolitan Desk section), was never pressed by her editors to identify her sources, even though her story contended, among other things, that a hardened, street-wise drug dealer let her watch him shoot up an eight-year-old. Cooke was not known for street smarts, and a number of *Post* reporters and editors said they did not believe her story from the start, but the editors who worked with Cooke extended their trust beyond reasonable boundaries.

On April 19, 1981, several days after the hoax was exposed, Bill Green— then the *Post*'s ombudsman—wrote a lengthy investigatory article about the story. Green interviewed forty-seven *Post* staffers for his article, although Cooke refused to talk to him. Green condemned the *Post* for its failure to short-circuit the fraud somewhere in the system and identified "the faith an editor has to place in a reporter" as "the jugular of journalism." Faith in this case is synonymous with trust. Green called the *Post*'s performance "inexcusable" because, among other things, "none of the editors pressed Cooke for confidential details on the identity of 'Jimmy' or his family." He also maintained that the "editors abandoned their professional skepticism."[38]

Metropolitan editor Bob Woodward said: "This story was so well-written and tied together so well that my alarm bells simply didn't go off. My skepticism left me." Woodward also said he was "negligent" in the Cooke case.[39] He was, but so were many others. Cooke was ambitious, and everyone knew it. She had told another *Post* reporter that she wanted a Pulitzer Prize within three years. She did not know the Washington streets and was known as strictly "uptown." The subject matter of the story was also recognized as explosive. City editor Milton Coleman, with an unerring eye for impact, told Cooke to pursue the eight-year-old addict as the focus of her story. It was so explosive and Cooke's credentials to write the story so doubtful that an editor's professional skepticism should have trumped all the trust that had protected Cooke.

Someone should have recognized that the paper's credibility was at stake and that the public's trust in the *Post* was on the line. Yet Cooke was never asked to persuade her editors that "Jimmy," his mother, or the mother's pusher boyfriend actually existed. She was also not asked to identify other sources for the story. Coleman's professional skepticism was not sufficiently aroused when Cooke said she was unable to find the eight-year-old mentioned in her notes but that she had located a second eight-year-old addict—"Jimmy" in her story—by leaving her business card with kids in slum playgrounds.

For over two years and in fifty-two previous stories, Cooke had not let them down. So why should she be challenged on this assignment? The answer, in part, is that the stakes were higher in the "Jimmy" story. The story would hit the streets with substantial impact, and mistakes could not be adequately rectified with a one-paragraph correction. But the high stakes were not the only reason that skepticism should have surfaced. Cooke's youth, her lack of knowledge of the Washington streets, her ambition, the nature of the story, and her unpromising technique of handing out business cards in slum playgrounds should have been enough to convince *Post* editors to lay ordinary trust aside and rigorously challenge their own reporter.

Hindsight, of course, is a powerful form of vision. Coleman's assessment is understandable: "It never occurred to me that she could make it up. There was too much distance between Janet and the streets."[40] When Coleman saw a name—Tyrone—on Cooke's first draft and took that to be the child's real name, it is understandable why he felt reassured. It also makes sense that he wanted to be reassured and that he needed to be reassured. Perhaps because he did not want to believe the story was not true, he did not ask the hard questions that might have revealed an inconsistency or brought to the surface some clue that the story was fictional. Bradlee, Woodward, and other editors were aware of the story and read it, at one stage or another, before publication. They also trusted Coleman, who had a hard-earned reputation as a smart and thorough editor. Furthermore, he was black, like Cooke, and thought to be much more savvy about the Washington drug subculture, although it really was not his world either. Coleman's opinion was that the other editors "kind of took it for granted that Coleman should know."[41]

So the story was published with no one at the *Post* knowing who "Jimmy" was. Predictably, it threw the city government into an uproar. The *Post* was immediately and sharply criticized for failing to identify the child so that he could get help. When city authorities were unable to locate the child, D.C. Mayor Marion Barry suggested that the story was at least in part concocted. Bradlee and Simons said they felt the pressure but were reassured by Coleman and Woodward that they had nothing to worry about. Green wrote: "The *Post* stuck by its story and what it described as its First Amendment rights to protect its sources." Coleman said he did voice some concerns to Simons but was told, "I more than anyone else had to stand by my reporter. At the point that I even began to hint to her that I thought she had not been truthful, her trust in me could be destroyed."[42]

In this case, however, the primary problem was Cooke's veracity, not her trust in Coleman or Simons. Her lie had passed all too easily through the system of checks because most editors tend uncritically to accept the principle of confidentiality and to trust their reporters when they present sources as anonymous. The journalistic virtue insufficiently in evidence was skepticism. Editors must challenge reporters; if they have any reason to think elements of a story are questionable, they must press the reporter to provide evidence and argument. As a result of not doing so in this case, the *Post*, at least temporarily, suffered a significant loss of public trust.

## Conclusion

Trust is not something journalists, sources, or editors either deserve or convey by moral right. They must earn it. Journalists merit the public's trust only if they consistently display fairness and competence, and they should grant their own trust to sources with good judgment and discretion. Stories that turn out to be in whole or in part false—like Janet Cooke's story about "Jimmy," *Time*'s erroneous paragraph about General Ariel Sharon, or CBS News's "Tailgate"—are bound to influence the extent to which the public trusts or distrusts the press. But the virtue of trustworthiness is based on consistency of action. An occasional, explainable mistake does not strip away that character trait.

Given the nature of the journalistic enterprise, it is perhaps surprising that the major media in the United States make as few serious errors as they do. But when mistakes occur from causes such as sloppiness or wish fullfillment, the public's trust is justifiably eroded. In some of the cases we have discussed in this book, the public was deceived, manipulated, or both. In others the public was unjustifiably harmed. In "Tailgate," for example, the public was deceived and the reputation of the U.S. Congress was maligned. In the Cooke story, the public was manipulated, and city government employees were searching vainly for a phantom eight-year-old, at taxpayers' expense, for no reason other than a reporter's ambition.

The *Post* was exemplary in the straightforward way it acted in the

Cooke affair to restore the public's trust. There were few options but to admit that the paper had been defrauded along with the public by its reporter and to accept full responsibility. But nothing required that the paper give its independent ombudsman the upper left-hand corner of page one and three and a half inside pages to examine what went wrong for the *Post*'s more than one million Sunday readers. This detailed admission of failure restored some measure of trust. *Time*, by contrast, was defensive, arrogant, and insensitive to the broad issue of public trust in the media as an institution in its response to its critics in the Sharon case, despite its publication of a limited correction (see Chapter 2, pp. 54–55).

Journalists often treat their privileges as rights that must prevail irrespective of values with which they clash. This unwillingness to recognize the merit of legitimate competing values together with a fear that admissions of error will invite legal sanctions or government control have created a situation in which the press is widely perceived as arrogant. This perception may not be a deep phenomenon, but a threatened, defensive press is not likely to perform in a way that will deserve the public's trust.

## NOTES

1. "White Paper of the Advisory Committee on Public Opinion," Sigma Delta Chi, Society of Professional Journalists, February 1984, p. 12.

2. All quotations are taken from Jonathan Friendly, "Editor Tells of 'Nightmare' at Wall Street Journal," *The New York Times*, May 11, 1984, p. 29.

3. Gannett Center for Media Studies, "The Media and the People," Columbia University poll conducted summer 1985, p. i.

4. But see Virginia Held, *Rights and Goods, Justifying Social Action* (New York: Free Press, 1984), pp. 62–85; Sissela Bok, *Lying: Moral Choice in Public and Private Life* (New York: Pantheon, 1978), pp. 17–32, and Bernard Barber, *The Logic and Limits of Trust* (New Brunswick: Rutgers University Press, 1983).

5. Frank Sutherland, "Anatomy of Murder Hoax—A Paper's Hard Decision," in *1985–1986 Journalism Ethics Report*, Sigma Delta Chi, Society of Professional Journalists, pp. 6–7.

6. MORI Research, "Newspaper Credibility, Building Reader Trust," study commissioned by the American Society of Newspaper Editors, April 1985, p. 13.

7. Ibid., p. 9.

8. Ibid., p. 13.

9. Clark, Martire and Bartolomeo, Inc., "Relating to Readers in the '80s," study commissioned by the American Society of Newspaper Editors, May 1984, p. 15.

10. Ibid., p. 12; and James R. Dickenson, "Poll Terms News Media Believable but Malleable," *The Washington Post*, January 16, 1986, p. A5. For a tough critique of the Times-Mirror poll (performed by Gallup), see Alexander Cockburn, "Gallup Comes Through for an Anxious Publisher," *The Wall Street Journal*, January 23, 1986, p. 31.

11. Seymour Martin Lipset, "The Confidence Gap: Down but Not Out," *Informing America: Who Is Responsible for What?* Donald S. MacNaughton Symposium Proceedings (Syracuse, N.Y.: Syracuse University, 1985), pp. 143–56.

12. See comments by Daniel Yankelovich in the "White Paper" of Sigma Delta Chi, February 1984, p. 12.

13. As quoted by Jonathan Friendly, "Reporter's Notebook: Trust and News," *The New York Times,* May 12, 1984, p. 29.

14. Ibid. Powell also allegedly said that journalists would "kick the brains out of public officials or business leaders but 'usually won't point [their] finger at the rotten apple in the journalism barrel.'"

15. Thomas Jefferson, "Letter to Baron von Humboldt," 1807, in *The Papers of Thomas Jefferson,* ed. Charles T. Cullen (Princeton: Princeton University Press), forthcoming.

16. As interviewed by Barbara Reynolds, in *USA Today.* April 11, 1985, p. 9A.

17. Institute for Econometric Research, "The Wall Street Journal's Stock Picks," Special Publication, pp. 1–2.

18. See Larry Elkin, "Court Upholds Winans' Conviction," *The Washington Post,* May 28, 1986, p. 63, and "Lawyers File Appeals for 3 in Winans Case," *The Washington Post,* November 27, 1985, p. D2.

19. "Ex-Reporter Says He Believed Leaks of His Journal Articles Weren't Illegal," *The Wall Street Journal,* March 19, 1985, p. 12.

20. "Winans Says He Knew Leaks Would Bring Dismissal," *The Wall Street Journal,* March 21, 1985, p. 10.

21. Editorial, *Business Week,* April 29, 1985, pp. 79, 128.

22. "Ex-Reporter Says He Believed Leaks . . . ," p. 12.

23. David Shaw, *Press Watch* (New York: Macmillan, 1984), p. 60.

24. Ibid., p. 59, 63–64; Editorial, "News Credibility," *USA Today,* April 12, 1985, p. 12A.

25. Gene Foreman, "Confidential Sources: Testing the Reader's Confidence," *Social Responsibility: Business, Journalism, Law, Medicine,* ed. Louis W. Hodges (Lexington, Va.: Washington and Lee University Press, 1984), p. 24. The quotation is partially rearranged in order.

26. As quoted in Shaw, *Press Watch,* p. 60.

27. See Ronald Dworkin, "The Rights of Myron Farber," *The New York Review of Books,* October 26, 1978, pp. 34–35.

28. James D. Squires, "When Confidentiality Itself Is Source of Contention," in 1985–1986 Journalism Ethics Report, Sigma Delta Chi, p. 7.

29. Milton Coleman, "18 Words, Seven Weeks Later," *The Washington Post,* April 8, 1984, p. C8. Commonly, "off the record" means not for any kind of attribution; "on deep background" refers to a general form of attribution such as "a source close to the negotiations"; and "let's talk black talk" is Jackson's way of saying to black reporters, "on background," which means the source may not be named, and the attribution may be something like "a senior State Department official."

30. Rick Atkinson, "Peace with American Jews Eludes Jackson," *The Washington Post,* February 13, 1984, p. A1.

31. See Sam Zagoria, "Reporting on Louis Farrakhan," *The Washington Post,* October 2, 1985, p. A24.

32. Meg Greenfield, "Must Reality Be Off the Record," *The Washington Post,* April 11, 1984, p. A21. Emphasis added.

33. Squires, "When Confidentiality Itself Is Source," p. 7.

34. Carl Rowan, "A Threat to a Reporter—And to All Blacks," *The Washington Post,* April 4, 1984, p. A23.

35. Telephone interview, January 14, 1986. Subsequent paraphrases of Ledeen's remarks are based on this interview and a second telephone interview on April 24, 1986.

36. Robert Sherrill, "News Ethics, Press and Jerks," *Grand Street* (Winter 1986): 115–33.

37. Associated Press, "Paper declines to accept award, saying story in column not true," *The Monitor* (McAllen, Tex.), January 30, 1986, p. 7A.

38. Bill Green, "Janet's World," *The Washington Post,* April 19, 1981, pp. A1, A12–A15.

39. Ibid., p. A12.

40. Ibid., p. A12.

41. Ibid., p. A12.

42. Ibid., p. A13. Emphasis added.

# Chapter 7

# Escaping Manipulation

The press sometimes abuses its power by manipulating public opinion. More often it is charged with being too easily manipulated by government officials, terrorists, professional image builders, and other publicity seekers. Michael J. O'Neill, former editor of *The New York Daily News*, has characterized the problem succinctly:

> The national media are now no longer just observers and messengers but lead actors in government, creating, shaping, and often distorting the informational base of decision-making, magnifying as well as reporting the conflicts of power, advocating, nagging, and harassing as well as explaining. They are the targets of manipulation by every party to every issue, the objects of guile and deception, the victims of conflicting pressures, witting and unwitting participants in the management of crisis and in the formation of policy, both the collaborators and adversaries of government.[1]

This chapter examines both the press's influence and influences by others on the press. Press power exists in a variety of forms. Here is just one example of the power of television news as described by a Palestinian journalist: "Every night on Syrian, Jordanian and Israeli television [Palestinian] young people [on the West Bank] received news of successful attacks against

Israeli soldiers [in Lebanon]. They saw the Lebanese get the Israelis out by making their lives hell and inflicting casualties. Many think: 'Why not do the same here?' "[2] The journalist was right. Television, including Israeli television, almost certainly played a part in stimulating what he called a "new wave of violence" by West Bank Palestinians.

Examples of how the power of the press is exercised range from editorial decisions on the amount of coverage to give a political candidate to decisions by trade journal editors on whether to review a new product. One review of a new computer program in a journal like *InfoWorld, Personal Computing,* or *PC World,* for example, can make or break a small software corporation. Plays, films, books, and careers of all kinds can be made or destroyed by the press. The press's power is formidable in political, economic, and social affairs. New York Mayor Ed Koch, after announcing that he was ordering a new investigation into some previously dropped charges of corruption at his medical examiner's office because *The New York Times* had put the heat on, said: "If you're asking me does *The New York Times* focusing on a particular matter get special attention, if I told you it didn't, I wouldn't be telling you the truth."[3] The same, of course, holds true on the national level. As presidential aide Michael Deaver said, "the President's staff would be 'crazy' if it didn't recognize television's influence and 'construct events or craft photos' to fit the network news programs."[4]

This ability to demand special attention translates into various forms of influence, including persuasion and manipulation. It is exercised mainly through the selection, treatment, and presentation of information. If the object of the exercise is simply to inform, few moral problems will result. Similarly, if the object is to persuade through reason, as in a column, editorial, or news analysis, there are not likely to be profound moral problems. But manipulation is the source of an unending stream of moral problems.

## The Concept of Influence

As a fundamental condition of human freedom, persons are entitled to expect that those who are in a position to influence them, such as public officials, corporate officers, stockbrokers, and those who report, edit, analyze, and package the news, will do so through a fair presentation of accurate information. No one wants to be manipulated by the morning paper, whether the reporters and editors are the manipulators or the unwitting tools of manipulation by others. If the press is to be trusted, the public must have good reason to believe that journalists are wary of being manipulated by sources and that they conscientiously avoid manipulating the public.

In a system like ours, in which a high value is placed on both a free flow of information and personal autonomy, the press ideally would be free of virtually all governmental or social control through manipulation or coercion, and the public would remain similarly free of control by the press. To understand what would be needed to approach such an ideal standard in practice requires some understanding of the broad concept of influence. Control is always exerted through some form of influence, but not all influences are controlling. Influences come in a multiplicity of forms, including threats of physical harm, promises of love and affection, economic incentives, reasoned argument, lies, aesthetic displays, press releases, and news stories. The degree of influence actually exerted can vary dramatically, and many forms of influence are easily resistible. Some types of influence have a major effect on an individual's ability to do things, while others make no difference. It is important, therefore, to recognize the kind and degree of influence at work.

Influence does not necessarily imply constraint, governance, force, or compulsion, although these concepts are essential to certain kinds of influence. Important decisions are usually made in contexts replete with influences in the form of competing claims and interests, social demands and expectations, and straightforward or devious attempts by others to bring about the outcome they desire. Some of these influences are unavoidable, and some may even be desirable. Clearly not all of them interfere with or deprive persons of autonomous belief and action, as when readers and viewers are influenced by news reports, or reporters are influenced by sources, without either being controlled.

However, some acts in journalistic contexts are partly or entirely controlled by the intentional influence of another person. If, for example, a reporter lies in order to obtain information from a source that the source otherwise would not have divulged, the reporter has deprived the source of free action. Control of this kind is not always unjustifiable, and media influence may not always be irresistible, but it can be difficult to resist and to justify. For example, CBS's "The Uncounted Enemy: A Vietnam Deception" inevitably influenced and shaped the opinions of many viewers with respect to Gen. William Westmoreland's integrity, competence, and trustworthiness. (See pp. 75-89) Depending on one's prior knowledge, beliefs, and critical faculties, the influence of this special report could have ranged anywhere from easily resistible to irresistible. This is often the case with documentaries, and even more so with docudramas in which fiction is seamlessly woven into the narrative to increase the dramatic impact, often strengthening the thesis in the process.

We are concentrating here on influence by manipulation, but journalists can also influence and be influenced by persuasion and coercion. Coercion—which involves a threat of harm so severe that a person is unable to resist acting to avoid it—is always completely controlling. Persuasion is never controlling. Manipulation, by contrast, can run from highly controlling to altogether noncontrolling. The moral ideal, of course, is to use only those forms of influence that leave persons free, informed, and generally in control of their beliefs and actions, but this ideal is extremely difficult to achieve. Because coercion of journalists or coercion by journalists is almost always unjustifiable and is relatively rare, it is given minimal attention here. (Coercion is far more important in medical, police, and business ethics.) Instead, we will concentrate on more subtle and pervasive problems surrounding informing, persuading, and manipulating.

## Informing and Persuading

The most common form of influence exerted by journalists is the augmentation or modification of a reader's or viewer's beliefs through the selective disclosure of information. When this influence is applied fairly and competently, it is unobjectionable because no control is exerted. But journalists often do more than inform; they attempt to persuade, which in principle is acceptable except in hard news and some kinds of feature reporting. Editorials, columns, reviews, analyses, documentaries, and other forms of presentation are designed to persuade and thereby to shape opinion. Persuasion, therefore, is not an insidious form of influence that has no place in journalism.

As we use the term, *persuasion* is restricted to influence by appeal to reason, and it is free of coercion or other forms of influence that deprive a person of free choice. Carefully reasoned editorials, theater reviews, and documentaries may not be entirely devoid of appeals to emotion, but if the decisive influence comes from reason rather than emotion, then the journalism in question is persuasive in our sense. Emotion-based influences are inherently manipulative, not persuasive. Consider, for example, the following introductory paragraphs taken from an editorial in *The Philadelphia Inquirer:*

> The question is not whether Marianne Mele Hall should be fired from her $70,000-a-year federal job as head of the obscure U.S. Copyright

Royalty Tribunal. Obviously she should be fired, and in the process President Reagan should condemn her in no uncertain terms for spewing divisive racist filth and then daring to take a fat salary from the multiracial, multiethnic taxpayers of this diverse nation.

A wise, just and humane president wouldn't hesitate to pinch this leech off the body politic, but don't hold your breath. Firing public servants of Ms. Hall's stripe is not what this administration is all about; hiring them is.[5]

This editorial proceeded to offer a few conclusions that might be described by a generous person as following from an argument, but the opening paragraphs capture both the tone and substance of the writing.

This kind of writing does not exemplify persuasion, because it is not primarily an appeal to reason. It exemplifies the use of emotional rhetoric rather than fact and reasoned argument to condemn a public official and have her fired. Words like "obviously," for example, are substituted for argument. We do not contend that a relatively brief editorial need repeat every argument implied or explicitly stated in the news coverage of an event like the firing of Hall. Our point is that editorials are most valuable if written to inform and advance the debate on important matters of public policy, not to inflame it by resorting to emotionally charged language such as "spewing divisive racist filth" and "pinch this leech off the body politic."

We agree with the *Inquirer* that Hall, who ultimately resigned, should have been removed from her position, but if the point of an editorial is— as we believe—an attempt to persuade the public, the above does not represent an appropriate way to do it. Instead, one needs a reasoned account of why the actions of the accused were inappropriate and should result in her dismissal. Anyone familiar with issues of public service, press freedom, and academic freedom knows that it is not obvious that the editor of a book tainted by racist assumptions is necessarily unsuited for public office, even if racism itself is obviously wrong. The *Inquirer* editorial, in short, is an example of failure to support a thesis with evidence and logical argument, relying instead on emotional appeals.

A similar and equally common problem in journalism is relying on unsubstantiated and questionable premises, without acknowledging their weakness, to generate a desired conclusion. Consider the following very typical introductory sentence of a *New York Times* editorial—this one titled "Inhumanity to Lab Animals": "Medical research would be impossible without experiments on animals, and most researchers treat them well, not least because badly kept animals make poor subjects."[6] This lead sentence stakes out the premises on the basis of which the editorial goes on to support a Senate bill to improve animal care, yet every element of the lead sentence is questionable, and at the time the editorial was published every element had been scrutinized by respectable critics of animal care in the United States (many of whom qualify in the *Times*'s sense, as moderates).

Consider each element, in turn. Certainly much—but far from all—"medical research would be impossible without experiments on animals" as that research is conducted today. However, many alternatives to research involving animals have been used in the past and are increasingly in use. A large literature on alternatives and trends toward their use seems to have escaped the editorial's writer.[7] More importantly, it has not been substantiated that "most researchers treat them well." The editorial itself goes on to note that "24 percent of one sample of research institutions were found to have major, repeated violations of minimum standards of care." Moreover, this finding derives from the Department of Agriculture's veterinary inspector reports, and many research institutions are not inspected at all. It is likely that in these uninspected institutions conditions are worse (although few data exist to support that broad a conclusion). Finally, it has not been shown that the statement "badly kept animals make poor subjects" is relevant to the real problems of cruelty to laboratory animals, which generally occurs in places conducting poorly controlled research.

The *Times* and *Inquirer* examples represent daily problems of communication and fairness for editorial writers, but these are not unsolvable problems. In both cases questionable premises have been treated as self-evident or axiomatic. In the *Inquirer* editorial it was the premise that a public official had demonstrated her unsuitability for office by editing a book, some of whose assumptions were racist. The *Times* editorial began with a set of basic but unexamined assumptions. In both cases, if the writers did not care to devote space to examining the premises, they could at least have indicated that their premises were questionable, or that in the view of the *Inquirer* or the *Times*, respectively, the preponderance of evidence supported their viewpoint.

This approach would be less satisfactory than a well-articulated defense of the premises, but at least it would make readers aware that the premises were not self-evident and that there was another side, albeit one that the *Inquirer* or the *Times* on balance rejected. The tone of such an editorial would be less authoritative but would benefit from increased credibility. The *Times* lead, for example, might go like this: "Much medical research would be difficult if not impossible without experiments on animals. There is evidence that a substantial number of researchers treat their animals well, partly because badly kept animals generally make poor subjects."

Although we have been discussing the importance of using bona fide forms of persuasion, we have yet to say what persuasion is. Persuasion can be defined as an appeal to reason that succeeds in getting persons to freely accept the beliefs, attitudes, values, or actions of the persuader. Persuasion, therefore, is always an overt form of influence; the persuader openly advances reasons for accepting or adopting what is advocated. Choices made and acts performed on the basis of persuasion are autonomous even when made under the influence of the persuader. By contrast, an emotional appeal may lure, coax, entice, or wheedle—thus confusing or disorienting the person. It alters perceptions through means that rob persons of their ability to make a free, autonomous choice, as in Vance Packard's *The Hidden Persuaders,* a book that describes some of the ways in which people are influenced without adequate awareness of the source of control.[8] Despite Packard's title, this is not what we mean by persuasion. Persuasion is not inherently more biased or controlling than informing and explaining, forms of presentation that are devoid of argued analysis.

An argued analysis may be entirely appropriate and even desirable in journalism. Just as we expect doctors to advise and recommend about health care, so we expect newspapers, news magazines, and television news programs to attempt to persuade us in a clearly designated format of the merit of political candidates, public policies, works of art, and a variety of other things. On television, arguments are often made more through pictures than through words, but for the presentation to be persuasive and not manipulative the visual evidence must be relevant and appropriately presented. It could be manipulative and therefore inappropriate, for example, for a television camera to dwell on the nervous gestures of an interview subject whose credibility is in dispute.

Reasoned argument is a way of logically ordering information and drawing conclusions from it, and it can be as important in promoting understanding as disclosure of facts. Often the real challenge for journalists is to restrict the influence exerted to explanation and persuasion, forms of influence that are not controlling and therefore not unjustifiable. A person may be caused to believe something by persuasion, but being caused is not necessarily being controlled. Just because an op-ed piece is both necessary and sufficient to persuade a person to believe something does not mean that persuasion is incompatible with free choice. Even if a person is powerfully persuaded, his or her personal acceptance of the reason or argument can still be autonomous.

However, editorial writers, columnists, and commentators often try to convince readers and viewers to accept a viewpoint by means that are as manipulative as they are persuasive. Moral argument by journalists is a good example of this problem. Joseph Epstein, editor of *The American*

*Scholar,* has wryly labeled journalists who urge moral conclusions "virtucrats":

> Our society seems to require a certain number of professional virtucrats: columnists, editorial writers, broadcast commentators. I recall a television editorial on the subject of black youth crime . . . delivered by Bill Moyers, who is one of our leading professional virtucrats. Mr. Moyers' raison d'etre . . . is demonstrating serious moral concern. He speaks, he is paid to speak, for virtue. Thus, toward the close of his editorial on black youth crime, Mr. Moyers concluded that no one is facing the issue "squarely. So it keeps ticking away." . . . Someone is facing the issue squarely; and that someone is Bill Moyers. If the clock runs out and the bomb explodes it sure as hell isn't going to be his fault. He has already told us what to do: create better education, more jobs, strengthen the black family, a few simple items like that.[9]

Epstein is criticizing Moyers for a kind of moral manipulation. Underlying Moyers's argument is the assumption that "society" should "create better education, more jobs, strengthen the black family," and so on. But even Moyers, who is among the best at television commentary, cannot make a reasoned argument in two minutes of air time. He therefore resorts to emotional exhortation—often accompanied by no less emotional pictures—hoping that his commentary will help keep the spotlight on a deplorable situation that he believes merits attention. Nevertheless, to the extent that his appeal is more to emotion than to intellect, it is manipulative rather than persuasive. Epstein's own presentation is often emotive. He asserts that opinion journalists are "virtucrats," a term he defines pejoratively as "prigs in the realm of opinion." Later, in a tone lathered in irony, he uses a fragmentary quote from and paraphrase of Moyers to support his characterization. He seems to appeal to reason, but his appeal is so liberally dipped in emotional rhetoric that it too qualifies as manipulation.

These examples suggest, among other things, that despite the distinction we have drawn between persuasion and manipulation, it is difficult to specify precisely where persuasion ends and manipulation begins. Ordinary usage, philosophy, and the social sciences provide no exact boundaries. But since our concern is only to be able to distinguish influences that leave us substantially free to act from those that do not, there is no need to stipulate precise boundaries.

## Manipulation and Being Manipulated

In mid-August 1985, President Ronald Reagan reacted in public to a speech by South African President P. W. Botha. Despite Botha's apparent resistance to external influence, Reagan said that he remained optimistic that change could be brought about in South Africa through "persuasion" rather than "coercion."[10] He seemed to suggest that his choices were limited to persuasion or coercion; finding the latter unacceptable, possibly because he thought it unlikely to produce results, he said the United States would opt for persuasion. What Reagan and his advisors neglected, or at least did not publicly specify as a possibility, was manipulation.

Manipulation is less well understood than weaker forms of influence such as persuasion and stronger forms of influence such as indoctrination and coercion. The word *manipulation* refers to a catchall category: deception, enticement, reward, punishment, seduction, propaganda, and so on, can all be forms of manipulation, and they can all come in varying degrees. Some of these manipulative influences are controlling, whereas others leave us substantially free to act as we wish. Minor manipulations, such as an advertisement for cold beer that makes you thirsty or a Bill Moyers exhortation to virtue, are largely inconsequential, while major manipulations involving pressure and deception can be significant and invasive. Many kinds of manipulation fall between these extremes.

Manipulation is any intentional and successful influence of a person by noncoercively altering the actual choices available to the person or by nonpersuasively altering the other's perceptions of those choices.[11] The essence of manipulation is getting persons to do what the manipulator intends without resort to coercion but also independently of reasoned argument. Manipulation in this sense may not be immoral (for example, a criminal might be tricked into surrendering), but the use of manipulative techniques almost always requires justification. In the context of journalism, this rough generalization holds true as much for those who try to manipulate the press as for those journalists who try to manipulate rather than to persuade the public.

The press is regularly manipulated by trade associations, politicians, bureaucrats, law-enforcement officials, corporate officers, lawyers, investors, and others who want to influence public opinion. The strategy in each case is to use the journalist as a means of influence. Here is a description from the financial press of how the process sometimes works. A *Wall Street Journal* "study of the short-sellers' [those who sell borrowed stock hoping to buy it back later at a lower price and thus profit] network indicates that short sellers cultivate their press relationships more skillfully than most other investors do. . . . As an active New York short seller put it, 'I'd rather make 30% in a week than in four months; the press helps.' "[12] Sources who trade in securities may provide accurate information, but they may also deceive more than they inform through, for example, partial disclosures and the spreading of snowballing rumors. According to the *Jour-*

*nal,* sources often try to manipulate its reporters by offering an exclusive story "for just a limited time" and through false reports that "another publication is working on the story."[13] The source's objective might be to get a reporter to write a story before investigating it adequately or to influence the timing of its publication.

The *Journal* reported on its own reporting in one instance, as follows:

> Speed is important because in many cases short sellers don't approach the press unless they are already in trouble—a stock they have sold short is rising. One such instance involved the stock of Sunrise Savings & Loan Association of Florida, which last October was the subject of several negative articles. The troubled thrift was declared insolvent this summer and was taken over by federal regulators.
>
> One short seller had "major unrealized losses" in the stock, which reached a high of $17.50 a share in October 1984, after trading as low as $10.25 the preceding August. "We were under severe pressure," he says, recalling that he felt it was important that the stock "be punished."
>
> Hoping to get a story published that would be favorable to his investment position, he says, "I urged a friend of mine [who purported to have] a good line into Barron's" to call the weekly financial magazine with the story idea. While the short seller did much of the research that his group presented to Barron's, "I never once talked to Barron's," he says. "They never knew the story came from me."
>
> *Wall Street Journal* reporters themselves had heard from short sellers that Barron's would be publishing a negative story in its next issue. The Journal, which treats Barron's as a competitor, rushed its own story on Sunrise into print the day before Barron's was published.
>
> Kathryn M. Welling, the managing editor of Barron's, says "four or five" individual sources, not just one, "mentioned the story to us" during the month it was being prepared. Ms. Welling says it is predictable that after any given story runs, many people will try to take credit for planting it. It would be erroneous to suggest that "all we are doing is running a free copier service," she says.[14]

An example of another common type of manipulation of the press is found in a pair of 1985 campaign stunts by Senator Alfonse M. D'Amato of New York. D'Amato and Representative Mario Biaggi staged a "Boston Tea Party" on the deck of a tall ship in New York Harbor to protest President Reagan's tax-reform proposals. They dressed up children as Indians, and they themselves heaved overboard cardboard boxes labeled "No Double Taxation" to protest the administration's effort to eliminate the federal deduction for payment of state and local taxes. This staged media event was calculated to influence by emotional impact rather than by reason. At about the same time, D'Amato also showed up on television and in the newspapers with federal agents as they moved in to make the largest hashish raid in New York's history. Before the raid, D'Amato's office called CBS News to be sure that cameras would record his presence during the raid. This too is an attempt to influence not by reason but by projecting an image, in this case that D'Amato was the embodiment of law and order.[15] In these examples, the press is simply the means to the manipulator's ends. The ultimate end is to manipulate the public, the government, financial markets, and so on.

We do not mean to suggest that these manipulations are always inappropriate, or unacceptable, but they are pervasive in journalism and deserve attention. In an insightful analysis, *Newsweek* reporters Charles Kaiser and Lucy Howard discussed the problems of "manipulative media handlers" such as politicians Robert Strauss and Jesse Jackson and theatrical figures Joseph Papp and Beverly Sills. In the case of such magnetic personalities, these reporters argue, there is only a "thin line between manipulating the public sensibility and simply doing something and being the magnet."[16] People with such special skills for charming or otherwise managing the press are able to maneuver reporters to see a situation in the desired way, to induce them to lay off a story, to use friendship to affect the coverage, and so on, often without providing any more evidence or more persuasive reasons than someone with an alternative point of view but less charm.

Manipulation has often been characterized as necessarily immoral because it uses another person to one's ends without the other's consent.[17] However, we find this argument unpersuasive. The moral character of offering an incentive that noncoercively alters a person's choices—such as a retirement bonus incentive program intended to make early retirement attractive to employees—differs markedly from the moral character of an act of deception that tricks a person into doing that which he or she otherwise would not do. Yet both are manipulative under our definition. Manipulation can also take many different forms, with many degrees of justifiability. For example, there is manipulation by offering rewards and by threatening punishments. But for our purposes the most important type of manipulation is manipulation of information, in which a person's perception of options is modified by affecting that person's understanding of the situation by a means other than truthful disclosure or persuasion.

## Manipulating the News

To manipulate through the selective or otherwise deceptive use of information, the manipulator does not change the actual options; only the conception or cognitive processing is modified as a result of the manipulation. For example, an automobile salesperson who intentionally suppresses a vital piece of information which, if known by a customer, would lead to a loss of a sale, has manipulated the customer into a purchase by controlling his or her understanding of the situation.

Manipulations involving the deceptive use of information generally require that the persons being manipulated be kept in at least partial ignorance or confusion. Sometimes it is even necessary for them to be completely unaware of the attempt to influence so that they cannot resist. If the manipulation does not cause the person to significantly misunderstand the range of available choices, then it may be compatible with free decision making. However, in the cases of interest here the manipulation will not be compatible with free action, and this incompatibility is the basic moral problem of manipulative influence.

An example of a drastically crude manipulation of information played a part in causing the resignation of Darren Tully, the publisher of two of Arizona's largest newspapers, *The Phoenix Gazette* and *The Arizona Republic*. Tully had spread false stories that he was a decorated veteran of the Korean and Vietnam wars. He had never even served in the military. When the stories were challenged by Maricopa County attorney Tom Collins, investigative reporters began to appear in Tully's papers that Collins was guilty of embezzlement and other offenses, accusations that also proved to be false. Tully had cleverly assembled highly selective information mixed with false statement both to enhance his reputation and to try to ruin the reputation of his accuser.[18]

Consider, by contrast, a more subtle example of the manipulation of information: *Newsweek* magazine's exceptional treatment of the so-called Hitler diaries. We quote here the first two paragraphs of a thirteen-page cover story.

> The writer, *we are told,* is Adolf Hitler. The words, most of them, are banal and cryptic, the mundane jottings of an unlettered man who seems at times to be less an evil genius than a petty civil servant. He frets about his digestion, carps about his friends and passes by in silence just when we expect him to bare his soul about something that really matters. And yet what he does write reeks of history. Here is Hitler on Munich, on Dunkirk; Hitler on Chamberlain, Churchill, Mussolini and Stalin; Hitler on the Jews, always the Jews. In all, 13 of the most hideous years in human experience are described by the man who did so much to make them vile.
>
> To the astonishment of Nazis who knew him and scholars who have studied him, it *now appears* that Adolf Hitler secretly kept a handwritten diary from mid-1932 until two weeks before his death in 1945. Through all those years, Hitler scribbled away on lined paper in hard-bound, black-covered notebooks. Most were sealed with a red wax imprinted with the eagle and swastika of the Third Reich. They were signed by Hitler and by his alter ego, Martin Bormann, or Deputy Fuhrer Rudolf Hess. The

diaries were flown out of Berlin just before the fall. When the plane crashed in what is now East Germany, a Wehrmacht officer picked up the books and hid them in a hayloft. Two years ago, *Der Stern,* a West German weekly magazine, began to buy the 60 volumes, apparently through one or more middlemen. This week, *Stern* and a string of clients will begin to publish *Hitler's odd archive* all over the world.[19]

*Newsweek* three times introduced questions about the authenticity of the diaries in boxes, headlines, and on the cover before beginning the actual text of the article. The cover carried a picture of Hitler, a red slash under the masthead announcing a "Special Report," a headline saying "Hitler's Secret Diaries," and a line one-half-inch high that asked, "Are They Genuine?" followed by two lines in identical type size that read, "How They Could Rewrite History" and "Hitler and the Jews." On the contents page a box at the top carried the headline "Hitler's Secret Diaries" and said the following in full:

> The mystery is *that they survived* at all—60 slim volumes bound in black and filled with archaic German script that *appeared to be* the handwriting of Adolf Hitler himself. Nearly four decades after the collapse of the Third Reich, *Hitler's secret diaries have come to light* in West Germany. The volumes span the years 1932–1945—the years of Hitler's rise and Germany's ruin, of Munich and Dunkirk, of D-Day and the Holocaust. NEWSWEEK's SPECIAL REPORT explores the diaries' cryptic reflection of the Fuhrer's inner life, *the question of their* authenticity and their treatment of Hitler's complicity in the murder of 6 million Jews.[20]

Then, at the beginning of the thirteen-page package, after a large bold-face headline announcing once again "Hitler's Secret Diaries," there is a far smaller subhead that begins, "*If they are authentic . . .*" Five pages into the main package on the diaries, there is an article spread over two pages, containing about one full page of type, that examines the debate over the authenticity of the diaries. The first third or so is devoted to evidence cited by *Der Stern* to demonstrate that the diaries are genuine. The rest of this article on the authenticity question is spent mainly on a discussion of how difficult it is to verify historical documents and questioning whether the Germans had seen enough to reach a definitive conclusion about their authenticity.

On the face of it, *Newsweek* appears to have met its obligations to its readers by notifying them prominently that the authenticity of the diaries is in question. On a more subtle analysis, however, *Newsweek* did not present the story as if authenticity were seriously in question. First, it was the cover story and was published in a highly unusual thirteen-page special report. Second, it devoted only one and a half pages of the thirteen to a discussion of whether the diaries were genuine, the headline references to problems of authenticity were relatively few, and in discussing whether the diaries were genuine, *Newsweek* treated the skimpy evidence in support of authenticity as at least as great or greater in weight than the much more formidable body of opinion arguing for skepticism about their authenticity and even for rejection of the diaries as fake.

Finally, and most importantly, the main text was predominantly written as if the diaries were genuine. After the initial sentence with the disclaimer, "The writer, we are told, is Adolf Hitler," the next few paragraphs are filled with assertions about the diaries, such as, "They confirm," "They shed new light," and "They provide glimpses of Hitler's innermost thoughts." Not until the fifth paragraph does *Newsweek* ask, "But are they genuine?" After two paragraphs of raising doubts (based mainly on *Der Stern*'s rush to put the volume into print), *Newsweek* says: "But that didn't mean that the diaries were fraudulent. Other experts . . . concluded that the material was genuine." With the exception of a few queries sprinkled throughout the coverage and three paragraphs summarizing the dispute about authenticity, there is no evidence of skepticism about the diaries, and the text reads as if they were genuine. It may be—although it seems unlikely—that the editors of *Newsweek* were sufficiently convinced that the diaries were authentic to present them the way they did. But if they consciously structured the presentation to create the impression that the diaries were authentic, they were manipulating the information—and through the information manipulating their readers—by presenting a story that was not even close to being verifiably true as if it were factual. Even the first two paragraphs quoted above were written as if they were reporting on what had actually happened, not what would have happened had the diaries been genuine.

This case may appear to be a relatively subtle form of manipulation compared, for example, to using a source's words out of context to make a point at variance with what the source was clearly trying to convey. But it is also a more pervasive form of manipulation in journalism—one that relies on deceptive treatment of the available information that is unsustainable by the evidence and by reasoned argument. Despite the strategically placed disclaimers, the substantive presentation takes what is highly speculative and presents it through the language of facts. Michael J. O'Neill has provided a useful example of this kind of manipulation in daily journalism:

> I remember being desperate for a story once when I was a United Press editor in Washington. So with few facts, but plenty of help from congressmen who cater quotes for any occasion, we produced a national scare about coffee prices, broke the coffee market, and started a wonderful row between the United States and Brazil.

> Creative activity like this is necessary because life simply doesn't supply enough sensations to meet the media's daily needs. When editors are stuck for a headline or producers need a lead for the evening news, they have to hustle up an expose, a new controversy, or a so-called news exclusive. This is called enterprise and enterprise stories appear by the gross to provide zest, sparkle, and shock to brighten even the dullest day.[21]

Deception in journalism uses intentional strategies such as withholding information and exaggerating that may lead readers and viewers to believe what is false. Earlier we referred to accusations in "The Uncounted Enemy: A Vietnam Deception" that William C. Westmoreland and others deceived the American public, manipulating public opinion as well as government action, by a process of deception. We have also noted that CBS seems itself to have been involved in manipulation of public opinion through deception in the way it presented its documentary. Some time after the trial, the program's producer, George Crile, avowed that "Gen. Westmoreland was a patriot. He was trying to win the war. . . . He was presumably acting in good faith. In a sense, I think we pushed too hard."[22] We interpret Crile's comment to mean that by failing (whether by design or inadvertently) to place Westmoreland's actions in a fuller context, while attempting to drive home a powerful thesis, CBS manipulated public opinion rather than merely attempting to persuade (by rational argument).

News organizations routinely use various forms of manipulation that alter the perceptions of and thereby the range of choices available to readers and viewers. Here is an example that was reported by the wife of a man held hostage in Iran in 1979:

> On the day the hostages returned from Iran, CBS asked me to join Dan Rather in the studio. At one point I remarked that while we were happy for the release of the hostages, we should also remember the eight who gave their lives in the aborted rescue attempt. Mr. Rather did not recall their names. However, since the camera was on me, he turned to an assistant off camera and mouthed the words "get me their names." In less than a minute the eight names appeared on a monitor. Never faltering, Mr. Rather continued, "Let us not forget . . . ," and he not only named each man but also included his branch of service and rank. I was shocked. I realized how all these years anchormen had impressed me as tremendously knowing, I never considered how the aura of savant is created. I have nothing against the technology that made the exchange possible, but I felt like Dorothy exposing the Wizard of Oz. It wasn't honest and the public has the right to know how the magic happens. If the audience does not understand the process, then news organizations exercise control and power without the audience's knowledge.[23]

Minor manipulations of this kind cultivate false beliefs about the anchorman's knowledge and trust based on illusion, which in turn fosters the network's goal of manipulating viewers into tuning in regularly to its news program.

Another type of manipulation by journalists involves a reporter impersonating someone else to get sources or subjects of stories to disclose something they would not otherwise disclose. Consider the deception Ben Bagdikian used in a major series of articles for *The Washington Post,* titled "The Shame of the Prisons." Bagdikian wrote the following in the second of eight articles:

> For three months I had looked at the American prison system as an outsider, observing men behind bars and talking about them the way a tourist visits a zoo. Prison experts agreed that perception of what it means to be imprisoned in America remains dim unless you are on the other side of the bars. They were right. Months of interviewing prisoners, former prisoners, corrections administrators and research scientists, as well as reading dozens of books and reports, had not prepared me for the emotional and intellectual impact of maximum security incarceration.[24]

Bagdikian judged that the only way he could convey to readers what it was like to be a prisoner in such an institution was to become a prisoner, and that in the context of a "serious look at the whole system" it was worth it. Short of committing a crime and earning entry, the only way to get inside was through deception. After much effort, Bagdikian persuaded J. Shane Creamer, attorney general of the state of Pennsylvania, to allow him to enter the Huntingdon State Correctional Institution in the guise of a transfer from a county prison who was awaiting grand-jury action on a murder charge. Using a false name, Bagdikian was brought to Huntingdon by two undercover state policemen. Once they had departed, no one in the prison, including the warden, knew his real identity. The risk was substantial. "I worry for a moment," he wrote, "if my project had been secret enough. Weeks earlier I was about to enter the Oklahoma State Penitentiary at McAlester when an ex-convict visited me and said, 'You'll never get out alive. Too many people know about it and the grapevine down there has picked it up.' . . . A prisoner entering under false pretenses is automatically assumed to be a planted informer, an occupation with high mortality rates."[25]

Deception was the only way to get the story in this case, but was there an adequate justification for the deception and consequent manipulation of the prison officials and prisoners who were deceived about Bagdikian's identity? In other words, was the story important enough to justify the deception used, and what harm, if any, might the deception have done to those deceived? The two questions cannot be answered independently. The importance of publishing the story would have to be weighed against the possible detrimental impact on the prison warden, the prison guards, the prisoners, and the enterprise of journalism. Bagdikian signed a waiver removing responsibility from prison authorities for anything, including death, that might happen to him while in Huntingdon. The prison was also selected for stability, and Bagdikian went in just before Christmas, usually a quiet time in prisons. But prison officials might still have lost their jobs or been demoted or transferred had anything happened to him. With respect to the value of the story itself, how important is it, for example, for ordinary citizens to read a graphic account of life inside a maximum-security prison? An adequate answer to that and similar questions is beyond the scope of this book, but a short answer is that a story like Bagdikian's, in the context in which it was presented, is potentially very important, because it could provide the public with a significant insight into the functioning of a key element of the criminal-justice system.

The available evidence and the outcome—Bagdikian emerged unscathed and wrote a compelling and informative account of his six days in Huntingdon—suggest that the *Post* made a morally justifiable decision in allowing its reporter to engage in this particular manipulation. It is a situation, however, in which the men of Huntingdon would be entitled if they sought it to an account from the *Post* of how and why the decision was made. (See Chapter 8 on accountability.) But even without this justification from the *Post,* we are persuaded that the manipulation was warranted, and we would not classify it as immoral merely because it was manipulative. Consequently, we do not believe the deception involved casts journalists in a bad light or in any significant way undermines their ability to do their jobs and serve the public.

Press conferences and news releases are also often used to manipulate the media and thereby public opinion. For example, corporations release selected financial information through the media to put the best possible face on their earnings and growth potential; terrorists who hold hostages release only what they want the world to hear about their objectives, while suppressing everything they want the world to forget or hope it will never discover. Leaks from sources, of course, often have similar goals.

High-level international meetings also may be specifically arranged to deliver a message through the media, as happened in September 1985 when U.S. Treasury Secretary James Baker called a meeting on short notice of the so-called Group of Five to do something about the inflated value of the U.S. dollar, which was having a distorting effect on international trade. The top finance officials of Britain, France, West Germany, and Japan met with Baker and issued a vague statement that played back in the press as a "major international effort to lower the [value of the] dollar." In the judgment of syndicated columnist Joseph Kraft, with whom we concur, this "brilliantly orchestrated media event" led to the following actions:

"Spurred by media stories, private holders of dollars sold out on a large scale and the Federal Reserve, this country's central bank, reinforced their action by also selling dollars. During the day, the dollar dropped by nearly 5 per cent." Kraft even interviewed a Federal Reserve official who said, "It's all a media hype," and who acknowledged that the media message had been organized by the U.S. Treasury.[26]

Similarly, world leaders are well placed to manipulate public opinion through deft use of the media. Commenting on an interview with Soviet General Secretary Mikhail Gorbachev in *Time*,[27] Jeane Kirkpatrick, former U.S. representative at the United Nations, wrote: "Gorbachev offered *Time* magazine an opportunity in exchange for an opportunity: *Time* would have its scoop, Gorbachev would have a credible means of direct communication with the American public." Kirkpatrick went on to accuse Gorbachev of "hyping" the level of tension in the world by calling it "explosive" while "the American media . . . hyped the hype."[28]

An example of the "hype" can be found in *Time*'s introduction to the interview, one paragraph of which said:

> The voice is extraordinary, deep but also quite soft. Sometimes Gorbachev talks for several minutes in a near whisper, low and melodious. Then, without warning, his voice can cut across the room. It is not angry or bullying, just stronger than any other sound in the room. Occasionally the eyes, the hands and the voice reach peak power at the same time, and then it is clear why this man is General Secretary.[29]

Substitute the word "God" for "General Secretary" and the rhetoric would almost seem more appropriate. No doubt *Time* is attempting to capture the man's considerable presence and power, but superman characterizations are more like advertising than reporting and can easily be manipulative. Gorbachev also controlled the agenda in this interview. He spoke of nothing he did not want to discuss. The subject of human rights, for example, was never addressed.[30]

As a rough generalization, the press reports whatever it can learn without a keen sense of or an effective way of determining how the reporting itself will play a part in the manipulation of public opinion. Governments sometimes covertly take advantage of this failure of the press to distinguish between persuasion and manipulation by sources. Soviet intelligence agencies, for example, frequently use a technique called *desinformatsia*, which involves planting carefully structured lies in the press. Soviet disinformation usually involves a distortion of the record intended to favor the Soviet Union, and it has involved various means to this end, including a forged State Department cable on El Salvador, ghostwritten stories released through Western journalists, or in one case a letter bearing the forged signature of the U.S. ambassador to Austria, which appeared to disclose that the United States was trying to persuade neutral Austria to develop military ties with the West.[31] In general, the purpose of Soviet disinformation is to undermine Western institutions by using journalists who can be manipulated. This goal is especially easy to achieve in the case of journalists who must depend on sources they cannot investigate for their basic supply of information.[32]

According to a study prepared by David Whitman, the United States used a covert method in 1978 that did not involve lying in an attempt to manipulate the Western European press into favorable coverage of the neutron bomb. Whitman reported: "The U.S. decision in January 1978 to institute a covert action program in Western Europe to build support for the neutron bomb was prompted by covert and semi-covert Soviet infiltration of the anti-neutron bomb movement in Europe, particularly in the Netherlands."[33] Whitman's study maintained that the plan had been developed by Leslie Gelb, director of politicomilitary affairs at the State Department, and George Vest, assistant secretary of state for European affairs. It was then approved by National Security Advisor Zbigniew Brzezinski and Secretary of State Cyrus Vance, as well as CIA Director Stansfield Turner. The point of the program was summarized by Gelb as an effort to

> get favorable newspaper articles in the Western European press. It was purely aimed at press coverage; we weren't trying to obstruct the renting of convention halls or anything like that. This campaign was chosen to supplement our overt activities, like having the embassies talk to European journalists. I don't know that I thought the covert action program would be decisive; I thought it would be reasonable to try to do.[34]

The covert campaign authorized payment to European journalists—itself a manipulation, of course—and attempted to promote the message that, compared to the Soviet SS-20 missile, the neutron bomb was a relatively limited weapon. The effectiveness of the U.S. campaign was evaluated by Whitman as follows:

> A sampling of British and German press coverage from the time indicates that the neutron bomb/SS-20 comparison, along with sharp criticisms of the Soviet propaganda campaign, began appearing frequently during February and March 1978. Newspapers, for example, like the Dusseldorf Rheinische Post, Die Welt, Bonn General Anzeiger, Freiburg Badische Zeitung, Rheinische Post, Suddeutsche Zeitung, Koblenz Rhein-Zeitung, London Times, London Daily Telegraph and The Economist, began either to contrast the dangers of the SS-20 vs. the neutron bomb or ridicule the Soviet propaganda campaign against the bomb.[35]

By working covertly to change the focus of the debate in Europe, the United States was doing what is done daily in Washington—selectively leaking or releasing information. Favorites among journalists were selected in accordance with the type and extent of coverage they could be expected to give to a particular story and in some cases by their potential for manipulation.

Perhaps the most pervasive tool used by government officials for manipulating the press is the carefully structured leak. Consider the following quotation of an unnamed source from a front-page story in *The Washington Post:* "There is no evidence that reporters were told anything we didn't want them to know." The source did not say that reporters were not told anything "classified" or anything that they "shouldn't know." [36] The source says directly that reporters were not told anything "we didn't want them to know." The leaks at issue in the *Post* story had to do with a matter debated among President Reagan's principal national security advisors— whether to launch U.S. air strikes against Syrian positions in Lebanon. The leak could have come from either those favoring the strikes or those opposing them,[37] but in either case the purpose of the leak would have been to manipulate opinion to influence policy by using the press as the agent of the selective disclosure.

Sometimes policy motives combine with personal motives in a campaign of manipulation, and it can happen that a reporter or small group of reporters is especially ripe to be manipulated because they share a bias with the leaking source. Jeane Kirkpatrick expressed how she had encountered the problem as follows:

> Undocumented allegations and anonymous sources link private ambitions to public policy in labyrinthine webs of personal and political relations. Two or three well-placed "sources" working together with two or three well-placed journalists can create an issue, shape an interpretation, build or destroy a reputation. From the perspective of political science, it is fascinating. From the perspective of public office, it is frustrating beyond belief.[38]

Kirkpatrick charged that lies were leaked to the press, and then eagerly published, about the advice she was giving Reagan on U.S. policy in Central America. If her allegation is correct, it is an example of a pervasive form of the manipulative leak, this time conceived by the source to mislead the public. In cases of this kind reporters may be disposed to believe that the information they are being fed is true, but the care they give to confirming it before publication will express their concern about being manipulated, and it may also say something about their ability to transcend personal biases.[39]

Still another form of manipulation of the public involves a complicity between journalists and advertisers in which advertising material is packaged to look like news. *Consumer Reports* has provided a number of examples drawn from the electronic and print media.[40] In a promotion for

Spic and Span, Procter and Gamble put fake diamonds in more than 2 million boxes of the cleaning product and real diamonds worth about $600 each in 500 boxes. Procter and Gamble's publicist, Hill and Knowlton, sent 90–second videotapes to television stations around the country with the story line that it is hard to tell fake diamonds from the real thing and that sales of the bogus diamonds were growing rapidly. The videotape was larded with "news" of the Procter and Gamble promotion. Hill and Knowlton said the videotape was used on the air in at least twenty-seven cities, including San Francisco, Dallas, Boston, and New York.

The television news directors who allowed this material to go on the air as "news," unidentified in any way as having been supplied by a public relations firm and with the sole goal of promoting a product—in this case, Spic and Span—are guilty of either being manipulated unwittingly or of participating in a manipulative scheme.

*Consumer Reports* also wrote that "In January [1986] *The New York Times* ran a special supplement on health in the form known as an 'advertorial.' In size and general appearance it resembled *The New York Times Magazine* . . . while the supplement was labeled as advertising in small, light print, the *New York Times* logo appeared on the cover, and the reader would have had to read carefully to discern that the *New York Times* news staff played no role in preparing it." By failing to clearly identify the supplement as advertising, the *Times* is guilty of complicity in a manipulation of the public. The use of small, light print designating the supplement as advertising hardly seems accidental. If the *Times* were concerned that the supplement be recognized as advertising, one would expect the paper to demand that it be more clearly identified as such.

Finally, *Consumer Reports* noted in the spring of 1982 that Eli Lilly launched a publicity package for its antiarthritis drug, Oraflex. The Lilly press package, however, omitted crucial information. Eleven days before it began its public relations campaign the *British Medical Journal* published several articles on severe adverse effects associated with the drug. Although according to the FDA this information was widely known in the medical community three days before Lilly sent out its publicity package, many television and radio stations used the public relations material as the source of their broadcasts. *Consumer Reports* wrote that "According to an FDA internal memorandum dated July 10, 1982, 'These broadcasts were of a uniform character; i.e. they all described Oraflex as being a potential remittive agent and as having a minimal potential for side effects. In fact, several broadcasts over different networks used nearly identical wording in these descriptions.' . . . The FDA's internal memorandum takes particular note of a report on ABC-TV network news on May 19. The report, the memorandum says, 'included a statement that physicians regard side effects related to Oraflex as being minor when compared to aspirin.' "

Oraflex was removed from the market in the United States in August 1982. Federal investigators maintain that it was a factor in the deaths of at least twenty-six Americans, and in the summer of 1985 Lilly pleaded guilty to charges of not informing federal officials that Oraflex had been linked to deaths and illnesses in foreign countries. The Oraflex case exemplifies the potential dangers when the press is manipulated through insufficient awareness.

## Reporting the News and Causing the News

Thus far we have largely been addressing manipulation, which is by definition intentional, but the press sometimes inadvertently causes news, a common and problematic phenomenon in journalism, whose consequences are often identical to those of manipulation.

Consider this example. *The Boston Globe* was accused by John R. Lakian, a Republican businessman, of intentionally sabotaging his political career in 1982 through a story by Walter V. Robinson about "discrepancies" in Lakian's personal history and business record.[41] Lakian, a conservative, alleged that the "liberal" *Globe* had engaged in character assassination and lies in an attempt to prevent him from being elected governor of Massachusetts. The *Globe*'s accusation was, in effect, that Lakian had lied in an attempt to gain public office, whereas Lakian's charge was that the *Globe* had lied in an attempt to prevent him from being elected by manipulating public opinion. It became clear during the course of the trial that Robinson's story contained significant errors, but not ones that clearly revealed an intent to sabotage Lakian's campaign. If the errors were intentional, a charge of manipulation against the *Globe* could be sustained. But even if they were inadvertent, the *Globe* and Robinson may have contributed to Lakian's defeat by distortion of the record. If they did, this is a case of the press playing a part in causing the news by improperly influencing the public's understanding and consequent action.

Here is another example, in which the press almost certainly played some role in causing the news. In May 1985, a rumor began to spread in Baltimore that Old Court Savings and Loan was in dire financial straits and might fail. Starting with a front-page story in *The Baltimore Sun* on May 9, the local press ran with the story, quickly spreading the news of potential disaster at that institution and implicating all Maryland savings and loan associations that were protected by a state rather than federal insurance system (FSLIC). The reporting spread from local Baltimore–Washington news sources to the national news media, which repeatedly carried—for several weeks—pictures of long lines of nervous investors outside the doors of Old Court and other savings and loan institutions, together with reminders of similarities with great bank failures of the 1930s. *Newsweek*'s headlines were simply "The Maryland S & L Panic,"[42] while *Business Week*'s asserted that "Washington Wrangles as the Thrift Crisis Deepens."[43] *Barron's* offered advice in its headlines: "When Bank Fails, Buy Bonds."[44] Perhaps the most important statement in its social impact came in a single line of a *Washington Post* editorial (a point of view present in subtle ways in other reports of this situation): "As a practical matter, the governor's emergency order limiting withdrawals to $1,000 a month will probably be the end of those S & L's with no federal insurance."[45] Panic mounted after this observation appeared in the region's most influential newspaper.

Little evidence for this editorial-page speculation had been provided by the *Post*. The "end" had not come for these institutions and was nowhere in sight for the vast majority of them. Many (not all) of these S & L's were financially sound, and others were able to merge with larger banks or S & L's. The *Post* judgment was hasty and its prediction unwarranted. It is undeniably true, however, that the savings and loan system in the United States generally rests in significant respects on investor confidence, because there are not now and never have been sufficient funds to cover withdrawals should all depositors seek them. This generalization is all the more true of a fairly weak insurance system such as the one then operating in Maryland. It is also true that there was a mounting problem about adequate insurance for thrifts in Maryland, and the day may have been inevitable when these weaknesses would come to light with the resultant panic and losses.

But a good case can be made that the crisis, panic, long lines at S & L's throughout the state, and massive state legislative and executive intervention were caused as much, if not more, by the media depiction of the situation as by any fatal weakness in the Maryland insurance system. Media presentations of panicky depositors, speculative evaluations, and flustered state officials, virtually all negative and with few reassurances, motivated depositors to do what they otherwise would never have thought of doing: removing their money from state-insured institutions in order to relocate the money, generally at lower interest rates, in federally insured institutions. The more reporters reported, the more news there was to report. Johnny Johnson, chief of staff to the governor of Maryland, berated reporters as follows (on May 10): "The name of the game in this is confidence. You make it very difficult. You become part of the story and no longer are reporters. The fact is you frighten people when you have pictures of lines."[46]

We are not suggesting that the media trumped up the entire story, thereby triggering the massive movement of funds and the resulting damage to the reputation of Maryland savings and loan institutions. Nor are we suggesting that the media should keep the public in the dark. But without widespread and sometimes misleading media attention there would not have been the panicked reactions witnessed during the last half of May throughout Maryland. To some extent, the media created the consequent legislative activity and did not merely report on it. Irrespective of intent, the consequence of the news reporting was to influence thousands of investors, as well as state legislators, to take new courses of action.

It would be inaccurate to describe the relevant media presentations in these circumstances as persuasive rather than manipulative. Little evidence was reported in the media to show that state-insured Maryland savings and loans in general were unsound. Moreover, as *Barron's* noted, it is ironic that the media presentation of the thrift crisis came at a time when most of the nation's savings and loan institutions—including those in Maryland—were recovering from a shaky period of bad loans. These difficulties had already been widely reported in financial periodicals but had not induced panic or withdrawals, probably because of the comparatively sober, analytical way in which that news had been presented by the financial press to its generally knowledgeable audience. Thus, at precisely the time when many savings and loan institutions were acting responsibly to protect themselves and their depositors against fluctuations in interest rates, the media presentation of a savings and loan crisis in Maryland began to turn public confidence against even the responsible institutions. Whether the redirecting of confidence was intentional or unintentional had no bearing on the outcome. The press became a player and therefore it deserves its fair share of the blame.

The press often justifies its reporting on sensitive issues on the ground that the outcome of events is unpredictable (whether or not the press reports on them), but the public needs the information in any case. This proposition sometimes but not always provides an adequate justification. Our point has not been that the savings and loan story ought not to have been reported, but rather that more care should have been exercised in presenting what was known and in drawing conclusions about the consequences that were likely to flow from the crisis. Unless it was a well-documented or foregone conclusion that those S & L's without federal insurance would collapse, why write that "as a practical matter, the governor's emergency order limiting withdrawals to $1,000 a month" would probably spell their doom? This is a moral issue, and not merely one about adequate documentation, because of the potentially harmful consequences that can flow from publishing such a sentence.

Another example of creating a controversy and then reporting on it developed in the British press. In July 1985 *The Sunday Times* was preparing a story about a pending BBC broadcast that would contain an interview with Martin McGuinness, alleged by some to be the chief of staff of the Provisional Irish Republican Army (IRA). Interviews with IRA representatives had been heard on British television before, but *The Sunday Times* apparently viewed the BBC broadcast as a potentially important news story and pursued it vigorously.[47] As the story was being prepared— on July 26, 1985—Prime Minister Margaret Thatcher gave a press conference in Washington. She was asked a hypothetical question by a *Sunday Times* reporter, who reminded her of a speech in which she had suggested that terrorists ought to be denied "the oxygen of publicity." The question concerned what she would say if British state-financed television "were to broadcast an interview with a leading terrorist like the IRA chief of staff." Thatcher, in ignorance of the pending broadcast and *Sunday Times* story, swallowed the bait and issued a volley of criticisms denouncing any such broadcast as improper. The next day—July 27—the prime minister's aides figured out what had happened and called *The Sunday Times* to remind its editors that Thatcher had responded to a hypothetical question, not to a specific question about the planned BBC broadcast. However, the reporter and editors at *The Sunday Times* were putting the final gloss on a story that suggested the reverse—that Thatcher's remarks were directly relevant to the planned broadcast. The aides' comments were held for the following week's paper.

The July 28 front-page headline was "IRA: Thatcher Anger at BBC." The story falsely implied that Thatcher had denounced and was in direct conflict with the BBC over the decision to air the interview with McGuinness. There ensued a particularly furious debate in Britain not over what *The Sunday Times* had done but over the alleged government attempt to censor the BBC broadcast. The BBC's board of governors eventually canceled the broadcast, following a request that they do so from Thatcher's home secretary, Leon Brittan. The board of governors denied that political pressure was the cause, citing instead "lack of balance in the programme."[48] Nevertheless, the British press almost uniformly denounced the BBC's board of governors for damaging the BBC's reputation for independence. The National Union of Journalists called for a strike, and the BBC's news department was silenced for the first time in its fifty-three-year history. Many programs normally broadcast by other departments were not aired because their staffs walked out in sympathy. Politicians were locked in dispute over the issue for days thereafter.

*The Sunday Times* then wrote an editorial in which everyone but itself was condemned for immoderate behavior. Yet it was *The Sunday Times* that had manipulated Thatcher into her first volley of denouncements and then compounded the problem by manipulating politicians and journalists into an unnecessary controversy in which everyone (except perhaps *The Sunday Times*) came up a loser. It caused the news and then reported on it as if it had played no casual role.

Part of the problem in journalism, as in the social sciences, is a simple lack of sensitivity to the potential effects of what is reported. Reporters are assigned or otherwise accept certain roles that are relatively free of restraints that we would expect of someone in a different role—such as that of a government official—but without appreciating the responsibility attached. Consider the example of David Hartman's handling of live interviews with an American hostage, Allyn Conwell, and the Shiite Moslem leader and Amal militia leader Nabih Berri, who was also Lebanon's minister of justice. Unlike his more polished ABC colleague, Ted Koppel, Hartman permitted his show to be transformed into a platform for statements from both Conwell, who professed considerable sympathy with the Amal movement, and Berri, the terrorists' spokesperson. Hartman even asked the Amal leader if he had any message for the president, thereby aggrandizing himself and offering Berri the status of a negotiator with the president of the United States as well as a live opportunity to impress the American public and possibly influence negotiations that were already underway. (Immediately thereafter ABC began to apply its news guidelines to Hartman's "Good Morning America," a program classified as part of the entertainment division.)

The public was subtly subjected in this broadcast to the viewpoint that the American and Israeli administrations were basically responsible for the plight of the hostages and for the failure to negotiate a settlement. Largely forgotten was how these men came to be hostages. In a similarly structured program on CBS, Dan Rather also permitted out-of-context, propagandizing statements from similar sources, but at least Rather raised questions about whether such interviews should be done at all, and he reminded viewers that they might want to bear in mind that the hostages spoke "as prisoners."

Jack Smith, Washington bureau chief and a CBS vice president, reviewed CBS and other networks' coverage, as well as print coverage, of the crisis and pronounced it had been "responsible, objective, and dependable." In reviewing CBS's reporting, he said, he had found "virtually nothing that I would want to take back or do differently."[49] A dramatically different estimate, however, was offered by *Newsweek*'s Jonathan Alter, who catalogued one troublesome and controversial aspect of the coverage after another, especially the scurrying about of the networks to comply with the terrorists' offers and demands. Alter's final judgment coincides with ours. "The networks fought bitterly for the honor of being manipulated most often by the Shiites. . . . The Shiite hijackers . . . got exactly what they wanted out of the news media: a conduit for their cause and their demands. . . . Television in particular crossed the line from covering the story to becoming part of it."[50] The press and the public were, in effect, being manipulated by the terrorists, who were in firm control of virtually every major dimension of the story.

More responsible, less manipulative coverage is not difficult to imagine. It would require a sense of perspective about the personalities and the stakes involved. It would be less repetitive and would give less air time to the terrorists and events staged by them such as press conferences, interviews with individual hostages, and contrived social events such as seaside lunches. It would also avoid mischievous interviews with so-called experts who second-guess the government even though they are aware of the constraints that prevent policy makers from following their advice and with family members who may inadvertently disclose information that endangers their captive relatives, and who are often exploited by openly personal and intrusive questioning.

We can point in this instance to a prime example of thoughtful, responsible, unmanipulative coverage in *Newsweek* (June 24–July 15, 1985). Although its covers were dramatic, *Newsweek*'s coverage showed admirable restraint, objectivity, comprehensiveness, and balance—the criteria of quality journalism we have discussed in previous chapters. *Newsweek* also placed the events in their cultural context and in proper sequence, explained the nature of the terrorism and Islamic fundamentalism involved (beyond Lebanon into other nations), analyzed the U.S. government's policy dilemmas, analyzed whether television helps or hurts, examined the public's reaction as well as the government's handling of the crisis, interviewed Nabih Berri without mindlessly promoting his interests, and offered an analysis of how terrorism can be fought rather than accommodated.

It does not require any special knowledge to report on terrorism without being manipulated. In the print media, covering terrorism is little different in this respect from covering other fast-breaking international stories like airplane crashes and border skirmishes. The challenge for television is greater because of the competitive nature of the networks and the perceived imperative that television must be entertaining (gripping, dramatic, moving). If the networks are interested in avoiding being manipulated, however, they will plan future coverage of terrorism principally in terms of the imperatives of good journalism such as getting the story straight, getting it in context, and weighing the potential harms and benefits of the various coverage options. In the case of TWA 847, use of these criteria would not have produced dull coverage. It might have produced less coverage, which on reflection, even network executives might agree, would have been an improvement.

## Conclusion

In Chapter 6 we referred to a poll showing that 42 percent of the American public believes that their newspapers "attempt to manipulate them." This suspicion is not entirely unfounded, but manipulation is not always the product of the press's intention to manipulate. The press is often an innocent instrument of manipulation by others, rather than the actual manipulator, and in some situations where manipulation effectively occurs there may be no intention to manipulate at all. There may also be some confusion over the distinction between manipulation and persuasion. Sometimes the press is viewed as manipulative when in fact it is only offering reasoned argument or analysis.

We have traced problems of news manipulation that are caused by media involvement in the newsmaking process and other problems that result from manipulation of the media by sources. Involvement of the media in the news-making process is sometimes unavoidable and not always undesirable or improper. For manipulation to be unacceptable, there must be not only a manipulative influence but an undue or unjustified influence. In general, however, manipulation of readers and viewers through the deceptive use of information cannot be justified by political, social, or financial considerations. Nor can manipulation be justified on the ground that the reporter or editor thinks the story will have more impact if the evidence is presented in an imbalanced fashion, as is commonly done in television documentaries and investigative stories in newspapers.

NOTES

1. Michael J. O'Neill, "Media Power and the Dangers of Mass Information," *Nieman Reports*, Summer 1985, p. 32.

2. Thomas L. Friedman, "Palestinian-Israel Fight: Arab Lands Now Spectators," *The New York Times*, October 3, 1985, pp. A1, A10.

3. As quoted by Sydney H. Schanberg, "Governing by Headline," *The New York Times*, February 2, 1985, p. 21. (Punctuation altered.)

4. Quoted in O'Neill, "Media Power," p. 30.

5. Editorial, *The Philadelphia Inquirer*, May 4, 1985, sec. A, p. 8.

6. Editorial, "Inhumanity to Lab Animals," as reprinted in *The International Herald Tribune*, August 2, 1985, p. 6.

7. For a journalist who did not miss the significance of alternatives at the time, see Boyce Rensberger, "More Research Using Lower Animals Urged," *The Washington Post*, May 13, 1985.

8. Vance Packard, *The Hidden Persuaders* (New York: Pocket Books, 1957).

9. Joseph Epstein, "True Virtue," *The New York Times Magazine*, November 24, 1985, p. 93.

10. David Hoffman, "Despite Botha Speech, Reagan Rejects Coercion of Pretoria," *The International Herald Tribune (Washington Post)*, August 19, 1985, p. 1.

11. See Donald Warwick and Herbert Kelman, "Ethical Issues in Social Intervention," in G. Zaltman, ed., *Processes and Phenomena of Social Change* (New York: Wiley, 1973), p. 409.

12. "A Reporter Who Doesn't Want to Be Used Must Consider the Sources of His Stories," *The Wall Street Journal*, September 5, 1985, p. 25.

13. Ibid.

14. Ibid.

15. See Ronald Grover, with Lee Walczak, "Why Senator D'Amato Isn't A Knee-Jerk Conservative Anymore," *Business Week*, June 24, 1985, pp. 106–7.

16. Charles Kaiser and Lucy Howard, "How to Handle the Press," *Newsweek*, April 19, 1982, pp. 93–94; see also Hodding Carter III, "On TV One Picture Is Worth a Thousand Lies," *The Wall Street Journal*, May 10, 1984, p. 35.

17. See Richard T. DeGeorge, *Business Ethics* (New York: Macmillan, 1982), p. 192.

18. Brenton R. Schlender, "Publisher Resigns over Statements on Veteran Status," *The Wall Street Journal*, December 27, 1985, p. 5.

19. "Hitler's Secret Diaries," *Newsweek*, May 2, 1983, p. 50. Emphasis added.

20. Ibid., p. 3. Emphasis added.

21. O'Neill, "Media Power," p. 33.

22. Associated Press, "CBS Producer Criticizes Westmoreland Program," *The Washington Post*, May 4, 1985, p. A5.

23. Barbara Rosen, "Hostage to the Manipulations of a Medium," *The Wall Street Journal*, September 12, 1985, op-ed page.

24. Ben H. Bagdikian, "The Shame of the Prisons," *The Washington Post*, January 31, 1972, p. A1.

25. Ibid., p. A12; and telephone interview, February 3, 1986.

26. Joseph Kraft, "A Positive Shock," *The Washington Post*, September 29, 1985, p. B7.

27. "An Interview with Gorbachev," *Time*, International Edition, September 9, 1985, pp. 10–17.

28. "Is He Creating the New Soviet Man?" *The Washington Post*, September 15, 1985, p. D8.

29. "An Interview with Gorbachev," p. 10.

30. See the criticisms by Stephen S. Rosenfeld, "Bargaining on Human Rights," *The Washington Post*, September 13, 1985, p. A25.

31. See Stephen Engelberg, "If It's Too Bad to Be True, It Could Be Disinformation," *The New York Times*, November 18, 1984, p. E3; Ladislav Bittman, *The*

*KGB and Soviet Disinformation: An Insider's View* (Washington: Pergamon-Brassey's, 1985), written by the former deputy chief of the disinformation department of Czech intelligence.

32. See Andrew Nagorski, *Reluctant Farewell: An American Reporter's Candid Look Inside the Soviet Union* (New York: New Republic/Holt, Rinehart, Winston, 1985).

33. David Whitman, "The Press and the Neutron Bomb," published by the Kennedy School of Government, Harvard University, 1983, p. 95.

34. Ibid., p. 96.

35. Ibid., pp. 96–97.

36. Lou Cannon, "Justice Probe Fails to Disclose Source of Leaks on Mideast," *The Washington Post*, December 16, 1983, p. A1.

37. See Lou Cannon, "FBI's Probe Fails to Turn Up Source of Leaks on Lebanon," *The Washington Post*, December 16, 1983, p. A10.

38. Jeane Kirkpatrick, "Pardon Me, But Am I That 'Hardliner' the Anonymous Sources Are Talking About?" *The Washington Post*, June 20, 1983, p. A11.

39. On this topic, see Richard Halloran, "A Primer on the Fine Art of Leaking Information," *The New York Times*, January 14, 1983, p. A16.

40. "Advertising in Disguise," *Consumer Reports*, March 1986, pp. 179–81.

41. "A New Spin on Libel at the Boston Globe," *Newsweek*, August 19, 1985, p. 69; and "Judge Dismisses Libel Case Against the Boston Globe," *The Wall Street Journal*, August 13, 1985, p. 4.

42. Tom Nicholson, with Rich Thomas, "The Maryland S & L Panic," *Newsweek*, May 27, 1985, p. 50.

43. Blanca Riemer, with Christopher S. Eklund, Alex Beam, Kathleen Deveny, and G. Dave Wallace, "Washington Wrangles as the Thrift Crisis Deepens," *Business Week*, May 27, 1985, pp. 128–30.

44. Randall W. Forsyth, "When Banks Fail, Buy Bonds," *Barron's*, May 20, 1985, pp. 13, 22, 24.

45. Editorial, "Maryland and the S & Ls," *The Washington Post*, May 16, 1985, sec. A, p. 22. The *Post* later moderated its prediction. See Editorial, ". . . And S & Ls in Maryland," October 4, 1985, p. A22.

46. As quoted in Eleanor Randolph, "Media and the S & L Crisis," *The Washington Post*, May 26, 1985, p. C5.

47. This claim and the account presented herein are based on Andrew Kull, "Did the British Press Create the BBC Controversy?" *The Wall Street Journal*, August 7, 1985, p. 17, reprinted as "The Sunday Times Scoop Was One Mear Feat," in *The Wall Street Journal*—European Edition (our source); George V. Higgins, "The Documentary the BBC Banned," *The Wall Street Journal*, August 14, 1985, p. 20; "The BBC's News Blackout," *Newsweek*, August 19, 1985, p. 68; and James M. Perry, "BBC Policies Generate Static in Britain," *The Wall Street Journal*, September 4, 1985, p. 28.

48. "A Statement by the Chairman of the BBC," distributed by the BBC, issued August 6, 1985, p. 5.

49. As quoted in Eleanor Randolph (Washington Post Service), "Ex-CBS Official Assails TV's Role in TWA Crisis," *The International Herald Tribune*, August 2, 1985, p. 3.

50. Jonathan Alter, "The Network Circus," *Newsweek*, July 8, 1985, p. 21; and Jonathan Alter, with Michael A. Lerner and Theodore Stanger, "Does TV Help or Hurt?" *Newsweek*, July 1, 1985, pp. 32–33.

# Chapter *8*

# Inviting Criticism and Being Accountable

If news is in the eye of the beholder, who beholds the beholder? To put it another way, are the checks and balances on our professional performance adequate when they exist at all? To whom are we accountable?

> Morton Mintz,
> Reporter,
> *The Washington Post*[1]

Newspapermen have a special obligation to retain public confidence through conscious and deliberate effort to open ourselves to the public, to pay particular attention to complaints of unfairness, inaccuracy, bias, vindictiveness—that is, to make ourselves voluntarily accountable.

> John B. Oakes,
> Editorial Page Editor,
> *The New York Times*[2]

Since our freedom rests ultimately with the sovereign citizens, we should be alarmed when the public shows the disaffection it has been showing.

There is a large public perception that we in the press regard our power as unlimited, our freedom as unchallengeable and our accountability as virtually nil. . . . One day, we may have to reinvent the National News Council or something like it, and we'll wonder why such an institution was allowed to fail.

> Robert Maynard,
> Editor and Publisher,
> *The Oakland Tribune*[3]

The quotations above suggest that journalists need to be more accountable than they are. Morton Mintz asks rhetorically to whom journalists owe accountability. John B. Oakes and Robert Maynard assert that it is owed to the public, while suggesting that the public's justified demand for press accountability often goes unsatisfied. Each suggests that if journalism does not provide more effective mechanisms of accountability and put them into practice, a price will be paid.

Eliot Freidson probably had physicians, not journalists, in mind when he wrote the following passage about the risks of granting too much autonomy to professionals and therefore not demanding enough accountability of them, but the unresolved problems he has outlined are also omnipresent in journalism:

> This is the critical flaw in professional autonomy: by allowing and encouraging the development of self-sufficient institutions, it develops and maintains in the profession a self-deceiving view of the objectivity and reliability of its knowledge and of the virtues of its members. Furthermore, it encourages the profession to see itself as the sole possessor of knowledge and virtue, to be somewhat suspicious of the technical and moral capacity of other occupations, and to be at best patronizing and at worst contemptuous of its clientele. Protecting the profession from the demands of interaction on a free and equal basis with those in the world outside, its autonomy leads the profession to so distinguish its own virtues from those outside as to be unable to even perceive the need for, let alone undertake, the self-regulation it promises.[4]

Arrogant, contemptuous, patronizing, and unable to see or unwilling to admit its own flaws—this is the kind of criticism the public has leveled at the American press in recent years. To a considerable degree the public has been right: The press has not shown sufficient interest in standards or formal structures of criticism and accountability.

In this chapter we will consider the nature and role of criticism and accountability in journalism, various current controversies over press accountability, to whom journalists should be accountable, by whom they may legitimately be criticized, and how and by whom accountability should be enforced (if it should be enforced at all). We also will examine procedural and practical questions, such as whether voluntarily giving critics access to one's airwaves or print space is an effective means of making television and print journalism more accountable, whether journalism and government should enter into agreements about the coverage of events such as terrorism, whether journalists use a double standard of accountability, and whether unredressed excesses of press coverage are necessary costs of democracy.

## The Concept of Accountability

Unlike the common practice of inviting criticism from outsiders, the concept of accountability is unclear and subject to many interpretations. In ordinary English *accountable* means "answerable" and "liable to be called for an accounting." These terms are essentially synonyms, however, and therefore unilluminating. The concept of accountability as we use it assumes responsibility of the sort captured by the expression "the buck stops here." The person owes an account in the form of a clarification, explanation, or justification. Any valid account generally entails a relevant and justifiable explanation of one's actions given to someone to whom it is legitimately owed. For example, an employee can be fired for legitimate reasons such as inadequate job performance, and this reason can be part of an account given to the employee for the firing. But the employer cannot legitimately use as part of the account that the employee's grandfather was a union member or that the employee's politics offend the employer. These might be the real reasons for the firing, but explanatory reasons, even if they are true, are not always justifying reasons, and the latter alone qualify as an account in the pertinent sense.

In journalism, the duty to give an account might involve explaining and justifying many aspects of the production and publication or broadcasting of a news story. For example, an interview subject might believe that his meaning was distorted by the selection, editing, juxtaposition, or some other manipulation of what he said. "Giving an account" entails explaining and justifying why the words or segments were used as they were. Similarly, if a public official was maligned by an unidentified source in a newspaper article and not given an opportunity to respond, then accountability might require a public explanation and justification of why the source was unidentified, how the source was qualified to make allegations about the subject of the article, and why the subject was not given an opportunity to respond.

To qualify as an adequate justification, the account given must meet broad moral standards like fairness and truthfulness, as contrasted with standards that are purely personal or that simply reflect an institutional belief. We must be careful, however, not to be overly demanding. Any responsible attempt at giving justifying reasons probably will qualify as giving an account in our sense (although not necessarily as giving an adequate account), and there can be alternative or even competing accounts that qualify as justifying reasons. Therefore, parties who offer rival viewpoints can both discharge the duty of accountability.

The kinds of standards that are generally relevant in giving justifying reasons rest on legitimate expectations. If, for example, a reporter promises that he will protect a source's identity but does not do so, the reporter has failed to meet the source's proper and rightful expectations. As a result, the source is entitled to an account, and perhaps to some redress if hardship, costs, or risks are involved. This is no different from the duty of a professional who fails to meet the legitimate expectations of a client, as defined by the codes of the profession and the laws or traditions of society, to give the client an account and, depending on the circumstances, perhaps some form of redress.

Many think of accountability in terms of legal liability. This linkage is hardly surprising in a world where lawsuits against physicians, corporate board members and officers, and others in positions of responsibility are society's common vehicle for enforcing accountability and providing redress. Journalists, of course, are sometimes sued for libel, and the multimillion-dollar suits, especially those with celebrity plaintiffs, make headlines. But overall the press is well protected against frivolous lawsuits by the First Amendment. This is as it should be. In any event, legal liability is outside the scope of our concerns. We will treat accountability as a moral problem.

An example of the moral rather than legal character of the issues that concern us is found in *Washington Post* columnist Colman McCarthy's charge that the press often operates under a double standard: "We demand openness from others but not ourselves. The public is weary of double-standard journalism." McCarthy's ire had been raised by *The New York Times*'s controversial dropping of a twice-weekly column by Sydney Schanberg (which, coincidentally, often focused on government accountability). The *Times* had dropped the column without comment, and without making available information sought by other newspapers interested in pursuing the story. McCarthy thought an accountable newspaper would do the following: "Make the case. Present some facts. Be as candid with the public as newspapers demand others to be with them. . . . Instead of trying to reach the ideal the press likes to say it strives for—the public's right to know—here is a paper hurting all the media by saying: You only have a right to know what we want you to know."[5] There is no hint of a legal issue here, but moral issues of fairness, consistency, openness, truthfulness, and—most prominently of all—accountability are conspicuous.

McCarthy is on the track of one of the major problems of press accountability. If the press holds other persons and institutions accountable for their actions, should the press not be held accountable under the same or similar standards? We will examine this question as we proceed, but first we will explore two cases involving accountability that introduce the complexity of the problem. The first example explores a decision by the Public Broadcasting Service (PBS) to air an hour-long rebuttal to one of its programs, and the second probes criticism of and accountability in the coverage of terrorism.

## Two Controversies over Accountability

On June 26, 1985, PBS television stations around the country began show-ing a fifty-seven-minute tape narrated by Charlton Heston that criticized a widely praised thirteen-program PBS series on Vietnam. Although Hod-ding Carter, Ted Koppel, and others had previously produced television programs sharply critical of other television news and documentary pro-grams, this videotape was unusual for several reasons. First, it was shown on the same network as the documentary series it criticized. Second, it drew on the dramatic abilities and box-office appeal of a movie star and used various Hollywood techniques to criticize the restrained, historical documentary series. Third, the videotape was produced with the financial support of the U.S. government, in the form of a $30,000 grant from a discretionary fund controlled by the chairman of the National Endowment for the Humanities. Finally, it was produced entirely outside the network by a politically conservative press-monitoring organization called Accuracy in Media (AIM).

Many journalists thought that PBS either had bowed to political pres-sure from the Reagan administration or had made a serious error of judg-ment in agreeing to air the tape. Richard Ellison, executive producer of the series, said, "I can't prove it, but I suspect there was political pressure from the Administration."[6] Stanley Karnow, the respected journalist who wrote the series and the accompanying book, *Vietnam: A History,* called it a "dangerous precedent" and asked, somewhat rhetorically, "Is PBS going to let AIM or any other group respond [on the air] whenever they have a complaint?"[7]

Barry Chase, vice-president of PBS for news and public affairs, de-fended the network's decision to accept outside criticism and to give the critics air time. He said, "We had been interested for a long time in finding a way to do letters to the editor on television."[8] *New York Times* tele-vision critic John Corry similarly praised the decision as "important be-cause it addresses a persistent problem in television: How can the medium present grievances against itself? Print journalism has op-ed pages, letters to the editor and other devices for this. With few exceptions—ABC's 'Viewpoint' for one—television has none."[9]

Economic and technical considerations make it easier for a newspaper to use its own op-ed pages and letters columns to expose points of view at odds with those previously published than for a television network to provide air time for responses, but, like Corry, we support the policy in principle. PBS set a defensible precedent by deciding to air AIM's critique of its series on Vietnam. The subject was controversial, and there was no reason to consider the PBS series definitive or beyond criticism. Airing an alternative view was a public service, not unlike the public service rendered in a news story that publishes various sides of a controversial issue. Nonetheless, the airing of the critical rebuttal was not an exercise in accountability. Airing the criticism of others, while useful, is not equivalent to giving an account. PBS did not answer the criticisms; it merely aired them.

A discussion of the two broadcasts that immediately followed the AIM presentation, in which both sides were represented, came closer to satisfying the demand for accountability. But the discussion format proved an inadequate mechanism for answering many of the questions that would have required a response in a genuine account in our sense. PBS provided a valuable public service, which we applaud, but not an account. We do not mean to suggest that accounts are always the most appropriate reactions. Sometimes providing a forum for criticism is the fairest approach, and a response to the criticism would be out of place. It would be both inappropriate and impractical, for example, for columnists to engage in running debates with readers who criticize their columns in letters to the editor. Our present point is not that the press should always give an account, but only that acting to invite criticism is not the same as accountability and that the two ought not to be confused.

By contrast, in our second example accountability and not criticism is the central concern. At about the same time that the AIM response was aired, TWA Flight 847 was hijacked to Beirut. The television coverage of this seventeen-day hostage crisis stirred a whirlwind of comment, much of it critical (see pp. 205–7). One problem was that the networks gave the hijackers and their sponsors virtually unedited access to the airwaves. After the incident had ended, with the loss of one innocent life and the rest of the hostages safely home, Britain's Prime Minister Margaret Thatcher called on journalists to better define the limits of their accountability by adopting a "voluntary code of conduct" that would "starve the terrorists and the hijackers of the oxygen of publicity on which they depend."[10] (See p. 204 above for more detail.) Two days later, U.S. Attorney General Edwin Meese told the American Bar Association meeting in London that he agreed with Thatcher and recommended that journalists be asked to agree to "some principles [on coverage of terrorism] reduced to writing."[11]

After these attempts by Thatcher and Meese to codify the limits of accountability in this sphere, *The New York Times* interviewed a handful of news executives who disagreed vigorously with them:

A. M. Rosenthal, executive editor, *The New York Times:* "The Constitution, with its guarantees supported by the courts, has historically been the best code ever drawn up, and I really don't see any need to tinker with it."

Edward M. Joyce, president, CBS News: "Throughout our coverage of this most recent crisis, CBS News believes it acted responsibly and exercised voluntary restraint in reporting dictated by our own judgment and news standards."

Timothy J. Russert, vice-president, NBC News: "Any attempt by the Government to promulgate principles or plans by which the United States should cover hostage crises obviously raises the gravest First Amendment concerns and, in terms of the networks, antitrust concerns."

Richard Harwood, deputy managing editor, *The Washington Post:* It is not "desirable for the government to be initiating proposals of this kind."[12]

Two days earlier, veteran television correspondent Morton Dean had written:

The competitive zeal with which the networks chased after the story of the hostages should be celebrated as an example of what's right about the democratic system, not what's wrong with it.

There were, to be sure, some unruly and odious excesses. But I believe that such indiscretions are a worthwhile price to pay for a precious freedom that does not exist for more than 80 percent of the world's citizens.[13]

Op-ed articles and letters to newspapers and television networks led to other examinations of the TWA 847 coverage, including a "Viewpoint" program on which the presidents of ABC News and NBC News were evasive about whether the mounting criticism would lead to changes in their news practices.[14]

Their caution is warranted. If the press were to enter into agreements with the government to limits its coverage of events, or to tailor its coverage to the government's requirements, the press would abdicate its responsibilities to monitor government by ceding too much control over what is published or broadcast. But this valid concern should no preclude measures of accountability internal to the press. One can be entirely opposed to the government or any other group having the authority to control the media, while being in favor of the public having some established means of focusing its legitimate demands for accountability.

The defensiveness common to the four news executives' statements above is symptomatic of how difficult it has been for those in their positions to focus on legitimate questions of accountability. Instead they dread the specter of government regulation. Nevertheless, unlike the rebuttal aired by PBS, the responses made by these executives were moves toward accountability in that they were partial justifications of the behavior of their organizations, however inadequate. The issues that concern us in examples such as this are not *whether* the networks gave an account—they did—but the reasons why they did so, the quality of the reasons they offered, and to whom, if anyone, they viewed themselves as accountable.

## To Whom Is Accountability Owed?

Aside from the general public and readers and viewers—whose needs and rights we have discussed in several earlier chapters[15]—the principal categories of persons to whom accountability is owed include subjects of stories, sources, and supervisors and employers. These relationships are so disparate that we need to examine the nature of accountability in each case separately. Our list of categories does not include accountability to journalists as a group (sometimes referred to as accountability to the profession) because we do not think journalists are accountable to journalists as a group. Journalists are not a self-employed, self-administering group of professionals. They may be accountable to various peers and colleagues, and they may be obligated to give accounts to regulatory or monitoring groups established within journalism (see pp. 224–29). But there is no accountability to the group per se.

*Accountability to Employers. Washington Post* reporter Morton Mintz once argued that, for practical purposes, reporters' "accountability runs upward [toward employers] not outward [toward the public]."[16] This rueful statement was made in full knowledge of how different the work of journalists is from, for example, that of advertising salespeople or financial managers. Although business executives of news organizations should be as concerned about profits as those who sell cars or soap, journalists should be indifferent to whether their daily work—reporting or editing—directly enhances profitability or otherwise affects an employer's interests. Otherwise journalists would regularly entangle themselves in conflicts of interest.

The classic example is an editor failing to publish a legitimate news story that is potentially detrimental to the interests of an important advertiser, because the advertiser has made it known that he will discontinue the advertising if the story appears. The publisher of a newspaper (or the stockholders if the media organization is publicly held) is not morally entitled to demand that editors or reporters be accountable to them for failing to promote the paper's business interests in ways that conflict with journalistic obligations. Similarly, a reporter would not be morally accountable to a publisher for failing to do what a former publisher of *The New York Times,* for example, used to demand of one of his reporters, which was to keep Jewish organizations from bothering him.

Although newspapers, magazines, networks, and local radio and television stations are businesses that will fold if unprofitable, the news business is not just another business. As Supreme Court Justice Potter Stewart once noted, the press is the only business specifically singled out for protection by the Constitution.[17] Because of what this implies, avoidance of conflict between an employee's journalistic responsibilities and an employer's nonjournalistic interests is imperative.

*Accountability to Subjects.* Subjects of stories are generally the parties most directly affected by their publication. Many will be unharmed by their moment in the spotlight, but others will be projected into the public eye in a manner harmful to their interests. Their private sorrows might be exploited; they might be defamed, made to suffer financial losses, or any number of other unpleasantnesses. There may be compelling reasons to cast a subject into the public eye against his or her will, even if risk to reputation, legal risk, or financial risk is inevitable; but there should be effective measures to ensure accountability for risks imposed, even on subjects whose interests are damaged as a result of the legitimate pursuit of news.

Some subjects, directly or otherwise, control major institutions, and they may court the press in order to publicize their activities and advance their causes or fortunes. Some are elected officials, others have been appointed by elected officials, others are civil servants on the public payroll, and still others are box-office stars. The public is entitled to know how well these public officials and public figures are carrying out their duties and performing in their roles. Because these persons are often directly accountable to the public, the press must have the freedom to report on how their conduct bears on the public interest. But even presidents and pop stars are entitled to the presumption that the press will treat them fairly—not with exquisite delicacy perhaps, and not always even politely, but fairly.

What form of accountability is appropriate if a public official or other public figure suffers from unfairness at the hands of the media? A libel action exacts a high price from both the plaintiff and the media organization, both economically and emotionally. Moreover, legal recourse does not resolve the moral issues of accountability. The law generally is not a promising device, because it permits journalists to be unfair in various ways to public officials and public figures, without having to give any account of their behavior. Once again, we acknowledge that there is good reason for this permissiveness: If public officials and public figures could sue for something as difficult to delineate as unfairness, they could too easily intimidate the press into avoiding a broad range of stories of potential public interest. But this risk does not excuse immoral conduct, nor does it argue for ruling out all forms of accountability.

Consider a case of accountability that involved no legal aspect whatever but raised significant moral problems. During a press conference soon after the hostages were released from TWA Flight 847, Uli Derickson, the purser, was misunderstood by several reporters to have said that she helped the hijackers select from the passenger list those with Jewish names. They wrote their stories accordingly. In fact, she had said just the opposite, but she had expressed herself somewhat ambiguously in response to a reporter's question, leading to the misunderstanding. Derickson later reflected on the matter as follows: "It was horrible really. I just can't understand why they did it—it's just like the media feeds the terrorists. I didn't know what to do—this is hard to take for a person like I am, an ordinary person. I've never had that kind of attention. And after I had only six hours of sleep after a 55-hour ordeal." [18]

There is little doubt that Derickson—actually a heroine of the hijacking incident—was misrepresented by elements of the media. We believe this kind of unintentional misrepresentation amounts to behavior for which the press should be held morally accountable, although such an error can easily occur. In the news business, decisions have to be made in quick succession, often with no opportunity to reconsider them, and ambiguities sometimes have to be resolved instantly. Misjudgments—even misjudgments that lead to defamation—under these circumstances may or may not be tantamount to negligence; certainly an error of this kind and its consequent harm is often excusable. But even the most valid excuse does not remove an obligation to accept accountability.

The obligation of accountability does not arise from the intentions of the journalist, but rather from the nature of the relationship between a journalist and the subject of a story. In this case, Derickson was legitimately entitled to the expectation that she would not be defamed, and she was owed an account and a retraction when she was. In this case, the press used its limited powers of self-correction to attempt to clear Derickson's name. Most of the media disclosed and corrected the error promptly and prominently. Although it is difficult and sometimes impossible to set the record straight adequately, at least this time a record was established that could be cited by Derickson.

*Accountability to Sources.* The relationship between a journalist and a regular news source bears some resemblance to the relationship between a fiduciary agent and a client. Over time it may become close; and trust, truthfulness, and confidentiality play central roles, especially if the journalist must protect a source against harm or invasion of privacy. But there are crucial differences. One of a fiduciary agent's main goals is to serve the interests of clients, whereas a journalist's main goal is to provide the public with information. The source's interest may or may not be identical with the public interest, and the journalist must determine when the two diverge and ascertain that the source's interest is not promoted at the expense of the public interest.

Reporters are also accountable to sources for other actions. A source can almost always legitimately expect a reporter to truthfully disclose the purpose of interviews and to report without distortion whatever the reporter and his or her editors deem newsworthy in the information the source provides. The source can also almost always legitimately expect a reporter to abide by whatever rules of attribution are agreed upon—or, in the absence of any agreement about attribution, that a rule of reason should apply. If, for example, all previous conversations with the source had been off the record, then the only reasonable assumption would be that the same conditions still apply. However, if an experienced news source with whom the reporter has had many interviews—in which the source set different conditions at different times—fails to ask for specific ground rules such as "on background" or "on deep background," the reporter is not obliged to raise the issue; under these circumstances the operating assumption, at least in Washington, is that the interview is on the record. The rule of accountability in each of these cases is that the source is entitled to an account (and perhaps to redress) if, but only if, the source's legitimate expectations are not met.

Finally, there is accountability with respect to confidentiality, which raises few if any controversial or complicated questions beyond those discussed in Chapter 1. When a source is promised confidentiality, reporters are accountable if they fail to keep their promises, as they would be for failing to keep any promise. (One potential reason to break a promise of confidentiality would be to prevent a serious crime; another would be to prevent an innocent party from going to prison; another would be to keep someone from suffering an unwarranted financial loss; and another would be a set of reasons comparable to or even more compelling than those cited in the Coleman–Jackson case or Claude Lanzmann's case in filming *Shoah*. See pp. 167–73.) While there may be a good reason for breaking a promise to a source, the source in general is still entitled to an account.

## Regulating, Institutionalizing, and Enforcing Accountability

Authors of a 1947 study by the Commission on Freedom of the Press said the following about accountability: "If the press is to be accountable—and it must if it is to remain free—its members must discipline one another by the only means they have available, namely, public criticism."[19] Anyone who follows the press carefully will be aware that with few exceptions—a notable case being David Shaw, press critic of *The Los Angeles Times*—print journalists rarely criticize other print journalists. Similarly, television rarely devotes time to serious criticism of television.[20] Although the Commission on Freedom of the Press appropriately recommended that members of the press need to discipline one another by public criticism, anything so sporadic and haphazard is bound to be an unsatisfactory method of imposing and enforcing accountability. There are better methods, however, including formal schemes and mechanisms, a few of which will be discussed after first examining the most publicly visible mechanism of accountability.

*Government and the Fairness Doctrine.* We have often expressed the view that government-imposed mechanisms of accountability are inconsistent with a free press in a democracy. Nonetheless, it is worth considering whether the preeminent contemporary mechanism of press accountability by government, known as the Fairness Doctrine (and under which the electronic media have long toiled), might be a justifiable, albeit carefully limited form of government control. The Fairness Doctrine is based on the theory that the airwaves belong to the public, not broadcasters, and that as long as the number of frequencies is limited the government has an obligation to guarantee that those frequencies are used to protect the rights of the owners of the airwaves. Associate Justice Byron White stated the purpose as follows in *Red Lion Broadcasting Co.* v. *Federal Communications Commission* (1969):

> Where there are substantially more individuals who want to broadcast than there are frequencies to allocate, it is idle to posit an unabridgeable First Amendment right to broadcast comparable to the right of every individual to speak, write or publish. . . . A license permits broadcasting, but the licensee has no constitutional right to be the one who holds the license or to monopolize a radio frequency to the exclusion of his fellow citizens. There is nothing in the First Amendment which prevents the Government from requiring a licensee to share his frequency with others and to conduct himself as a proxy or fiduciary with obligations to present those views and voices which are representative of his community and which would otherwise, by necessity, be barred from the airwaves.[21]

In this opinion the Supreme Court held that a Pennsylvania radio station that had broadcast a sweeping personal attack on a journalist, Fred Cook, had to provide Cook with the opportunity to respond. Such a rationale has traditionally been confined to broadcast rather than print media, on grounds that there is virtually unlimited access to printing presses, whereas the airwaves are limited resources that must be allocated and that are publicly owned.

The Fairness Doctrine holds that "important" issues must be aired and that if these issues are controversial, "important" contrasting views must be presented. It was expanded during the 1940s to provide that if "during the presentation of views on a controversial issue, an attack is made upon the honesty, character, integrity, or like personal qualities of an identified person or group," that person or group would have an opportunity to respond on the air. The FCC also held that if a station endorsed a political candidate, or if a candidate was criticized on the air, then that candidate would be given air time to respond.[22] These requirements of fairness do not demand that journalists give an account; they simply mandate a right to respond and defend one's views.

Both sides of the political spectrum in the United States have at times fought the doctrine: conservatives because it is perceived as an expendable form of government regulation (the doctrine has been invoked infrequently) and liberals because it is perceived as a means of intimidating or even silencing journalists.

The main argument for the Fairness Doctrine is that it is the only mechanism providing for public response that has any teeth, and therefore it is the only effective mechanism for controlling abuse by journalists and station owners. Congress has repeatedly accepted moral arguments based on fairness and equal opportunity as appropriate grounds for protecting the public against imbalanced reporting. Representative Timothy Wirth (D–Colo.) has defended both the actions of Congress and the opinion in *Red Lion* on grounds that the doctrine poses no threat to the First Amendment rights of journalists and provides enormous public benefit. Representative John Dingell (D–Mich.), chairman of the House committee charged with overseeing the FCC, has argued that the Fairness Doctrine is "absolutely fundamental" to preserve free speech on the airwaves because it protects responsible journalism from irresponsible journalists, whose activities invite federal control and intervention.[23] The Mobil Corporation has also campaigned vigorously in defense of the Fairness Doctrine on the ground that it protects the viewer's (and should protect the reader's) right to a balanced presentation, which Mobil construes as a right correlative to the press freedoms guaranteed by the First Amendment.[24]

The main argument advanced in opposition to the Fairness Doctrine is that the government is effectively permitted to define how freedom of expression is to be understood and practiced. Defenders of the doctrine note that some government officials go even further by supporting tough, enforceable regulations. Richard V. Allen, former national security advisor to President Reagan, has written, "The overwhelming majority of Americans resent attack and ambush journalism, and demand higher, enforceable ethical and personal standards from the news media. . . . The answer is simple: Don't let them get away with it."[25]

Opponents of the doctrine also deny that there is any real scarcity of the airwaves. They point out that in many cities listeners and viewers can pick up dozens of radio and television stations and have access to only one significant press. Moreover, with the advent of cable and satellite broadcasting, which offer the possibility of an almost unlimited number of broadcast channels, opinion has now shifted in many quarters toward the view that the Fairness Doctrine has been rendered obsolete. The worry that it does conflict with the First Amendment's guarantees of press freedom also persists, because it cannot be denied that a federal policy and agency must impose coverage requirements and scrutiny, all of which translates into regulation. Influential figures at the FCC have themselves said that the Fairness Doctrine no longer serves the public interest, because it inhibits expression of unorthodox beliefs while inviting government intrusion.[26] s the number and diversity of the media have increased, press and political pressures have mounted to strike the doctrine from the FCC's regulations and to begin treating the broadcast media in exactly the same way as the print press is treated.

The Fairness Doctrine has at times succeeded in inhibiting radio and television stations from endorsing candidates when there are large fields, which is neither necessarily good nor necessarily bad. It has also been invoked to restrict virulent racism, uses of the airwaves to intimidate certain groups, and concerted attacks on persons and institutions.[27] But overall the results have been modest. The Fairness Doctrine has also proved of little or no relevance in promoting accountability for documentaries such as "The Uncounted Enemy: A Vietnam Deception" (see pp. 75–89) or network coverage of fast-breaking events such as the hijacking of TWA Flight 847 (see pp. 205–07). At least there has been little effect for the past fifty years.

However, the FCC ruled—on July 12, 1985—that federal law permits government agencies to file Fairness Doctrine complaints against the media, and these could have the effect of reversing some past precedents and also of requiring more accountability for actions taken. This 1985 ruling resulted from a complaint filed by the CIA charging that ABC's "World News Tonight" had three times distorted the news in broadcasting allegations that the CIA had tried to arrange the assassination of Ronald Rewald, a Honolulu businessman who was under indictment for several crimes. The FCC rejected the CIA complaint on grounds of inadequate evidence but effectively issued an open invitation to government agencies to file Fairness Doctrine complaints. Two days later an editorial in *The Washington Post* cogently expressed the press's viewpoint that there must not be intimidating regulation by the government: "Allowing one agency of government to haul a broadcast news organization before another (one capable of extracting huge financial costs) is a formula, intended or not, to intimidate the press and dry up the free flow of news."[28] Ironically, ABC had been the only major network to oppose elimination of the Fairness Doctrine.

Whatever the drawbacks and advantages of the doctrine, to date there is no reason to believe that it has significantly improved either accountability or public access to the airwaves or that it is needed to discourage wrongdoing or insensitivity. The advent of cable and satellite television has so increased the availability of air time that the doctrine as a federal enforcement mechanism has probably outlived whatever usefulness it once had. This judgment does not mean, however, that the principles the doctrine represents—that a broadcast licensee does not own the airwaves and that citizens, whether they are politicians or otherwise, are entitled to fair treatment on the air—are not valid. But our quest here is for an efficient and workable mechanism or institution, and we doubt that any government-imposed scheme is likely to work sufficiently well to justify the risks it inherently carries. Rules and policies such as those in the Fairness Doctrine are justified if and only if, on balance, they promote the public utility more than they endanger it. We do not deny that the principles represented by the Fairness Doctrine can serve the public well. What we question is the claim that the service is so vitally needed that the risks to a free society of such an instrument in government hands justify it.

There are, however, other forms of fostering criticism and accountability that have been generated by the press itself. Criticism can, of course, be found in institutionalized forums the media provide such as letters to the editor, columns in newspapers and magazines, and programs such as ABC's "Viewpoint," which periodically airs a discussion of media performance. Although some of these entail giving accounts, the public would be better served by an institutional commitment to responding to criticism of the particular medium's policies or behavior (or some significant sample thereof) that goes beyond brief replies or boxes, which rarely have any effect on the behavior and practices of journalists.

*The Idea of a National News Council.* If the government is an undesirable institution to impose accountability, is there a better one? The National News Council represented an attempt to answer this question positively. This now-defunct body was originally suggested by the Commission on Freedom of the Press in 1947 and finally established in 1973 in the middle of the Watergate scandal. The first question the council investigated was whether President Richard Nixon was right when he said (at a news conference on October 26, 1973) that "he had never seen such outrageous, vicious and distorted news coverage as the television coverage of his office in recent weeks."[29] The council concluded that the White House had failed to substantiate the charges. Tellingly, though properly, a body that had been organized to promote opportunities for criticism of the press vindicated the press in its first decision. The council said it was "seriously detrimental to the public interest for the President to leave his harsh criticism of the TV networks unsupported by specific details that could be evaluated objectively by an impartial body."[30]

The National News Council lasted just over a decade. It met in various cities three times a year and had a staff that researched complains about alleged unfairness and inaccuracy. The staff investigated its last complaint on June 20, 1983, and shut its doors early in 1984. It came into being without much fanfare and went out of existence with even less. In the intervening ten years few people outside of journalism knew of its existence, and few people in journalism cared. One major reason for its failure was that leading news organizations such as *The New York Times, The Chicago Tribune,* and NBC News would not cooperate. They attributed their unwillingness to fears that the council would be manipulated by special-interest groups and that its existence would encourage an atmosphere that might eventually lead to creeping government regulation of the press.

There is nothing in its ten-year history, however, to suggest that they are right. When the council disbanded, former member Robert Maynard of *The Oakland Tribune* gave a terse summary of what we regard as an essentially correct assessment of this council's potential: "In the two years I was able to devote to the work of the council, I became convinced such a mechanism, if ever accepted by the press, could be a benefit to journalism and society. Unfortunately, I also became increasingly pessimistic about the likelihood the press would ever accept it."[31] We agree that some mechanism resembling a news council could play a pivotal role in providing a framework of accountability in journalism. Vigorous self-monitoring, not self-censorship, is a promising way to provide a barrier against the threat of federal encroachment, to deliver candid criticism, and to help make journalists accountable.

One problem with the National News Council was that its founders and leaders were too timid, which is understandable considering that they lacked the full or even substantial support of the media. In the council's series of case reports titled *In the Public Interest,* it declared that "all of its monitoring activities are rooted in a determination to preserve and strengthen press freedom."[32] Few question the worthiness of this goal, but the emphasis for such a body should not be on defending the press but rather on strengthening it through criticism and accountability. The power of the institution was too limited, and the criticism it leveled against individual newspapers, magazines, and networks was too tepid. For example, after citing numerous damning examples of flaws in *The Washington Post* series on the experimental drug program of the National Cancer Institute (see Chapter 3), the council said it "cannot accept the broad charges of complainant against the useful and important series."[33]

The demise of the council was inevitable not only because it lacked institutional backing but also because it lacked the means to achieve its ambitious goal of vigorous investigation and criticism. To be successful, a news council would have to have funding to carry out its investigations properly; it would have to have the independence to censure offenders, including the right to demand responses from the media; it would have to have the support of the power centers of the media; it would have to be insulated against any kind of outside pressure or interference, ideological or otherwise; and it would have to have a monopoly on deciding press questions much like the Supreme Court's monopoly on interpreting the Constitution. The last condition would be necessary to prevent any body outside the press—governmental or other—from insinuating its way into the business of press accountability and to give the council the authority of an unchallenged and uniquely sanctioned body.

Most importantly, a new news council would have to have institutionalized access to space or air time in all of the media to guarantee that, unlike the original council, its findings would be well publicized. It is critical that such findings be of the highest quality and that they be circulated to the widest possible audience, because they would be the primary product of media accountability. Summaries of the council's decisions would have to be published or broadcast in full by all members, including the member or members found guilty of transgressions. The full council decisions would be treated as news, which is to say the media would be free to write stories about them, carry texts, write editorials, run op-ed pieces, or ignore them.

Without almost universal acceptance by the media, the effort would be prone to failure. To be effective, acceptance would require the council's membership to reflect the interests of large and small newspapers, news magazines, television networks and local TV stations, radio networks and radio stations, and wire services. A news council must not represent a first step toward increased press regulation by the government. The best way to achieve this objective is to guarantee that control of the body remains in the hands of journalists and publishers who are dedicated to achieving what Bentham, Mill, Madison, Jefferson, and other free-speech theorists believed the press exists to do. Of course, the responsible journalists, publishers, and broadcast media would be free to appoint—and we would encourage them to appoint—enough public members to make a difference in the deliberations of the council. In the interest of credibility, the council might even be composed of a majority of nonjournalists (appointed or elected by journalists).

A council conceived along these lines would be able to field complaints from the public, sift out those deserving serious examination, and turn them over to a professional staff that could conduct thorough investigations, including hearings with testimony by accused, accusers, and others, and write detailed reports to the council, which would have ultimate authority over their content and release. Having working journalists on leave from their news organizations perform the staff work would ensure a level of professionalism, strengthen the commitment of the member organizations, and reduce out-of-pocket costs to the members. We recognize that some journalists assigned to this duty might be tempted to go easy on their colleagues for fear either of creeping self-censorship or that they might subsequently be judged harshly themselves. But there are enough self-confident, rigorous, and concerned journalists to minimize that concern.

*The Ombudsman Practice.* Although a council established and maintained by the media is needed if journalists and news organizations are to be made accountable to the public in a manner that reinforces rather than tears at the fabric of press freedom, other current practices are also desirable, each in its limited way, and therefore should be retained and in some cases made more widespread. Independent ombudsmen, for example, provide a more efficient means of public access to local news media than would any national news council. The rationale of the ombudsman—for the press and for other institutions—is to provide an independent source for receiving complaints from aggrieved parties in order to probe the justifiability of the complaint and to make recommendations for change, if needed. There are at present only about three dozen ombudsmen at newspapers around the country, although there are about 1,700 dailies in the United States. The use of ombudsmen is more widespread in Canada and is growing at a faster rate in many countries than in the United States.[34]

In the almost two decades that *The Washington Post* has had an ombudsman, several have made genuine contributions in their columns to the debate on the credibility and responsibility of the press. It is harder to say with assurance, however, that they have changed the character of the *Post* or that they have made the *Post* more accountable for its actions. The same is true with respect to other papers that have ombudsmen. Because the *Post* grants its ombudsmen independence by signing them to a two-year nonrenewable contract, they are free of concern about criticizing any aspect of the *Post*'s performance. Sam Zagoria, a recent *Post* ombudsman, reflected on the advantages of the institution—as seen by its advocates—

as follows: "Ombudsmen provide a ready ear to an aggrieved resident; their work is less costly and confrontational than a lawsuit and results are quicker and . . . [there is] less risk of runaway verdicts."[35]

There are potentially many advantages to the press in having an ombudsman. Here is a case where a published column by an ombudsman could have been useful in sorting out for the public what had happened. The paper in question, *The Louisville Courier-Journal,* has an ombudsman who only writes internal memos and does not write for publication. *Courier-Journal* sports editor Billy Reed wrote a column on the search for a basketball coach at the University of Kentucky. Among other things, he wrote, "There will be a Martian in the White House before there's a black coach on the bench where Adolph Rupp sat." This comment, and an incorrect interpretation of what it meant, were circulated widely in the American press, along with a report that a distinguished black coach had been highly offended by the column. These reports were damaging to both Reed and the *Courier-Journal.* As it turns out, Reed had intended to poke fun in a barbed way, and the black coach had actually expressed admiration for the forthrightness and courage of the columnist. But by the time these facts emerged, Reed and his paper were deluged by criticism, doubt, and misunderstanding.[36] We do not suggest that an ombudsman's article could magically dispel these public misperceptions and doubts, but a report by a respected, genuinely independent ombudsman could have mitigated the situation.

Of course, ombudsmen are hired by editors, which suggests the possibility of a conflict of interest, especially if the ombudsman uncritically shares the editor's outlook about how the paper should be edited. Ombudsmen also have little power, even if they are granted some status. Although they have access to the public through regular or occasional op-ed columns, and to the staff through memos and personal contact, they are not empowered to order changes, to introduce formal reviews, or to demand accounts from editors. And their published statements do not represent a commitment by the publication.

Despite these limitations, ombudsmen are in a position to make a useful contribution to media accountability by regularly writing about issues of press behavior that are demonstrably of public concern, while internally calling issues to the attention of reporters and editors. The fact that the issues are aired and the public is given a chance to evaluate journalistic behavior is a valuable service and also a step toward accountability. Once again, however, such institutionalized criticism is not accountability; accountability would require that journalists offer justifications for their conduct. The selective publication of responses to criticism by editors and reporters could profitably supplement the ombudsman's column. Accountable journalists or news organizations will not merely invite and willingly receive criticism or external evaluation, but will volunteer documentation and reasoned justification for controversial behavior.

Many of the journalists we know—at least those who work for what the British like to call the "quality press"—are as devoted to the objective of truth as the best scholars we know. Why, then, are journalists more in need of encouragement to receive more criticism and to become more accountable even under their own terms? And why is it so difficult to find workable and appropriate means of making them accountable? The primary answer bears repeating. Apart from the fact that accepting accountability will inevitably be burdensome, journalists are afraid that demands for accountability will turn into formal regulation and that regulation will endanger press freedom. This concern is not idle, but if the right model of accountability is developed, objectionable control is not inevitable.

## Conclusion

If the obligation of accountability is to have any meaning, journalists must agree on a framework for enforcing it. Accountability is essential for credibility, and with diminishing credibility come increasing demands for the limitation of liberty. Polls in the mid-1980s provide some evidence that a substantial fraction of the public finds the press credible in much that it does, but also arrogant, unreliable, and unfair. In time, such judgments could be translated into restrictive judicial decisions, antipress legislation, and other changes that could cripple the media.

But, independent of these disturbing possibilities, the press has a moral obligation to invite criticism and promote its own accountability. The public will always expect more of journalists than they can deliver, because few who have not worked in a newsroom or watched the process of news gathering and preparation for publication can begin to grasp how chaotic a process it is. But if the public will accept that journalists care enough about what they do and how well they do it to allow them to regularly pass judgment on their own errors (often excusable errors that are inevitable despite all the competence and good will in the world), the enterprise of journalism will come closer to the public's legitimate expectation of accountability. Producing a newspaper or the evening news on television is, in the words of one editor, a daily miracle. Being accountable for the mistakes that are made in the process ought to be a source of pride rather than a mark of shame.

NOTES

1. Morton Mintz, "Professionalism in the Newsroom," 2d Annual Consumers Union Lecture, delivered at the Graduate School of Journalism, Columbia University, May 18, 1972, p. 2.

2. John B. Oakes, in Morton Mintz and Jerry S. Cohen, *Power, Inc.*, (New York: Bantam Books, 1976), p. 422.

3. Robert Maynard, "It's Time the Press Listened to Critics," *USA Today*, April 5, 1984, p. 10A.

4. Eliot Freidson, *Profession of Medicine: A Study of the Sociology of Applied Knowledge* (New York, Dodd, Mead & Co., 1970), pp. 369–70.

5. Colman McCarthy, "The Journalistic Double Standard: The Squashing of Sydney Schanberg," *The Washington Post*, September 8, 1985, p. H8.

6. Fox Butterfield, "A Critique on PBS of Vietnam Series Sets Off a Dispute," *The New York Times*, June 13, 1985, pp. A1, C33.

7. Ibid., p. C33.

8. Ibid.

9. John Corry, "Television's Vietnam: The Real Story," *The New York Times*, June 27, 1985, p. C22.

10. Karen DeYoung, "Thatcher Tells Media: Starve the Terrorists on Publicity," *The Washington Post*, July 16, 1985, p. A1.

11. R. W. Apple, Jr., "Meese Asserts U.S. Favors Press Code," *The New York Times*, July 18, 1985, p. A7.

12. Ibid.

13. Morton Dean, "TV's Duty to Cover Terror," *The New York Times*, July 12, 1985, p. A27.

14. Ted Koppel, with guests Roone Arledge and Lawrence Grossman, ABC, "Viewpoint," July 30, 1985.

15. In earlier chapters we have, in effect, argued that journalists are accountable for furthering specific social goals specified in the definition of the profession, including providing the requisite information to the public. Journalists are also accountable for a level of competence sufficiently high to satisfy the legitimate expectations of a reasonable reader (see Chapter 2) and for a high level of care and concern in guarding the public interest.

16. Morton Mintz, "Press Power," Speech at Fifth Annual Symposium on Coordinating Clinical Trials, Arlington, Va., May 25–26, 1978, from the Final Draft, July 19, 1978, p. 8.

17. Yale Law School Sesquicentennial Convocation, November 2, 1974, as found in Marc A. Franklin, ed., *Mass Media Law*, 2d ed., (Mineola, N.Y.: Foundation Press, 1982), p. 39.

18. Victoria Churchville, "TWA Purser Dericksen Speaks Out About Ordeal on Hijacked Plane," *The Washington Post*, July 19, 1985, p. A3.

19. Robert D. Leigh, ed., *A Free and Responsible Press*, (Chicago: University of Chicago Press, Midway Reprint, 1974), p. 94. The study was funded by *Time* and by *Encyclopedia Britannica*.

20. Although the print press does criticize television news, it often does so ambivalently and without a clear sense of holding a reporter accountable. Newspaper commentary on television's coverage of the hijacking of TWA Flight 847 (see pp. 205–7) is a good example of ambivalence. Television critics like *The*

*Washington Post*'s Tom Shales were highly critical of the networks for their treatment of the story, while reporters such as Lou Cannon, the *Post*'s White House correspondent, came to their defense. Cannon's defense is typical of the press defending the press: "Several freed hostages thanked reporters for keeping the public focus on their plight. . . . [And television] refrained from . . . airing information that could have been damaging to the hostages." Cannon argued further that Lebanese Shiite leader Nabih Berri's "frequent appearances on television may have exposed Americans to some self-serving propaganda, but they also gave the Amal leader a highly publicized stake in solving the crisis." Lou Cannon, "A Convenient Double Standard," *The Washington Post,* July 8, 1985, p. A2.

21. Marc A. Franklin, ed., *Mass Media Law,* 2d ed. (Mineola, N.Y.: Foundation Press, 1982), pp. 658–59.

22. Ibid., p. 652.

23. See David Burnham, "FCC to Examine Fairness Doctrine," *The New York Times,* April 12, 1984, sec. C, p. 26; Peter W. Kaplan, "Fairness Doctrine in Broadcasting," *The New York Times,* February 7, 1985, sec. C, p. 25; and Michael Isikoff, "End to 'Fairness Doctrine' Urged," *The Washington Post,* February 8, 1985, p. B1.

24. Advertisement, Mobil Corporation, "Freedom of Speech Does Not Exist in a Vacuum," *The New York Times,* October 4, 1984, sec. A, p. 31.

25. Richard V. Allen, "Control the Media to End their Abuses" (guest column), *USA Today,* April 5, 1984, p. 10A.

26. Jeanne Saddler, "FCC Says Fairness Doctrine No Longer Is Needed, but Will Keep Enforcing It," *The Wall Street Journal,* August 8, 1985, p. 46.

27. See "FCC Due to Rule on Radio Station's Fairness," *The New York Times,* April 15, 1983, p. A16; and Wayne King, "Kansans Protest Broadcasts of Hate," *The New York Times,* May 18, 1983, p. A18.

28. Editorial, "CIA and FCC (Cont'd.)," *The Washington Post,* July 16, 1985, p. A14; and "FCC turns down fairness complaint lodged by CIA against ABC," *Broadcasting,* January 14, 1985, p. 65.

29. Richard P. Cunningham, "Why the News Council Failed," 1984–85 Journalism Ethics Report, Sigma Delta Chi, Society of Professional Journalists, p. 4.

30. Ibid.

31. Maynard, "It's Time the Press Listened."

32. National News Council, *In the Public Interest,* Vol. III (New York: National News Council, 1984), p. 500.

33. Ibid., p. 362.

34. Sam Zagoria, "Learning from the Swedes," *The Washington Post,* November 6, 1985, p. A22.

35. Ibid.

36. See John Feinstein, "Thompson Upset by Column," *The Washington Post,* March 28, 1985, pp. C1, C5; and John Feinstein and Michael Wilbon, "AP Names Ewing Top Player," *The Washington Post,* March 29, 1985, p. C1.

# Appendix

The following excerpt from George Crile's interview with Navy Commander James Meacham is reproduced verbatim (with corrected spelling) from a transcript of the full interview that was produced by CBS News and made public in connection with Gen. William C. Westmoreland's libel suit against CBS. The full transcript, dated March 6, 1981, totals fifty-seven pages. We have reproduced only pages 28 through 44. This excerpt is sufficient to provide the context for the part of the Meacham interview that was aired on the documentary "The Uncounted Enemy: A Vietnam Deception." We reproduce it to show Crile's technique in an on-camera interview and to provide a sense of the complexity of the interview, very little of which was eventually broadcast. Material that was aired appears in boldface type. Here is the excerpt:

*(Meacham overlapping indistinct)* On April first . . .
MEACHAM:   You're gonna have to speed things up here . . .
CRILE:   O.K. Give me a little more time 'cause otherwise we'll be in a pickle. On April first, you probably remember very well, the end of March, the president resigned. And afterward, you were called to a meeting in General Davidson's conference room; it was a meeting attended by all of the key people in the intelligence section. And at that meeting, Colonel Graham called on—on you and Colonel Wyler to help him erase the computer's memory.
MEACHAM:   Yeah.

CRILE:   What was he asking you to do?

MEACHAM:   Well, again, the specifics of this are fairly complex. We had a—

CRILE:   In its simplest form.

MEACHAM:   —a running account of enemy in the country that we kept on a computer, for which we had a couple of fairly good anchors way back in antiquity, and some checks since then that indicated we were basically on the track, or we thought we were basically on the track. One of the problems of doing this on a computer is it's fairly simple to go back at any one specific time way back in—several months or even years ahead of time, change the base line then, and automatically, without any—any effort, changing all the figures since then. Up to that time, even though some of the current estimates and the current figures had been juggled around with, we had not really tinkered with our data base, if I can use that jargonistic word. And—and Danny Graham was asking us to do it. We didn't like (?) it.

CRILE:   Was the [sic] the equivalent of burning government records?

MEACHAM:   No, no. Not at all. It's—wasn't equivalent of burning anything. All . . .

CRILE (Overlapping):   (Indistinct) destroying . . .

MEACHAM:   No. I wouldn't say it was equivalent destroying anything at all. It was—we had a long series of accounts, a running . . .

(cut)

CRILE:   Maybe you could just explain it a little bit, which is that—that there comes a time when Colonel Graham asked you and Colonel Wyler to tamper with the computer's memory, to change the data base in some way.

MEACHAM:   That's it.

CRILE:   You said no.

MEACHAM:   Well, no—we didn't say no. I mean, this thing wasn't our private property; it belonged to the intelligence directorate. We were the custodians of it; we didn't like what Danny Graham proposed to do. We didn't want him to do it. At the end of the day, we lost the fight and he did it.

CRILE:   He did it.

MEACHAM:   He did it.

CRILE:   With your help?

MEACHAM:   Never (?) got my help. I mean—he took the—insofar as we were the custodians of the records; well, we gave them to him; we were ordered to give them to him, we did. And some of my computer people went up to instruct him in the—in the techniques of—of doing this.

CRILE:   This was Bernie Gattozzi.

MEACHAM:   This was Bernie Gattozzi.

CRILE:   What exactly did they do?

MEACHAM:   Well, they changed the data base way back. We have this running record that started years before, where there were additions and subtractions each month, retrospective corrections, and ideally we came up with a—with an accurate figure at the end of the month, certainly we came up with a figure at the end of each month. (indistinct) even though we had, on occasion, tinkered around with the monthly figures, all of which were pretty soft and which were estimates—

it got harder as time went on, but on any given day, our figure for that day was a pretty soft figure. We tinkered with those, but we never really compromised the overall system because we could always go back and start from ground zero and work forward again. And indeed, if we tinkered with this figure today, as long as we didn't change it permanently, why at the end of the day, it would work out. And we would still get a—six months from now, we'd get a better figure for today, regardless of what we changed, how we changed this estimate; there was nothing permanent here. Now what Danny Graham was proposing to do was to go back and—several years before, and change this data base, which would've changed the figure for every single month from then on.

CRILE:  And why did he want to do this? What was he worried about?

MEACHAM:  I don't know that I can recall the specific issue. I suppose it was that—that the figures were getting too far out of balance at that time, between what we thought was true and what he thought should be true. I think I—it's only fair for me to say at this point, of course, that Colonel Graham had access to lots of different kinds of intelligence that we didn't—my section didn't.

CRILE:  I understand. But there was a—this was in—this was for you a moral dilemma. You had done a number of things that you didn't like doing before.

MEACHAM:  Yeah, we didn't want—we didn't want to tinker with the data base at all.

CRILE:  That was tantamount to what? In your mind? It was something you—you couldn't get yourself to do, but why? How could you have been criticized had you participated in it?

MEACHAM:  Well, I don't know. I don't know if I coulda been—coulda been criticized for it. I mean, to a certain extent, all of these figures were estimates; they were—they were—it's not like going out and counting a whole—whole bunch of people in a football game.

CRILE:  Would it, for instance, have been against military regulations to do that?

MEACHAM (overlapping):  No, no. It was certainly not a falsification of official records, if that's what you're asking.

CRILE:  Was it—but you drew the line and said no.

MEACHAM:  Didn't want to do that; didn't want to do that. But we didn't have any choice. At the end of the day, why, my people had to go up and—and assist him to do this.

CRILE:  And was it a hard thing to do? Was it easy just to go in and (indistinct crosstalk) . . .

MEACHAM (overlapping):   . . . well, there wasn't—there wasn't anything—no, I mean, physically no; there wasn't anything to it. It was, you know, a couple hours work for a computer programmer.

CRILE:  You know, you—you wrote to—to Adams saying, "I'm glad you got hold of Bernie Gattozzi; he was the key man in the great computer hassle. As I think I told you, about the end of my tour, he was a more or less seconded (?) to Danny Graham to tinker around with the whole historical basis of the thing."

MEACHAM:  That's right. That's correct.

CRILE:  Now, if that had gotten out at the time, if Secretary McNamara had been told that somebody had gone and done this to *(word)* these computers, what would the response have been?

MEACHAM:  Well, I don't know. I mean, you're trying—you're trying to make something harder than it is here. We didn't like this because we thought our data base was right, we thought we had some fixes back there on some—with some very reliable documents; we'd spent months of our lives working that system; we thought it was okay. We didn't want it fiddled with. However, we wouldn't'a had—I think we could've lost an argument before an objective jury about this; officers senior to—to me and to anybody in my section would've said, "We have seen other evidence that justifies—" Indeed, this is the argument Danny Graham made, "We've seen other estimates that now justifies our correcting our data base; this is why we have it on a computer; we realize now that we were wrong three years ago; therefore we—we choose to reset the system, based on our estimates." At the end of the day, of course, their estimates were the estimates. I mean, the— every estimate starts out at the bottom and filters up to the top, and various people can put in their judgment of the—on these things. It wasn't our judgment, and we didn't like it. But I don't think that it was hard and fast enough that any one of us could've gone to Secretary McNamara and say—and said, "Danny Graham is tampering with official records." And—and made a case that he would've believed.

CRILE:  Can I express a certain amount of wonderment? You're now a reporter. You were then an intelligence analyst. You were writing home to your wife . . .

MEACHAM:  Yeah.

CRILE:  . . . very clear-cut language. "I'm not talking about the confusion and inefficiency, which to a certain extent are products of all wars." You said that you were "talking about cover-your-ass orders, lies, from the very highest levels." Your letters are filled with talk of lying. Isn't it clear that something stronger, more questionable was happening than you are now allowing yourself to *(word)*?

MEACHAM *(overlapping)*:  Well, it's not all clear that that—that—that these particular sentiments were applying specifically to these sets of numbers that we're talking about. It's not clear in my mind even that—that that's what I was talking about. We were all disillusioned with the way we had to operate in that war out there. And—and we didn't like it.

CRILE:  You know, let me read you another section: "We shall see if I can make the computer sort out the losses since the Tet offensive began in such a manner as to prove we are winning the war. If I can't, we shall, of course, jack the figures around until we do show pro-progress." You wrote that.

MEACHAM:  Well, so what?

CRILE:  So, aren't you saying that you were manipulating figures to come up with preconceived notions as to what the estimates should be? Faking intelligence.

MEACHAM:  No, no. I'm not saying that at all.

CRILE:  You say, anyhow, "We are winning the war, and now I can prove it, having received sufficient, adequate guidance from my leaders."

MEACHAM:  *(indistinct)* Well, we certainly weren't faking any intelligence. Nobody that I have any connection with ever faked any intelligence.

CRILE:  What—what were you doing? How do you describe this?

MEACHAM:  How do I describe what?

CRILE:  Your own characterization of the process that you were pursuing.

MEACHAM *(overlapping)*:  Look (?), the—the problems that we had are as follows: we had a set of numbers that we tried to keep in balance. When we had large numbers of losses, these had to come from somewhere. Now, I started to—to outline this system before, and I didn't quite get finished with it, but the fact of the matter is whenever we would have a large loss, it's almost invariable in that system—it may have been a bad system; it was just the best we could think of—that we wouldn't know where to take these losses from.

CRILE:  Gee, I hate to do this. This is you again, to your wife: "Dear Dorothy: You should've seen the antics my people and I had to go through with our computer calculations to make the February strength calculations come out the way the general wanted them to. We started with the answer and plugged in all sorts of figures until we found a combination which the machine could digest. And then we wrote all sorts of estimates showing why the figures were right. And we continue to win the war." What could be clearer than that? You're not producing honest intelligence reports.

MEACHAM:  Well, there isn't such a thing as an honest intelligence report; there's my view and somebody else's. We quite clearly didn't agree with the figures that we were having to use, but it's not a question of honesty or dishonesty, and I think it's wrong of you to try to use those words.

CRILE:  I was only asking you to try to tell us what happened.

MEACHAM:  Well I've been trying—I've tried two or three times, and I have yet to get to the end of the story. It's a long, complicated story, and I'm not trying to force it on you if you don't want to hear it, but the fact of the matter is when you have a large number of losses, you have trouble finding where these guys have come, because invariably you haven't got all the additions (?) that should go with that number of losses into the system at that time.

CRILE:  Pardon me, but let's take El Salvador, or the Soviet Union today. If—if the DIA (?), military intelligence is told to prove that there are 3,000 missiles aimed at us, and they start with the answer, what's the point of having an intelligence service? Shouldn't we be . . .

MEACHAM:  I don't have any idea of what you're talking about, or what the connection has to . . .

CRILE:  Let me make an analogy: if you're trying to figure out how many guerrillas there are in El Salvador today, you should begin, I presume, in a classic sense by adding up the reports of the different units and coming to a total.

MEACHAM:  Not necessarily. I mean, there's two or three ways to go about this. We're getting in an area that's very, very complicated here.

CRILE:  Well, please—please help me, because it's not a mystery what—*(indistinct crosstalk)* . . .

MEACHAM *(overlapping)*:  I mean, you're trying to—*(indistinct)* get me to say that we all falsified intelligence, I'm not gonna say it 'cause we—I don't have any sense of having done that.

CRILE:  What do you have a sense of having done?

MEACHAM:  I don't know how to answer . . .

CRILE:   Are you proud of the—of your performance, of Mac-V's performance—?

MEACHAM:   Well, of course not. But I mean, I don't see the connection.

CRILE:   What we're really trying to do is just to determine in your own mind what actually happened. Is this something which—which should cause people to be concerned about the reliability of our intelligence reporting? Or not?

MEACHAM:   I think—you mean at that time? You mean the reliability of our intelligence reporting at that time?

CRILE:   Yeah.

MEACHAM:   I think certainly we ought to be—you know—be concerned about it. It's certainly open to doubt that—that we (?) were getting the—the correct answers out of it.

*(cut)*

CRILE:   Do you understand that the—I mean, what Sam and I are both trying to say right now.

MEACHAM:   I understand perfectly well what you're trying to say.

CRILE:   And . . .?

MEACHAM:   I don't agree with it.

CRILE:   Well not—not that—agree with it; it's a question of—of whether there isn't some way to—to reach a—well, I would love to have you present this history with some perspective which would be . . .

MEACHAM:   Well I've done the best I can do. I'm sorry that it's not satisfactory to you.

CRILE:   Well no, it's not—it's not that; it's just that I—you know, I'm—I'm sorry just to have had to have been a hectoring (?) force here. I would've liked something different.

MEACHAM:   Well, I mean, you—quite clearly know what you want me to say, but that's not the perception that I have.

CRILE:   No, that's not. I really was only trying to—well, we'll wait a second. . . . Let me try to give you a little bit of a sense of what seems to have emerged. Do I—in this whole exercise, you know, we've talked to a number of different people, and what—what has happened to many of them—Colonel Morgan, I grant you, you're not altogether sure about how formidable a man he is . . .

MEACHAM:   Well, he wasn't there through much of this.

CRILE:   Well, but different people at different levels have all felt very badly about what happened; they don't think it was right. And—

MEACHAM:   Well, I didn't think it was right, but—there's no reason to say that—the thing is, you know, any different from the way I actually saw it, or remember now that I saw it.

CRILE:   Yeah.

MEACHAM:   You see, you've missed this one point that I keep coming back, and I've been over this with Sam, and he—you know, we don't agree on this. But the fact of the matter is: each—at the end of each month, we didn't have much faith in that figure anyway. And if some guy says, "Look, we want to change this," why (?) there's—there's hardly any way to argue about it, really.

CRILE:   Except when it comes to something as—as really basic . . .

MEACHAM *(overlapping)*:   As long as we didn't—as long as we didn't tinker with the data base, you see, this would all wash out, sooner or later. This is a temporary figure. As long as you don't tinker with the—with the antecedent dates. This is all—this is all temporary, and it all washes out. These—a figure for this month changes each month for six or eight months.

CRILE:   But the data base is something different.

MEACHAM:   That's it.

CRILE:   Because then—then you're doing something permanent.

MEACHAM:   That's it.

CRILE:   And you can't get back.

MEACHAM:   Well I suppose you could keep a duplicate record, but basically what you say's true. That's right.

CRILE:   So it's really—it's like going back through the files and creating a separate set of records, and then burning the originals.

MEACHAM:   Yeah, except I think records is probably too strong a word for this.

CRILE:   The memory of the computer.

MEACHAM:   Yeah. Yeah. Yeah. Well, I mean, these weren't records in the sense that you said—I wrote a check for 17 dollars and 52 cents on this day. They were all a little softer than that. Although we thought—the—you know, the early records were pretty good; we thought the data base was not too bad.

CRILE:   But you took what was a principle stand at that point, which was no . . .

MEACHAM:   No, we didn't like that.

CRILE:   No dice.

MEACHAM:   And—and we didn't do it. And then he had to do it on his own. He had to get Gattozzi up there and do it on his own. We didn't do it.

CRILE:   Did that compromise Gattozzi?

MEACHAM:   Well, I don't know compromise. I mean, you know, he—he's—here's a lieutenant in the army that's ordered to do a specific job on a computer, and he did it. That's all. Whether (?) he's compromised by it or not I don't know. But—

CRILE:   Would—would Danny Graham feel embarrassed by this if he were asked about it?

MEACHAM:   I doubt it. I imagine he would—he'd say he had good reasons to do that.

CRILE:   But would you feel . . .?

MEACHAM:   He said—he said at the time he had good reasons to do it.

CRILE:   And you challenged that.

MEACHAM:   We didn't challenge that he thought he had good reasons; we just thought we had better ones for him not to.

CRILE:   *(word)* remember, he went off to—well, when he went off to Washington earlier, to defend the figures, with you as a part of the team, didn't *(word)* actually tell the DIA (?), "Look, this is an issue of a battle between the civilians and the military, and you've got to line up on our side."

MEACHAM:   *(word)* I think he probably did, yeah. I think he probably did.

# Index

# THE VIRTUOUS JOURNALIST

## STEPHEN KLAIDMAN

## TOM L. BEAUCHAMP

This book combines the insights of a seasoned journalist with those of an expert on philosophical ethics to provide a penetrating and comprehensive analysis of the ethics of news reporting. It sheds much light on the character traits and professional virtues needed for fair, truthful, and competent journalism. The book will be essential reading for anyone interested in the role the press plays in influencing social, economic, and political choices in modern society.

Drawing on a wealth of real-life cases, *The Virtuous Journalist* melds for the first time a conceptual analysis of the critical moral problems in journalism with a solid understanding of the constraints and possibilities faced by the print and electronic media. The authors are not First Amendment absolutists but believe nonetheless that, in a democracy, the media should be subjected to minimal legal restraint. They also argue that freedom from legal restraint requires increased moral responsibility.

Among the specific topics treated in the book are notions of morality and fairness, journalistic competence, standards of objectivity and accuracy, avoiding bias, avoiding harm, notions of public service, and maintaining public trust. Specific cases discussed include the controversy surrounding the CBS documentary "The Uncounted Enemy" and recent reporting on the AIDS epidemic.